# Bodies in Revolt

# Bodies in Revolt

*Gender, Disability, and a Workplace Ethic of Care*

## Ruth O'Brien

*Foreword by* Martha Albertson Fineman

**Routledge**
Taylor & Francis Group

NEW YORK AND LONDON

Published in 2005 by
Routledge
Taylor & Francis Group
270 Madison Avenue
New York, NY 10016

Published in Great Britain by
Routledge
Taylor & Francis Group
2 Park Square
Milton Park, Abingdon
Oxon OX14 4RN

Printed in the United States of America on acid-free paper
10 9 8 7 6 5 4 3 2 1

International Standard Book Number-10: 0-415-94534-8 (pb: alk. paper)
                                 0-415-94533-X (hb : alk. paper)
International Standard Book Number-13:  978-0-4159-4534-9 (pb : alk. paper)
                                 978-0-4159-4533-2 (hb : alk. paper)

---

**Library of Congress Cataloging-in-Publication Data**

---

O'Brien, Ruth
Bodies in revolt: gender, disability, and a workplace ethic of care/Ruth O'Brien.
Includes bibliographical references and index.
1. People with disabilities—Employment—United States. 2. People with disabilities—Employment—Law and legislation—United States. 3. Sex discrimination in employment—United States. 4. Age discrimination in employment—United States. 5. Industrial relations—Social aspects—United States. 6. Quality of work life—United States. 7. Feminist ethics. I. Title: Gender, disability, and an alternative ethic of care. II. Title.

---

Taylor & Francis Group
is the Academic Division of T&F Informa plc.

Visit the Taylor & Francis Web site at
http://www.taylorandfrancis.com

**and the Routledge Web site at**
**http://www.routledge-ny.com**

For Martha Campbell

# TABLE OF CONTENTS

# PREFACE

Early one Monday morning in Maine, I was talking with a former disability rights litigator, Sharon Miller. We were headed toward the airport, having just finished a weekend-long session editing legal commentary for *Voices from the Edge: Narratives about the Americans with Disabilities Act*. Feeling good that we had accomplished so much over the weekend and that I had profited greatly from Sharon's input, I hesitated spoiling the atmosphere by telling her about my new "theory" project. Then I spilled it. As I quickly conveyed the argument, I could feel her bristle.

"You know" she said cautiously, "what you're arguing is precisely what employers already think—that the Americans with Disabilities Act gives employees too much power in the workplace."

"I know," I said. Then added, "But Sharon, this is *theory*, not reality."

Elaborating, I explained that I well knew that the Americans with Disabilities Act (ADA) has given too little relief to persons with disabilities, whether in the work force or seeking employment. Indeed, my first book on disability, *Crippled Justice: The History of Modern Disability Policy in the Workplace*, had explained how and why federal court judges had interpreted the ADA's Title I, or employment provisions, so narrowly that they, in effect, had gutted this part of the law.

But still, I told Sharon, having studied both labor law and civil rights law helped me understand just how significant a departure from American law the ADA is. What I wanted to explore here was how in theory the ADA has tremendous potential to bridge the individual rights and collective divide in American law. Hence this book should not be interpreted as anything more than a vision, and a utopian one at that.

Like all utopian visions, the motive behind this one is to cast light on existing problems. I hope that this vision reveals the tribulations that most employees face since American labor laws have become so feeble and the federal courts have effectively eroded Title VII protections for women and persons of color under the Civil Rights Act.

Another reason I gave Sharon for writing this book is to make some readers aware that they harbor biases against persons with disabilities. By labeling every person as having a disability, or in all likelihood going to have one, I hope to make those readers feel uncomfortable. Perhaps by demonstrating that the very proposition that experiencing disability is a universal part of life and living, this book will help them discover their own prejudices (conscious or not) against persons with disabilities.

Seeing my point and yet still fretting that some employers might pick up this book and inappropriately use it as evidence to defeat persons with disabilities in the workplace or trying to find work, Sharon came up with a clever idea.

"You ought to add a disclaimer," she said.

So here it is—a disclaimer—not for Sharon, a defender of disability rights, but for all those who would purposefully mistake theory or this utopian vision for reality.

There is no small number of people to thank for helping me write a theoretical book. I owe Winston Fisk, my undergraduate thesis advisor, my first debt of gratitude. Winston encouraged me to think theoretically about ideas and action in a way that was particularly unorthodox at Claremont McKenna College. He gave me free range in writing my undergraduate thesis about how the former Yugoslavia's system of worker self-management was based on Hegelian Marxism, Husserlian phenom-enology, and Heideggerian existentialism. Although a mouthful, the thesis itself is entirely forgettable. What I do remember and draw upon is the courage he instilled in me to explore how the realm of ideas affects seemingly mundane policies and programs.

It is to Martha Fineman that I owe another debt of gratitude. She enticed me into exploring a universal notion of an ethic of care. Martha opened the door for me to feminist theory, exposing its universal applications. She encouraged me to think big and expansively about the ADA. And of course, I'm grateful to Martha for gracing this book with an elegant foreword.

I must thank Michael Dooner, who showed me how he experienced quadriplegia while working in a high-powered law firm long before I knew I'd be writing about disability policy. I'm only sorry he's not here to read it. Linda Findley, his partner at the time, offered me inspiration, showing me how disability represents difference, not a physical malady.

My colleagues, family, and friends also gave me the requisite guidance to write the book. Judith Baer, Alyson Cole, and Gretchen Ritter offered shrewd comments that helped me turn this into a better book. Meanwhile, Chloe Atkins, Marshall Berman, Mark Blasius, Jane Cohen, Nancy Hirschmann, Eileen McDonagh, Sally Engle Merry, Jill Norgren, Corey Robin, Philippa Strum, and Joan Tronto offered insightful criticism about different aspects of the overall argument. A Professional Staff Congress award gave me some much needed release time and funds for computer equipment. Two Ph.D. students in political science at the Graduate Center of the City University of New York—Joe Cleffie and Jason Schulman—did a terrific job tracking down sources. I was thankful that my editor, Rob Tempio, also picked up this project with as much enthusiasm as his predecessor, Eric Nelson.

My family remains a great source of support. I thank Max and Theo, as very energetic "boy" boys, for forcing me to think and rethink every stultifying stereotype that ever pops into my head about gender. Watching Rudi Matthee parent our sons never fails to surprise and delight me, giving me hope about how warm and nurturing men can be. My sister, Kathleen O'Brien, and my mother, Virginia O'Brien, put up with a great deal more explanations about political theory than they would undoubtedly have preferred during the holidays. I'm also grateful to have a wonderful circle of friends—Rouba Abdel-Malak, Nadine Cohen, Mark Hillary, Carol Hutchins, Jasmin Kraemer, Stephen Kuusisto, Marta Lauritsen, Robin Boyle-Laisure, Susan Martin-Marquez, Shawn Casey O'Brien, Nancy Rao, Nancy Solomon, and Arlene Stein—who listened without showing fatigue to the ever-developing argument underlying this book.

It is to one special friend, one of the most giving, open, creative people I've had the good fortune to find—Martha Campbell—to whom I dedicate *Bodies in Revolt*. While I must claim any of the book's mistakes, it is because of Martha's wisdom, encouragement, and insight that I could write this.

# FOREWORD
# Averaging at the Edges

Ruth O'Brien has given us a great deal to think about in this important and challenging book on disability. In the first instance, it becomes very clear that the American approach to defining equality is narrow. In this foreword, I begin with briefly describing a more expansive and creative approach to issues raised by human differences—the "Universal Design" movement. I follow this with a contrasting description of the anti-discrimination model of traditional equal protection jurisprudence, which is firmly based on an assumption of sameness. Universal Design is inclusive of differences while equality jurisprudence is not.

One of the many wonderful insights O'Brien offers us is that law need not be so restrained. In fact, the Americans with Disabilities Act (ADA) breaks free of the strictures of formal equality and sameness of treatment, to offer an ideology of inclusion that resonates with the direction of contemporary design.

## Universalizing Design

My son Benjamin, who recently finished his Masters in Design at Carnegie Mellon, informed me that, increasingly, designers are recognizing the commercial value of accommodating differences across the range of potential consumers. While, historically, the manufacturers of everything from dining room chairs to computer programs tended to build their models around an "average" user, the trend of the future seems to be in breaking down large groupings into smaller, more defined units and bundling together multiple averages across the spectrum of differences. Rather than concentrating on only the grossest part of the aggregate that leaves both tails of the Bell Curve dangling in designers' no-man's land, proponents of Universal Design begin with the premise that "no one is average" and, thus, no product is appropriately conceived in a one-size-fits-all mode.

xiii

As a legal scholar interested in differences, accommodations, and affirmative action, I was intrigued by this movement. It takes as its starting point the challenge presented by difficult and complex problems arising from the inevitable variations in human physicality, mentality, ability, and so on. Rather than ignoring such differences in an unrealistic pursuit of one standard or norm, Universal Design proponents embrace diversity as presenting creative opportunities for creative thinking about inclusiveness.

In addition, rejection of the idea that we can identify one norm or average range of characteristics upon which to focus helps to undermine the idea that those who fall outside those realms may be considered somehow deviant and, in turn, that recognition of their needs can be considered caving in to an undemocratic form of "special treatment." In the parlance of human rights discourse in Europe and elsewhere outside of the United States, Universal Design "mainstreams" differences, normalizing them by not only making them visible, but central to the design task at hand. There is no condescending notion that tackling differences may be a nice thing to do for persons with disabilities, for example the approach of a "niche market" mentality. Rather, inclusive design sets out a system that mandates accommodations because it recognizes that every individual has unique and special needs. According to one advocate's Web site, the movement seeks to "design products and environments to be usable by all people, to the greatest extent possible, without [the need for] adaptation or specialized design."[1]

## Disability Studies and Discrimination

In this important book, O'Brien explores the revolutionary potential of the Americans with Disabilities Act. The approach to disability—the history of which she describes—must be placed in the context of the typical method for determining equality in American jurisprudence. Just as Universal Design has the potential to change the way designers approach their task, the ADA provides a theoretical alternative to the American legal system's construction of the concept of equality and what constitutes discrimination.

Our understanding of equality is based on a premise of basic sameness, in which most forms of discrimination are forbidden. The doctrine of formal or rule equality dictates that, unless there are relevant legal differences, people should be treated the same. The equal protection inquiry, therefore, is into the legitimacy of classifications, considering the extent of similarities and differences between or among individuals and groups.

[1] http://home.earthlink.net/~jlminc/products.html

Reasoning through making analogies, comparisons and distinctions is the legal methodology employed by judges in an effort to see if the differential treatment set out in legislation is warranted. Some categories, such as race or sex, are considered inherently suspect and prompt serious (or stricter) scrutiny by courts and, therefore, make differential treatment difficult to justify. Other classifications need only be rational to survive scrutiny.

Making inclusion in the larger (average or standard) group the norm, by not questioning the status quo and valorizing sameness of treatment as the most appropriate measure for equality, means assimilation is the preferred option. Labeling as discrimination any differentiation in treatment and requiring it to be justified as against an ethic of formal equality tends to render invisible and incapable of compensation through law the fundamentally unequal circumstances many individuals and groups in society experience. An antidiscrimination approach presumes that remediable legislation and affirmative action programs, designed to address unequal economic and social positions, are illegitimate in most instances and makes them vulnerable to attack.

Under a formal equality system, in which different treatment is inherently suspect, setting aside some category of persons for differential treatment can provoke a charge of discrimination from those who perceive it as conferring an unfair and unegalitarian advantage of another person or group. Ironically, differential or "special" treatment may also be rejected by those receiving it, because it is viewed as stigmatizing and, by implication, an assertion of inferiority when compared with the standard against which they have been measured. An antidiscrimination approach to civil rights places those set off as different in the position of arguing for their relative sameness to the untargeted population. Any perceived difference from that group is deemed to be legally irrelevant. By contrast, those seeking to uphold the differential treatment bear the burden of showing that the differences do justify differential treatment, that the treatment is not arbitrary or unwarranted.

Of course, in an antidiscrimination model of equality, some differences might result in the application of affirmative action schemes. But affirmative action is viewed as a temporary deviation from the basic principle that everyone should be treated the same under law. Affirmative action might be necessary to remedy past discrimination, but once the effects have been addressed in this way, the playing field is once again assumed to be level and differences in treatment considered suspect.

## Disability and Ideology

O'Brien characterizes the ADA as an "ideology" in this book. Considered as such, the basic objective of this ideology is a different, more nuanced version of equality, one which is to be achieved through adherence to principles of inclusion and accommodation, rather than sameness of treatment. As an ideology of equality, the ADA expresses a series of assumptions and aspirations that, together, stand as a critique of the antidiscrimination approach of most civil rights legislation. For one thing, the ADA does not begin with the premise that bodily differences are irrelevant. In fact, the recognition that there are vast differences in bodies forms the basis for the Act. Difference is the norm—the natural state of things to be assessed and addressed by law and policy.

The ADA, in recognizing that differences are individual, inevitable, and pervasive throughout the population, acknowledges that those differences will never disappear from the population. Nor will the need to treat people individually and unequally in light of those differences fade away at some future time.

O'Brien shows us how many of the core beliefs and essential assumptions of our legal system are shaken when the vulnerability of the body intrudes as a central organizing concept in policy making. The ADA embraces difference and encourages different treatment. It does so in the service of a more expansive notion of equality than that found in the formal equality model, which adheres to sameness of treatment as the norm. The ADA's version of equality is more substantive in nature. It starts from the premise that there are inevitable and extensive differences among people, some of which must be specifically addressed by different or unequal treatment so that equality of result can be attained.

The provision of the ADA that best conveys this ideology is its reasonable accommodations mandate. Reasonable accommodations can be understood to impose on employers an obligation to do what is necessary to mold the workplace so it is compatible with the needs of individual employees. Importantly, the Act is focused on the individual—not groups—as the unit of concern. It looks to identify and address individual needs, and not to identify impermissible categorization or classification. In this way, the ADA is affirmative or positive, in that it gives the individual power, due to the requirement that the employer must engage in a process of accommodations. It is not merely a prohibition on discrimination, but mandates reaction on the part of the employer.

As the book details, the revolutionary potential of the ADA has been severely curtailed in operation by court interpretations reigning it in. However, in viewing the ADA as an ideology of equality, this book carries us forward to consider the values and beliefs it advances, even as the courts do in its legislative manifestation.

In tracing the development and potential of the ADA, this book creates a vocabulary to match the new concepts. We are to look to our "animality," rather than describe certain differences as disabilities, and therefore, assume they are unnatural or unusual. In addition, different capabilities (disabilities) are not properly thought of as establishing an "identity." Our animality is universal and cannot serve as a characteristic to distinguish us, in any meaningful way, one from another. Quite the contrary, animality is a universal that cuts across traditional identity markers such as race, gender, class, and orientation. Also, distinguishing animality from identity is the recognition that it is fluid in its manifestations for any given individual, and not an immutable characteristic. The concept of animality references the cluster of physical, emotional, psychological and other potentialities that, together, define the scope and nature of "the human condition."

The ADA encapsulates a way of thinking about the body—about all of our bodies. It suggests that it is not only appropriate, but also necessary for us to think of our bodies as things that have needs and that are engaged in a process of decline and decay, and will one day cease to be. In addition, the ADA seems to anticipate that this process can and will occur in myriad ways over time. The ultimate destination is universal, but there is no standard path on which to travel.

An individualized and embodied notion of equality could prove to be a truly radical tool for social transformation. The mandate of equal treatment could translate into individualization. In fact, this is exactly what the ADA attempts, by placing the concept of the diversely vulnerable body together with the responsibility of the workplace to ensure equality of treatment. The ADA situates this body in the workplace context and demands accommodation of its needs. In doing so, the ADA sets forth objectives that undermine the tendency, established under early industrialization, to think of workers and work as susceptible to standardization and conformity.

In shaping demands on the state under this approach, we would think not in terms of our "rights," but in terms of our "needs." Rights are based on the concept of sameness. Needs are rooted in an appreciation of differences. The concept of needs is not negative in this regard, but indicative of variations in the experiences and conditions humans may face.

## Lessons of Universal Design

Universal Design has taught that, focusing on the needs of the non-average customer results in better products for everyone, even those with average abilities, because we are all "disabled" at times. Curb cuts, designed for persons in wheelchairs, make life easier for travelers with suitcases, parents with strollers, delivery persons with hand trucks, and so on. Oxo good grips kitchen tools, designed for persons with arthritis, have become hugely popular because they are more comfortable to use for everyone.

Universal Design incorporates the truly radical idea of disability: that our abilities vary—all of us—not just over the course of our lives, but over the course of the day. We have limited cognitive capacity when we are driving a car, distracted by our children, or wake up in the middle of the night for a snack. We have limited mobility when we are carrying a heavy package or wearing uncomfortable shoes. We have limited vision, hearing, and attention, that we must divide between all of the things that we do all at once.

Hands-free cell phone headsets were not designed for persons without hands; they were designed for persons whose hands, vision, and attention are largely preoccupied with driving a car. Universal design recognizes that persons driving a car, and persons without the use of their hands, share certain characteristics and that a product designed for one could benefit the other. O'Brien reminds us that the law, as well as American society, would benefit from taking such insights to heart and following the lead of the ideology of disability.

**Martha Albertson Fineman**

# CHAPTER 1
# A Subversive Act

## Introduction

In 1990, the U.S. Congress and President passed a law—the Americans with Disabilities Act (ADA)—that included revolutionary employment provisions. By providing workplace accommodations, the ADA's employment provisions make employers take into account the ongoing needs of their workers with traditional and nontraditional disabilities alike. The law defines a physical or mental impairment by virtue of what a person cannot do rather than in terms of a specific medical condition or disease. It is not that Jane has epilepsy, but what she cannot do as a result of how this disease specifically affects her unique mind and body.

This definition of disability is vast, expansive, and indeed almost universal. It transforms disability from a medical category that involves a limited group of people into one that describes the human condition. Over the course of a lifetime, a physical or mental impairment or condition such as cancer, high blood pressure, or pregnancy, will affect most people at one time or another. Hence, the ADA turns disability into an open-ended category that is nonessential, ever-evolving, and socially constructed.

Offering an expansive view of disability is nothing new. In the 1970s, Irving Zola suggested that everyone was temporarily able-bodied.[1] Thirty years later, the feminist disability theorist Rosemarie Garland-Thomson argues that disability is about identity. Instead of creating a new identity group, she contends that disability is a fundamental aspect of our human identity.[2] What Garland-Thomson, and other disability theorists such as Mariam Corker and Eve Sedgwick maintain is that disability offers us a

1

"universalizing view"; or in Simi Linton's words, it constitutes "a prism through which one can gain a broader understanding of society and human experience."[3]

What is new in this book is that by recognizing the breadth of the ADA's new definition of disability, its employment provisions could undermine one of the most basic tenets of capitalism. American business rationality generally dictates that employers use profits, not human need, to determine who receives better work conditions. By contrast, the ADA's employment provisions, which require employers to make reasonable accommodations, take into account human need. These provisions therefore have the capacity to humanize the face of capitalism. No other provisions within labor law or civil rights law compel employers to pay heed to the individuality of their employees.

Mandating that employers address workers' needs alters the logic underlying American business rationality not just because of the particular accommodations that those workers receive. As workers with disabilities engage with their employers in what the ADA calls an "interactive process," requests for reasonable accommodations could undermine managerial prerogative power. The interactive process mandates that workers negotiate over the essential and nonessential tasks of a position to determine accommodations, thereby challenging what their employers (and employees without disabilities) perceive as a "normal" workplace. Employees with disabilities can scrutinize a position's duties and responsibilities, gaining insight into workplace rules and regulations that other employees do not have. Requests for accommodations can help persons with disabilities understand the logic behind the operations of an entire workplace, something that most employers prefer to keep ambiguous.

What is more, nothing prevents employees with either permanent or temporary disabilities from sharing this perspective with other employees. Accommodating one person could well set a precedent for another. Recognizing the physical or mental individuality of a person does not mean accommodations must be constructed for each individual. For example, the scanner, designed for someone with severe vision problems, need not be reinvented for everyone who cannot see. Hence, the ADA's employment provisions could help employees bridge the classic divide between individual rights and collective action. While unions sometimes work for the collective good at the expense of the individual, requests for accommodations further the individual *and* the collective good.

Finally, tying human needs to accommodations individualizes the workplace and challenges what Max Weber described as the force of rationalization in modernity.[4] In the twentieth century, the labor process became increasingly formalized and standardized. Time–motion studies, initiated by scientific management during mass industrialism in the early twentieth century, have continued to affect more employees under

Fordism during postindustrialism after World War II, and beginning in the mid-1980s, neo-Fordism within global capitalism. Whether it is on the assembly line, at a chain restaurant that sells hamburgers, or an office providing a service such as insurance, employers have created more and more precise rules and regulations that govern the work performance of the self-disciplined "standardized" body. If employers accommodate their employees, taking into account the individual peculiarities of their bodies, these employers would be undercutting the standardization of the workplace.[5]

What should concern employers is that technology has now changed so that making standardization in the workplace is no longer necessary. While management may still seek standardization, computers help managers compile data that evaluate each employee's performance. The number of keystrokes an employee makes, for instance, can be monitored on a minute-by-minute basis. Computers can gather so much information that what distinguishes neo-Fordism from Fordism is that these machines can replace the managers. Employers, however, still demand that the individual conform to the workplace. The ADA's employment provisions could turn this around, making the workplace conform to the individual.

## The Radical Potential of the ADA

While the revolutionary character of the ADA's employment provisions was little noticed during the legislative debate, the federal courts spotted it immediately. The courts observed that these provisions undermined the discretionary power of an employer's right to manage. Between 1992 and 1998 almost 94 percent of all litigation was decided in favor of employers.[6] In many rulings the federal courts emphasized how the employment provisions unnecessarily interfered with managerial prerogative power.[7] Then, in 1999, the Supreme Court handed down three rulings that upheld and extended the lower federal court decisions, curbing the ADA's capacity to transform the workplace.[8] These federal courts did so, however, not by disturbing the logic or the workings of the interactive process, but by ensuring that few people fell under the ADA's jurisdiction. In 2002, the Supreme Court rendered three more decisions that limited the scope of the employment provisions.[9]

What, then, is the point of studying a revolutionary yet extremely ineffectual law, a law that is itself largely unavailable to persons with disabilities? This book argues that the ADA should be viewed as an ideological law in the tradition of critical legal studies, one that is constitutive and reflective of a system of values and beliefs. Feminist legal theorists and critical race theorists regard law as an ideology in an approach that has become known as "perspective" scholarship. As Martha Fineman explains in her path-breaking book, *The Neutered Mother*, this type of scholarship shows us how to challenge "the traditional notion that law is a neutral, objective, rational set of rules, unaffected in content and form by the passions and perspectives of those who possess and wield the power inherent in law and legal institutions."[10] Perspective scholarship criticizes the dominant ideology underlying American law. Fineman, for instance, examines existing family law, arguing that it is based upon a sexual bond between husbands and wives when it should be premised upon children and those who nurture them, whether they be male or female, blood relatives or not. Perspective scholarship like this tries to speak for, at least in theory, "certain groups that have been unrepresented (or underrepresented)."[11]

Placing the ADA in perspective scholarship, this book shows that it is a unique piece of civil rights legislation in that it recognizes a fluid identity. To be covered under the ADA one must have a substantial impairment that rises to the level of a disability, and given how a person's health can change, this identity is not based on a static or staid category. To qualify for this category, the person in question must be individually assessed. This person's status is altered if his or her condition changes. The ADA is therefore similar to other civil rights laws in that it is based on someone's identity. However, it departs from these laws because the identity of a person is fluid and individual rather than static and part of a group. With both common and statutory law relying on analogies, the precedent that the ADA sets in terms of creating a fluid identity may affect those with fluid or multiple identities, such as transsexual, intersexual, or multiracial individuals. Also, medical procedures like cloning, surrogacy, abortion, and *in vitro* fertilization question the most basic issue of identity: what constitutes a human being. Late twentieth and early twenty-first century science focuses not on the whole body, but on its ever-changing components.

The ADA is also the first civil rights law that is not based upon a traditional rights orientation. These provisions interject a dynamic concept of need into the workplace. They make employers take into account the individuality of their employees, and by so doing, the employment provisions rest on a feminist morality—an ethic of care. Essentially, the focus on need turns employers into "caregivers," albeit unwilling ones, who must negotiate with their employees regarding reasonable accommodations. Moreover, as employers are obliged to maintain negotiations that acknowledge the organic character of the mind and body, this care is ongoing given the changing and potentially perpetual nature of disability.[12]

Women indeed could use the ADA as a means of feminizing the workplace. In many places of employment, pregnancy is already treated like an illness or a short-term disability, allowing women to take leave with pay. This leave policy, however, does not alter the workplace culture, quite aside from raising women's concerns about having pregnancy labeled a sickness or disability. By contrast, an expansive definition of disability recognizes the organic nature of the human mind and body, and would include most women (and men who have physical or mental needs), offering them a means of pursuing justice in the workplace. Under the ADA, many employees could negotiate over work conditions based on concrete considerations of human needs. Using a broad conception of disability would simultaneously help minimize the stigma and bias that persons with traditional disabilities face.

Studying the ADA sheds new light on the limitations of both civil rights law and labor law. Title VII of the Civil Rights Act does not get to the heart of employment discrimination. It gives women no mechanism like the ADA's interactive process that could change the male-dominated workplace culture. Also Title VII has faced a backlash of opposition because it prevents employers from discriminating against people in specific categories. Safeguarding a group—a protected class—from discrimination does not take an individual into account, making this protection vulnerable to criticism when it is unnecessary or should be more inclusive of those who fall outside of the class.

While the National Labor Relations Act (NLRA), which is based on the majority rule principle, offers workers the ability to fight for better work conditions with collective bargaining, this legislation has failed to foster difference in the workplace.

Organized labor has not served women well.[13] This stems in part from the fact that labor laws require that individuals who join unions that bargain on their behalf surrender their identity. Union leaders gain concessions for a group of employees or the collectivity with no respect for the employees' individuality, including their gender.

## Rationality, Morality, and Animality

As it is neither based on individual rights nor collective bargaining, the ADA nevertheless offers both persons with disabilities and women a new means of humanizing the workplace. If able-bodied workers could either overcome misconceptions they have about disability or the resentment they harbor against employees who receive accommodations, they would discover that the ADA gives them a means of gaining concessions for an entire work force that civil rights and labor laws under the limited American welfare state have failed to provide. Yet to do so, the able-bodied work force must recognize its own mental and physical vulnerability. A more universal notion of the organic mind and body or "animality" should be substituted for the concept of disability in the ADA.[14]

Whereas an ethic of care interjected morality into the discussion about an ethic of rights based on rationality, animality introduces the mind and body into the debate. Animality underscores that *Homo sapiens*, the human being, is made up of flesh and blood and that needs can be derived from this. Laws, in turn, can be based upon fulfilling these needs.

By substituting the term "animality" for "disability," this book purports that there is no such thing as a normal healthy mind and body. This image does not reflect reality. Nor should a normal mind and body constitute an ideal to which members of society should aspire. Creating such an ideal turns human needs into weaknesses.[15] It transforms physical and mental needs into aspects of one's frailty or vulnerability, rather than one's humanness. Armed with a vision of the ideal normal healthy mind and body, the American state and society then judges all those who fall short of it, categorizing them as subnormal or abnormal. It reveals one's inferiority as a human being.

Starting with the premise that people have physical and mental needs turns this proposition around. The term animality demonstrates that these needs do not reflect human imperfection. They reveal the human condition. As Joan Tollifson describes it:

> Organic life is vulnerable; it inevitably ends in disintegration. This is part of its beauty.[16]

By examining our animality, we can avoid the (dis)able-bodied and the (ab)normal binaries that plague the modern state and society, holding everyone down.

## PART I: Interpreting a Statute as Ideology

*Law as Ideology*

The idea that legal doctrine reflects ideology is now commonplace.[17] From the 1970s, critical legal studies examined how legal doctrine was part of existing social structures that constrain individual behavior and thought; yet discovering how a statute—not a law in practice or a legal doctrine—reflects ideology has been the focus of few studies.[18]

The notion that law is ideological has been construed by scholars in two distinct ways. Marxists and neo-Marxists view ideology in a pejorative way. To them, ideology involves false consciousness. They see ideology as a delusion or a screen that conceals reality. Perceiving law as ideological therefore means that Marxists and neo-Marxists consider it tainted: it represents illegitimate or ill-begotten formal power.[19]

Cultural anthropologist Clifford Geertz, who has greatly influenced legal scholars, conceives ideology in an utterly different way. To him, it is not a screen or a mask but rather an "aspect or slice of culture located within a particular institutional arena. An ideology is a set of categories by which people interpret and make events meaningful."[20] It includes both explicit rules and implicit schemes that enable actors to generate a wide variety of practices.[21] An ideology is thus a legitimate set of categories, rules, and schemes that are generally organized into a constitutive structure.

Following Geertz (as well as Pierre Bourdieu), legal anthropologist Sally Engle Merry observes that envisioning law as ideology helps us uncover layers of meaning and belief. Ideology is complex in that it can highlight questions of harmony, integration, and consensus, whereas, when it is viewed in terms of power, it underscores conflict, control, and hegemony.[22] Viewing law as ideology shows both how it frees and restrains people. Nowhere is this better seen than with the civil rights movement and law. Similarly, the anthropological view of law as ideology can illustrate how the ADA has helped and hindered people in the same way.

Given both the liberating and constraining connotations of considering law to be ideological, some scholars have questioned whether it might be transformative. Merry concludes that law could change politics since it produces cultural meanings and identities, which are an integral aspect of power. Courts, for instance, provide a forum where problems are labeled and categorized and solutions determined. Law has the capacity to structure discourse and talk. Taking a broader view of law than the first critical legal theorists, Merry argues, demonstrates that it creates a language and a locale for resistance that can be transformative.[23]

To Merry, everyday resistance to law can bring about political transformation. Similarly, Michael McCann's groundbreaking book, *Rights at Work*, shows how even though the pay equity movement lost most of its courtroom battles, this movement created a discourse and a consciousness that facilitated resistance.[24]

In what McCann calls the legal mobilization framework, he analyzes the constitutive role of legal rights as both a strategic resource and as a constraint for collective efforts to transform or reconstitute relationships among social groups. Legal practices and rights discourses, he suggests, are not limited to formal state forums. Both state officials and citizens who engage "in everyday struggles" are engaged in resistance. Social movements begin with someone like Rosa Parks who refused to fit into social categories like segregation that define our lives.

Giving more weight to the legal mobilization framework, Merry contends that "resistance within, by means of, and through law" does exist for three interrelated reasons. First, actions that seem to be individual and idiosyncratic emerge from distinctive cultural understandings embedded in particular worlds. Cultural understandings inform all actions; one does not act in isolation. Second, resistance can reshape how identities and communities are understood. At the very least, it can "disrupt prior understandings" of the identity of a group of people.[25] Third, it shows that no sharp line can be drawn between individual and collective action.[26]

Political theorist James Scott discusses how resistance should be understood in terms of conscious collective actions like peasant uprisings, sabotage, and subversive songs. Sabotage and foot dragging are forms of resistance. These activities challenge a law's definition of personal problems in courts, following the emergence of new notions of power generated in discourses, political institutions, and social relationships.[27] Scott's idea of resistance parallels Foucault's emphasis on how power is exercised in daily life.

## A Statute as Ideology

Analyzing the ADA as ideology—the statute itself—shows how it has affected, and will continue to affect, legal discourse and practice far beyond the courtroom. The federal judiciary interprets a statute, altering its meaning. A plaintiff who brings suit under the statute wins or loses the case depending on how the judiciary interprets its legal merits. Nonetheless, the statute frames the legal discourse, introducing the very concepts and provisions that the judiciary interprets. The statute cannot be studied in a vacuum; it was the legislative authors who interjected the fundamental ideas behind it.

What is more, an examination of the ADA's transformative potential in terms of law as an ideology reveals a methodological nexus between this legal literature and the path dependency literature in political science.[28] Why did the ADA's legislative authors adopt this particular policy path? On the one hand, the ADA could have included a definition of disability that depends on physicians and experts.[29] Indeed, some disability rights activists have called for the ADA to be amended so that it relies on a medical definition of a physical and mental impairment, because the federal courts have interpreted the functional definition so narrowly that few persons with disabilities are prevailing in Title I employment cases.[30]

On the other hand, the employment provisions within the ADA could have mandated that employers hire a quota of persons with disabilities. Creating this type of policy would have followed a well-worn path established by most European nation states. The U.K., France, and Germany, for example, mandates that employers hire a certain percentage of persons with disabilities.[31] This policy reflects a charitable model of disability. It asks employers to be charitable toward persons with disabilities. At what level employers hired persons with disabilities would be irrelevant. The charitable model is therefore well illustrated by the fictional errand boy who worked on the 1980s television drama *L.A. Law*, who was used as a foil to humanize the high-powered glamorous lawyers who simultaneously felt sorry for him and were inspired by his humanity. Charity-based public policies, many experts in disability studies have observed, help make members of the nondisabled society feel good about themselves.

Although political scientists consider the U.S.'s welfare state weak in comparison with its European counterparts, this charitable path would not have been out of character with American disability policy history. After all, one of the first national welfare state social policies involved giving pensions to Civil War veterans and their dependents.[32] Until the 1950s, most policies that provided benefits to persons with disabilities were modeled on veterans' benefits, which were based on the principles of charity and designed to honor the "deservingly disabled."

The drafters of the ADA, however, followed neither the medical nor the charity model. Instead, the legislative authors modeled Section 504, which created the blueprint for the ADA, after Title VI of the Civil Rights Act.[33] The civil rights model, however, does not adequately describe the ADA provisions. Civil rights laws offer women and people of color negative rather than positive rights. That is, the legislation protects them from discrimination, but it does not mandate that an employer offer women and people of color anything substantive like a reasonable accommodation.

By contrast, affirmative action policies do give people of color a positive right. These policies provide that if a person from an unprotected class and one from a protected class are equal, an employer should hire the latter. Yet, the analogy between affirmative action and reasonable accommodations does not hold. In 1985, the Supreme Court held that reasonable accommodations were not tantamount to affirmative action.[34]

The ADA is therefore a unique piece of legislation. It recognizes both the individual and the needs that this individual has, instead of categorically giving him or her an identity. It offers an expansive definition of disability in a way that few activists predicted would be opposed by the courts.[35] The fact that these courts have not created their own medical definition—while not letting more persons with disabilities prevail—shows that the medical model path has been closed off. The ADA should therefore be viewed as an ideology that has had an effect on legal practices and discourses about persons with disabilities. The path this legislation has taken will affect future pieces of disability rights legislation, although the American polity is still in the midst of determining what a disability actually is. Equally important, the ADA could have an impact on other rights laws and policies like those affecting transsexuals or the identities of those who are affected by high-tech medical procedures.

## A Functional Ideology

The ADA is the first federal statute that recognizes that someone's identity must be assessed individually and how this identity can change. This represents a significant departure from other civil rights laws, which are based on racial and gender binaries. Part of a vanguard, the ADA should be placed in context with the move away from such binaries as white and black, or male and female, toward the intersecting and dynamic identities that activists in other social movements have sought. Since the ADA's passage in 1990, activists fighting for the rights of transsexuals, intersexuals, and multiracial identities have all fought for a less static conception of identity than other groups pursuing civil rights.

The definition of a disability, which cuts across all the ADA's substantive provisions, has liberated persons with disabilities from what could be described as an identity box. This definition sends a bold message to physicians and rehabilitation experts who helped categorize and label persons with disabilities throughout the nineteenth and twentieth centuries. Some activists have gone so far as to argue that this legislation gave persons with disabilities their human rights or their dignity as human beings.[36]

To be sure, lawyers might call upon physicians, psychiatrists, and rehabilitation experts to provide evidence of how a physical or mental impairment substantially limits the life of a person with a disability. Nonetheless, these experts have lost their monopoly power. The ADA does not make persons with disabilities solely dependent on diagnoses rendered by medical or rehabilitation experts. Persons with disabilities have their own voice and their own agency when they address a school official or a judge in a courtroom. What this means for those people who are employed or are seeking employment is that employers must individually assess how a physical or mental impairment affects their substantial life activities. The person is no longer defined by his or her condition, illness, or injury.

When the ADA first became law in 1990, neither the business community nor the disability rights community realized its potential. The federal courts, however, recognized it immediately, and set out to dramatically decrease the number of persons eligible for protection under the law by rendering a narrow interpretation of the definition of a disability.[37] Most importantly, the Supreme Court perceived the employment provisions in the ADA as an attack on managerial prerogative power, going so far as to hold that an employer can refuse to hire someone with limiting, but not substantially limiting, disabilities.[38] As Justice Sandra Day O'Connor ruled in the lead case, *Sutton*, about the ADA's employment provisions:

> An employer is free to decide that physical characteristics or medical conditions that do not rise to the level of an impairment—such as one's height, build, or singing voice—are preferable to others, just as it is free to decide that some limiting, but not *substantially* limiting, impairments make individuals less than ideally suited for a job.[39]

Instead of providing antidiscrimination protection, the Supreme Court and many lower federal courts have turned the employment provisions on their head, giving employers cause for letting someone go.

While the federal courts' interpretation of the statute's definition of disability has limited the recourse that persons with disabilities have against employment discrimination, their rulings have produced some odd results regarding identity. These results show how the statute has framed the debate about disability. The federal judiciary has not discouraged people with nontraditional disabilities, like those with back injuries, from pursuing litigation under Title I. In fact, the functional definition that the Supreme Court used to restrict disabled persons opened the door to people with nontraditional disabilities, particularly around reproductive issues. The judiciary has not underscored a division between traditional and nontraditional disabilities or "deserving" and "undeserving" persons with disabilities.

This stems in part from the fact that the ADA is based on a functional definition of a disability. This means that someone has a disability by virtue of what he or she can or cannot do, not by what medical category the physical or mental condition falls into. When the Supreme Court increased the threshold of what one must not be able to do to be perceived as having a disability, it relied on categories that were almost absolute. If a store clerk using crutches could get around a workplace, he or she might be deemed to have no disability and therefore would not be entitled to take a shortcut through the store open only to management; yet someone with a disease that meant he or she could not procreate without infecting his or her offspring was regarded as having a disability. People with asymptomatic human immunodeficiency virus (HIV) and hepatitis C, for instance, are considered disabled, whereas someone with cerebral palsy is not.[40] This definition captures the fluidity of an individual's corporeality, undermining the idea that identities are static or fixed.

Persons with similar disabilities do not all receive the same accommodations. Employees who use wheelchairs do not necessarily receive desks adjusted to the height of their chairs. One employee, for instance, might not use a desk at all. Every "body" is unique.

## PART II: An Inclusive Statute

### Open Doors

Rather than undermining or making light of persons with disabilities, extending the breadth of the definition of a disability creates an opportunity for activists to open a discussion about the universal nature of human impairment. The disability rights movement has a long history of supporting a sociopolitical or a socially constructed definition of a disability rather than a medical one. Feminists and disability rights experts could well work to include temporary disabilities, like pregnancy, in the definition. The federal courts could recognize new people with three types of health needs as having a disability under the ADA. An expansive functional interpretation of disability could make them applicable for coverage under the law. These three groups could join forces with the disability rights movement, thereby opening the door to the idea that all people are temporarily able-bodied.

### Door Number 1: An Ethic of Maternal Care

In the U.S., women composed nearly half of the work force by the late 1990s.[41] Almost 75 percent of all women work outside the home.[42] Many women work up until two weeks before giving birth. Most companies allow women to use their sick leave policies to cover part of their maternity leave. However, after the birth, the health of the mother and that of the child are considered distinct. Physicians give new mothers six weeks to recover from the birth. What the baby needs from the mother beyond that period is no longer taken into account.

In 1993, President Bill Clinton and Congress passed the Family Medical Leave Act (FMLA) giving women *and* men 12 weeks of unpaid leave to take care of a child or another family member. Essentially, this leave means that an employer cannot fire someone who takes it.[43] Before this legislation passed, the federal courts would not recognize a woman's request for maternity leave. As law professors Stewart Schwab and Steven Willborn describe, the court ruled that an employee could not "dictate managerial decisions affecting the employment relationship."[44]

Despite the FMLA, many new mothers return to work after the six-week medical leave since they cannot afford an extended unpaid leave. "For every woman who quits her job after childbirth," said one reporter, "four return."[45] Furthermore, not all women have their six weeks pregnancy leave covered since they do not have that much sick pay.

Meanwhile, the pediatricians caring for the babies urge women to nurse them for six months because of the long-term health benefits associated with breast milk. Pumping breast milk at work is therefore an option that most women would prefer existed; yet what many women find is that there is no private place to pump the milk. The one existing room that provides privacy is a restroom. While many women resort to using this room, it is unhygienic.

But what recourse do women have to help them balance the demands of new motherhood and work? The FMLA permits women and men to exit, but does not alter, the workplace. Moreover, the federal courts have found no protection under Title VII of the Civil Rights Act for breastfeeding women.[46] "The courts' hostility to accommodation in these cases," Schwab and Willborn maintain, "contrasts sharply with the serious way in which courts in ADA cases investigate whether employers can alter job schedules to accommodate workers with disabilities."[47] The reasonable accommodations model of discrimination helps women feminize the workplace by creating private places for them to breast pump. This physical place links the woman's health with that of the child, creating a very expansive notion of accommodations based upon physical needs. Creating the space for one nursing employee, employers could not deny it to others.

### Door Number 2: An Aging Work Force

Americans live longer than ever before. Medical technology has increased life expectancy dramatically. In 1790, only 2 percent of the population was over the age of 65. By 1890, this figure had doubled to 4 percent. However, by 1990, the number of people living past 65 had tripled to 12.6 percent. This figure is expected to double again in another sixty years.[48]

Despite these increases in human longevity, Americans do not work longer. Some scholars anticipate that by 2030, 167 million workers will support 82 million retirees on Social Security, which is almost a two-to-one ratio of employee to retiree. This represents a dramatic increase since 1960, when 73 million workers supported 14 million retirees, just under a five-to-one ratio.[49]

These data also show that American employees retire earlier than ever before.[50] The number of workers 65 years of age or older has declined by 40 percent—from 70 to 30 percent—from 1950 to 1990. Less than 15 percent of those over 65 return to or seek employment.[51] The irony about those who stay longer in the work force is that they do not have the broadest training. Rather, they are those in manual occupations who could be replaced more easily by younger workers.[52]

Anticipating the burden this will impose on the Social Security program, the federal government raised the age at which someone qualifies for full benefits from 65 to 68 years of age. Convinced that this increase was not enough, Alan Greenspan, chairman of the Federal Reserve Board, maintains that it must be increased to 70. Meanwhile, the American Academy of Actuaries recommends that the retirement age be raised to 73.[53]

Industry also recognizes this change in U.S. demographics and the relatively new pattern of early retirement as a crisis in the making. For instance, Judith Mazo, a senior vice president at the Segal Corporation, said that "manufacturers will have to come up with incentives to keep people from retiring."[54] Going further, another executive explained that the business community should create an age-friendly environment to induce employees to remain on the job. What this type of environment included, he explained, are flexible work options such as part-time work, job sharing, flexitime, or telecommuting.[55]

An age-friendly work environment might well convince employees over 60 years of age to stay in the work force longer. As one management study showed, between the ages of 40 and 49, workers value money first. These workers ranked enjoyment and usefulness second and third, respectively. This ranking changes, however, when employees prepare to exit the work force. Between the ages of 50 and 59, employees suggested that enjoyment at work comes first, with their salary dropping to last.[56] A work environment that suits the needs of older workers, like providing them with flexitime or part-time work, would enhance their enjoyment.

In 1967, President Lyndon Baines Johnson and Congress passed the Age Discrimination Employment Act (ADEA) to combat the prejudice that employers might harbor against older workers. "Half or more male workers lost ground as they aged from their 30s into their 40s, 50s, and 60s," observed economist Jeff Madrick, and to be sure, employers discriminate against workers in their fifties and sixties.[57] Many managers believe that "aging workers are less competent with technology" in addition to being less flexible and having less potential for learning.[58] They also believe that there are greater costs, such as health care, associated with hiring older employees. Identifying older employees with these traits means that the onus is on them to show that they do not have them. One of the items on this list—greater costs associated with employment—is not a perception of a work habit or a trait, but an empirical expense. Employers fear that an older worker's health care premiums could be higher than those of younger workers, driving up the overall costs of the firm. In fact, the ADEA was passed to prevent employers from keeping older employees out of the work force on this basis as well as to counteract prejudice based on stereotypes of older employees.

Whether it is prejudice or higher health care costs, the deficiency within the ADEA is that it does little to alter the workplace, making it an "age friendly" environment. Like other pieces of antidiscrimination legislation, the ADEA offers employees negative rights, protecting the rights of all workers over 40 years of age. Employers cannot discriminate against this group. Like the Civil Rights Act, the ADEA does not mandate that employers make any accommodations that would make it possible for older people to work. Only the ADA provides this option.

Age-related diseases and conditions that inhibit older workers from doing as much as their younger cohorts are already covered under the ADA's employment provisions, yet older workers rarely identify with this legislation and reach out to the disability rights movement.[59] If disability were broadly conceived as a need, so that as workers age they would anticipate receiving reasonable accommodations like flexitime or job sharing under the ADA, more employees might stay in the work force longer.

### Door Number 3: Life's Secrets

The discovery of DNA has increased the pool of people who can be identified as having a genetic predisposition to a disease. Focusing on the promise of finding genetic therapies that can cure diseases like multiple sclerosis or Alzheimer's disease, the Human Genome Project has decoded, mapped, and sequenced all human genes. Indeed, President George W. Bush, an antiabortionist who fought for passage of the ban on partial birth abortions, issued an order accepting some stem cell research because of the promise of curative genetic therapies.[60]

Knowing that someone has a genetic predisposition toward a disease makes this person vulnerable to discrimination in the workplace. While no national legislation exists, all 50 states have some antidiscrimination legislation that both employers and insurance companies must abide by.[61] However, given that genes are inherited traits, knowledge about mutant genes opens up a whole family to job discrimination. What is more, scientists have already found correlations between gene mutations and specific ethnic communities. Thus Africans and African-Americans have a genetic predisposition toward sickle cell anemia.[62] The number of correlations will undoubtedly increase as scientists discover more races and ethnic groups that are predisposed to genes that cause certain diseases, and many employers conscious of keeping down their health benefits might well discriminate against individuals from these communities.

The whole issue of genetic testing—prenatal and postnatal screening—raises issues about society's emphasis on perfection. As law professor Deborah Hellman recently argued, the practice of basing insurance and employment on genetic traits implies that some people have "intrinsic flaws that render them less good, less worthy and less fit to be part of our community."[63] To better understand the ramifications that genetic testing will have on the ADA, the issue itself should be explored.

While no therapy has worked thus far, the Human Genome Project has produced a number of genetic susceptibility tests that do screen mutations. Huntington's disease, a rare inherited autosomal dominant neurodegenerative condition that develops in midlife with no cure, was the first disease that genetic testing spotted.[64] At present, genetic testing can identify 400 conditions. Prenatal testing screens everything from Tay-Sachs disease to a genetic mutation that gives someone an extra finger.[65]

The tests that affect the most people are arguably those that screen for breast and ovarian cancer. Approximately 5 to 10 percent of these cases are inherited, with 50 percent as a result of the mutation of one of two genes. Eighty to 85 percent of those with the gene for breast cancer and 30 to 60 percent of those with the gene for ovarian cancer will get sick.[66] There is also a correlation with certain ethnic groups. The Ashkenazi Jewish community, for instance, has a high rate of breast/ovarian cancer susceptibility.[67]

The benefits of genetic testing are not universal, however. Prenatal genetic screening gives parents information that could convince them to terminate a pregnancy. It is not an unwanted pregnancy, the disability studies expert Adrienne Asch elaborates, but an unwanted child that is at issue. Hence, the interests of the fetus and the parents can be at odds. Disability rights lawyer and activist Harriet McBride Johnson, for example, argues that if genetic screening existed when she was just a fetus, her mother might well have aborted her.[68] Turning her very existence into a powerful political statement, Johnson speaks out on behalf of a fetus's right to live. In fact, prenatal testing raises concerns about eugenics. Many countries use ultrasound equipment for sex selection, mainly aborting females. In Mumbai, India, one study showed that of 8,000 abortions, 7,997 were female.[69] What is more, the large number of abortions has caused the number of children with Down syndrome to decline in the U.S. from 15 to 10 of 10,000 births.[70]

Clearly, eugenics—the strategy to orchestrate human evolution through programs aimed at encouraging the transmission of "desirable" traits and discouraging the transmission of "undesirable" ones—is practiced in the U.S. The difference between eugenics today and what occurred in the early twentieth century is the absence of state sanction. Women decide to undergo prenatal genetic screening. If the screening yields positive results, they determine whether or not to bear a child with Down syndrome. This said, however, the women in this position are not making this decision alone. Genetic counselors, physicians, and insurance companies provide both the mother and the father with information about genetic diseases and conditions. Although the genetic counselors are instructed to offer "neutral" information, Hellman argues "The fact that prenatal testing programs exist and are common suggests that the 'normal' response to a positive test result for disability is abortion."[71]

One of the primary problems with prenatal screening is that it fosters a society based on what the ethicist Kelly Childress calls the "perfect child syndrome." As she elaborates, this type of society "buys into the mistaken idea that human dignity and worth is dependent upon the state of one's genetic 'health.' "[72] As disability studies expert Marsha Saxton explains, genetic screening claims that it is "better not to exist than to have a disability."[73]

Diagnostic investigation raises questions about the status of the fetus, parental rights, and essentially an understanding of the normality/abnormality binary. Without delving any further into this complex controversy, genetic testing can show people who previously thought that they were able-bodied that they may well become debilitated further on in life by the specific condition or disease detected. For those with diseases that can be cured, like ovarian and breast cancer, the tests can forewarn those with the mutated genes. Having this knowledge in advance can increase someone's chances of "beating the odds."

More importantly, how much control does the person with a genetic mutation have over this information?[74] Information about one family member affects the entire family. In Hong Kong, for instance, a court ruled that it was unlawful for the civil service to discriminate in employment against persons with a family history of mental illness.[75] This is not just a concern for people outside the U.S. In 1996, an insurance company threatened to cancel a family's insurance because one of the children had a genetic disorder that causes mental retardation.[76] Taking this one step further, another insurance company demanded that a woman abort a fetus with the gene for cystic fibrosis. The Health Management Organization (HMO) argued that the mother must have the abortion or it would no longer insure the family. The HMO justified its position by stating that it had already covered one child in the family with cystic fibrosis. Only after the family threatened legal action did the HMO drop its demand for terminating the pregnancy.[77]

Since specific ethnic identities can be associated with certain mutations, how will this information affect these groups? While Ashkenazi Jews can obtain vital information that could help them fight ovarian and breast cancer, will employers concerned about increased health insurance premiums decide they can ill afford to hire women from this community?

The U.S. is an anomaly in the industrialized world in that it lacks universal health care.[78] This not only has consequences for one's individual health, but also affects how larger issues like genetic screening and eugenics are decided. There is a four-way relationship between private insurance companies, employers, and employees, as well as their dependants receiving health care. One way of ensuring that the issues surrounding this complicated relationship are addressed—short of enacting universal health care—is to better utilize the ADA to help direct the routine activities of those in the workplace.

With health and employment intertwined in the U.S., the laissez-faire notion that the workplace and the home constitute two independent, private spheres no longer rings true: employer-paid health care links the two spheres. State and federal governments must take this linkage into account. This becomes most apparent when health insurance companies raise the issue of cost. It is not that insuring persons with disabilities and specific physical health benefits costs too much, but that insurance companies hope to avoid paying the bills. The question is: Who pays? If persons with disabilities as well as those with genetic mutations or their family members who have not been tested are kept out of the work force given the high cost of health care, who loses? Should insurance companies have the right to rid themselves of this calculable risk? Should Medicare and Medicaid pay the bills? Or should society at large bear the cost?[79]

No national antidiscrimination legislation exists for people with a genetic predisposition to disease. Insurance companies can charge an ill person much higher rates than someone who is not ill. The company obtains this information from a physician who has given the patient medical tests. So how is this information obtained from doctors qualitatively different from the information provided by genetic screening?[80] What is more, the very principle underlying insurance is that companies depend on individually based actuarial rates that predict the likelihood that a given person will use it. They gain their information from the individual's physician. How then is genetic testing any different from other types of medical tests?

The relationship between health insurance and employers means that the greatest fear most Americans have about genetic testing—that the information could be used in discriminatory ways—cannot be allayed. Health insurance companies have a right to medical information and while the employee has certain rights to privacy, they do pass along sensitive information that could make employers think twice about hiring individuals predisposed to certain illnesses. In the current system, the easiest way for someone to make sure that their genetic information is not misused is to refuse all tests. Unless an employer mandates genetic testing, employees can decide against any screening. But as Hellman convincingly shows, if people reject using this technology it will undoubtedly diminish the health benefits provided by the Human Genome Project. Not only will some people deprive themselves of possible therapeutic benefits, but a refusal to participate in genetic research hinders the development of other therapeutic remedies.[81]

Genetic screening is a double-edged sword. On the one hand, it makes people vulnerable to discrimination. On the other hand, genetic testing has tremendous therapeutic potential. Genetic screening places the American state and society in a dilemma. Do the tests make human perfection obtainable? Or will they be used to underscore human imperfection?

This book argues that people with a genetic predisposition to disease should identify with those with disabilities. First, genetic screening shows how many people will encounter a serious condition or illness. Second, genetic testing underscores a desire for a perfect society, which remains an illusion. This desire has consequences in that it fosters a public policymaking atmosphere that is unwelcoming and even hostile about human fragility and imperfection. The desire for the perfect human race also indirectly challenges one of the fundamental issues within an ethic of care—the myth of independence. Finally, with most Americans receiving their health insurance from their employers or the employers of their spouses or parents, genetic testing is a workplace issue. Many of these people will contract illnesses or have injuries that they can live with. Physical and mental conditions and impairments are as varied as the human mind and body.

*Fluidity for Every Body*

The groundbreaking idea behind the functional definition of disability included in the ADA is that it affects persons with temporary or permanent disabilities. The flexibility of the identity of persons with disabilities may well have significant ramifications for other groups of people. In particular, it resonates with the debate that law professors Lani Guinier and Gerald Torres have initiated about political race.[82] As historian Tricia Rose explains, "Political race is not identity politics in the traditional sense ... it is about doing, not about being." Rather than subscribing to the black and white binary, the term "political race" links race to power. This power, moreover, is "not just individual power, but the distribution of resources and the ways in which the distribution of resources are so clearly racialized in an unequal way."[83] The example Rose provides is how a white working-class person incorrectly assumes that he or she profits from being white. "[I]n fact," she explains, "a white, working-class person ... would not be reaping those benefits" if he or she lives in the African-American neighborhood that has poorly funded schools. Just as the ADA is both functional and universal, so is the concept of political race.

Similarly, the debate about transsexualism, which is not about sexual orientation, but rather sexual identity, undermines the male/female gender binary.[84] "The United States," law professor Jennifer Marie Albright explains, "has always adhered to a system of sex binaries as a way of classifying individuals."[85] "Transsexuals," she continues "are people who feel that their physical gender attributes do not reflect their internal gender identification." For this reason, many transsexuals "seek to align their 'inner self' with their 'outer self' through hormone treatments, psychological therapy, and surgical procedures."[86] The state courts, however, have been reluctant to recognize a postoperative female's identity, rejecting her request to change her male birth identity.[87] Meanwhile, some federal courts have issued mixed rulings, allowing postoperative females some protection from discrimination under Title VII of the Civil Rights Act.[88]

Unlike the concept of political race, the transsexual identity debate does not follow a liberal/conservative continuum. It has different political implications; for example, since a transsexual can have an outward appearance of marrying someone of the same sex, because the birth identity has not changed, this marriage would be legal.[89] To avoid this problem, two states—Florida and Texas—have allowed licensed lesbian transsexual marriages.[90] Meanwhile, other state courts suggest that a transsexual marriage that appears to be an opposite sex marriage can be declared null and void on the basis of its being a same sex marriage, which is prohibited in 48 states.[91]

The transsexual movement rejects the idea that sex or gender is biological. Law professor Katherine Franke argues that sex is regarded as a product of nature, while gender is understood as a function of culture, and that "we must consider the social processes that construct and make coherent the categories male and female." The body, she argues, is "not an independent biological given which emits its own meaning but a socially constructed organism to which meaning is assigned through interpretation."[92] People should have the right to change their legal identity to reflect their inner nature.

Another sexual category that has emerged in the 1990s is intersexuals. This term describes the 1 in 2,000 people who are born with ambiguous genitalia.[93] By the 1990s, a small movement of intersexuals formed to protest against the operations their parents and physicians had them undergo to assign their identity when they were toddlers. Beginning in the 1950s, medical experts decided that children born with this type of genitalia should have one set of sexual organs removed before they reached the age of two. The children, they argued, would accept their sexual assignment, possibly not even knowing their own medical history. However, research completed in the 1990s demonstrated that this assumption was wrong. Some of the adults who had been operated on as children demanded that a moratorium against this type of surgery be instituted for all intersexual children born in the future.[94]

Like transsexuals, intersexuals argue that they must have the right to decide their own identity. According to law professor Julie Greenberg, gender should not be lumped into just two boxes. The gender categories of "male and female," she writes, "occupy the two ends of the poles, and a number of intersexed conditions exist between the two poles."[95]

Finally, the very identity of who is human has come into question since the 1973 *Roe v. Wade* decision written by Supreme Court Justice Harry Blackmun. This liberal member of the Court brought into play the idea that scientific and medical breakthroughs help define legal categories in the abortion debate by demarcating the line between what is human and what is a fetus. In the thirty years since Blackmun rendered this opinion, scientific breakthroughs in surrogacy, artificial insemination, *in vitro* fertilization, and cloning have made many state and federal lawmakers question earlier assumptions about the fixed identity of a human being.[96]

While legislation concerning abortion does raise the question of when a fetus becomes a person, no federal statutes make any references to political race or the rights of transsexuals or intersexuals. It was the ADA that introduced the notion that a federal statute could individually assess someone's identity. When the lower federal courts and the Supreme Court began interpreting the ADA's definition of a disability, instead of making the individual assessment categorical, the judges and justices on these courts made it more functional.

If the stigma associated with these variations in the human mind and body is removed, persons with and without disabilities might be able to recognize disability rights for what they are: a means of making employers address their individual needs in the present and the future. A broad definition of disability could give those with and without disabilities more control over their lives at work and help extend an ethic of care to the workplace.

## PART III: Dynamic Needs

### Each According to Her Needs

As a statute, the ADA introduced the idea that identity is not staid and static. Another way that the statute itself is constitutive of ideology is how it has affected workplace dynamics. Employers must take into account the individuality of employees and employees must use this information to engage in an interactive process with employers that could alter the context of the workplace.

Introducing a dynamic concept of need into the workplace, the ADA's employment provisions cover virtually every workplace, since any office, shop, or factory with over 15 employees must follow it.[97] These employment provisions provide that an employee or prospective employee cannot be discriminated against because he or she has a physical or mental impairment. Because making a workplace accessible typically requires accommodations, this right is not a negative one. An employer must provide some *thing*—an accommodation—that transforms this right into a positive or substantive civil right. Employers must accommodate employees on the basis of their individual needs. Rather than creating a rationalized workplace that is staffed by standardized bodies, the individual peculiarities of all people could be addressed.

Accommodations take many forms. They can be goods or products, such as a special computer keyboard for someone with carpal tunnel syndrome or a scanner that reads text for an employee with vision problems. They can also be specially modified work conditions. A worker who has suffered a head trauma may need a day shift because he cannot drive and the bus system does not run at night. Since the human body itself is variable, accommodations can vary and take different forms as someone's needs can change over time.

What makes the ADA not about disability per se, but about *needs*, stems from the fact that this statute insists on matching a person's condition with his or her accommodations. As discussed in the last section, the law does not use classifications or categories like other civil rights legislation does. Instead, the ADA's employment provisions are based on an "individualized assessment" of each person's situation.[98]

*An Interactive Workplace*

Although a physical or mental impairment is individual, organic, and socially constructed, accommodations made for one person can benefit others. Recognizing the physical or mental individuality of a person does not mean that the solution that makes a place accessible—the accommodation—must be constructed for each individual. The wheelchair need not be invented and reinvented. While the ADA rests on the idea of an employer and an employee understanding needs after an individualized assessment, nothing prevents the accommodations devised from helping the entire work force.

Given the ADA's capacity to transform the workplace, the authors who drafted this legislation realized that they must delineate carefully who should have the power to determine someone's condition and his or her needs. On the one hand, if this power rests solely in the hands of employers or prospective employers, they might figure that few persons with physical or mental impairments could be fitted with accommodations because of the cost. On the other hand, if the ADA offered employees a unilateral means of gaining reasonable accommodations, some employees might inflate their needs. Most important, the creators of the law based their version on the premise that employers, not employees, have a better understanding of what is available. An employee might not understand what accommodations could be made and ask for too little help in the workplace.[99]

To circumvent the problems associated with giving either side unilateral power, the ADA's employment provisions establish an "interactive process."[100] That is, both employers and employees must consult with each other about what reasonable accommodations are necessary. Ultimately, the two parties negotiate about what accommodations an employer can provide the employee without imposing any "undue hardship" on the firm or company.

The term "undue hardship" has nothing to do with the actual expense of a particular accommodation. The authors of the ADA were very careful to explain that undue hardship means that the accommodation must not put a company or business into financial peril.[101] This means that large corporations, which employ 41 percent of the private work force, would have great difficulty proving that an accommodation caused them undue hardship.[102]

Another operative term is "essential functions."[103] Not all tasks that an employee performs, the ADA provides, are essential. A professor must teach, but does this mean that he or she must write on a blackboard? This same professor must attend committee meetings, but must he or she take notes at the meeting like everyone else? Together, the employee and the employer delineate what are a job's essential and nonessential duties.

Whereas the nonessential duties can be modified or even excluded, the essential duties cannot.

Yet, how can employers and employees separate the wheat from the chaff in terms of essential duties? Employers must share information about the entire production process or the logic of how an office operates. People requesting reasonable accommodations have the chance to scrutinize all workplace practices to help determine what is essential and what is not. For instance, when a lawyer with diabetes asked if she could arrive one hour later than her colleagues to ensure that she had the requisite sleep for her to manage her disease, both she and her firm analyzed how the hours of operation affected the entire practice. Was her presence at a set hour in the morning an essential or a nonessential duty? The firm was concerned that other lawyers, too, would ask for more flexible hours. But, the federal court decided that the arrival time was not essential.[104]

Requests for reasonable accommodations give persons with disabilities the authority to evaluate and assess the logic underlying work conditions. Thus, the ADA would be making employers address the human needs of all employees, not just those with disabilities. The employment provisions would require employers to treat their employees as individuals or human beings, not units of production necessary for maintaining and increasing profits. Put differently, a standard that juxtaposes difference and similarity actually means that there is no standard. What will be called a standard of difference could compel employers to change one of the fundamental issues about need that is counter to the whole concept of capitalism.

A number of decisions in the lower federal courts have set legal precedents that have imposed a significant duty on employers to provide accommodations. Federal court judges have done so by arguing that requests for accommodations trigger an "interactive process" between an employer and an employee. First, the courts have ruled that an employer must accommodate a person with whatever tools, equipment, or schedules that he or she needs to fulfill his or her job.

Second, if a person with a disability can no longer perform the essential functions of a position, an employer must reassign him or her to a new position.[105] As long as a reassignment does not mean that a disabled person receives a promotion or that a job was created specifically for him or her, an employer must retain this employee. It is then the employee's decision whether or not to accept the new job. This reassignment could also involve a demotion in terms of pay or status. An employee, for instance, might decide to work only on a part-time basis.

Third, the federal courts have ruled that it is the employer's decision, not just the employee's, to anticipate the employee's needs. While the employer can act only on the basis of information, a company must help to accommodate an employee. Federal court judges assume that employers are much more knowledgeable about the type of accommodations that could be made.[106]

Overall, although the federal courts have limited who is legally disabled and therefore deserving of antidiscrimination protection under the ADA, they have offered an expansive notion of what it means to have reasonable accommodations. The idea that accommodations must cause a company undue hardship, as the federal courts have interpreted it, means that the accommodation must put a business or a company in absolute financial peril. The interactive process, therefore, has retained its potential to provide those who qualify for protection under the ADA with comprehensive reasonable accommodations.

## PART IV: Existing Legal Protection

### Hierarchies in Common Law

Giving persons with disabilities power through an interactive process in the workplace represents a significant departure from common law in the U.S. The economic rationale for managerial control has been well sustained in common law.[107] Most notably, the employment-at-will doctrine gives managers prerogative power.[108] This legal doctrine, which was developed in England during feudalism, provides that employers have "the right to fire employees for a good reason, a bad reason, or no reason at all."[109]

No other industrialized nation (including the U.K.) uses it today, causing some legal scholars to argue that it shows how hierarchical the American workplace is. As one legal scholar describes, "If employees could be dismissed on a moment's notice, obviously they could not claim a voice in the determination of work or the use of the product of their labor. . . . Employment-at-will," he elaborated, "is the ultimate guarantor of the capitalist's authority over the worker."[110]

Ironically, the group of people who chipped away at this common law precedent was not women or people of color, but white men in mid-level white-collar business positions. Beginning in the 1960s, the courts modified the employment-at-will doctrine, providing reasons for common law exceptions. If a personnel handbook, for instance, created some system about hiring and promotions, an employer could no longer fire an employee willy-nilly or without cause.[111]

Employment-at-will has been most affected by the public policy exception. Since the 1960s, 40 states have adopted the public policy exception, which does not allow employers to fire employees if it "jeopardizes a specific public policy interest of the state." These exceptions are broken down into three categories. First, an employee cannot be dismissed if he or she refuses to "commit unlawful acts such as perjury and antitrust violations."[112] Second, an employee cannot be terminated for performing significant public obligations such as jury duty or whistle-blowing. Third, an employer cannot terminate an employee for using an employment statute such as workers' compensation or joining a union.

In the 1990s, employers began gaining ground in enforcing the employment-at-will doctrine again in the courts. Many judges gave employers the discretion to terminate people under this doctrine by allowing them to include at-will clauses in hiring contracts or in personnel handbooks.[113] Hence, the employment-at-will doctrine remains strong, although employers have made some concessions.

## Humanizing Capitalism under the Social Welfare State Statutes

Although employment-at-will still stands, employers have lost some discretion in the workplace during the twentieth century with the passage of labor and civil rights statutes. These statutes were passed rather late in the century in comparison to those passed by European nation states. The U.S. has never had a strong welfare state and few social policies have been enacted that have helped humanize capitalism. Most notably, the Fair Labor Standards Act (FLSA) of 1938 set minimum wages and maximum hours and imposed limits on child labor. In 1970, the Occupational Safety and Health Act (OSHA) became law, safeguarding workers from occupational hazards. Also, the Civil Rights Act of 1964 limited the reach of the employment-at-will doctrine prohibiting employers from dismissing workers on account of race or gender.

None of these laws, however, provides the individual with a power structure for negotiating with an employer.[114] First, the FLSA and the OSHA are enfeebled by a weak administrative structure that leaves a person who underscores problems in the workplace vulnerable to an employer's discretion. For this reason, few suits (if any) are initiated by employees themselves. This indicates that the power differential between the employer and the employee has not been addressed seriously. If workers blow the whistle on unsafe work conditions or minimum wage violations, their employers will discover their identities during the trial and most likely terminate them. In fact, the FLSA and the OSHA enforcement agencies are so weak that administrators concede that workers have reason to fear employer retaliation.[115]

Second, although the Civil Rights Act has produced more litigants, this law does not interfere with the nature of the hierarchical relationship between employers and workers.[116] Instead, civil rights laws eliminate two particular reasons that an employer could otherwise use as cause for 1termination. An employer still retains the prerogative to fire employees as long as they were not targeted because of their race or gender.[117]

What is more, the Equal Employment Opportunity Commission (EEOC), which enforces the Civil Rights Act, is a notoriously weak agency since it relies on the federal courts for enforcement. The EEOC can pursue its own cases, but it depends on funding from each administration. Those in a Republican administration, for instance, who are less eager to pursue civil rights, may keep the EEOC's funding low, limiting its ability to try cases for plaintiffs who cannot afford to do so on their own.

While women have gained entrance into the workplace, they have not fully succeeded in "feminizing" the employment context or changing the culture to reflect women's concerns. Issues unique to women like childbirth, or that have disproportionately fallen to women, like childcare and elderly care, are rarely reflected in the workplace's overall atmosphere. Asking for an extended lunch hour to solve a childcare problem might be considered more of an infraction than leaving early for a baseball game.

## PART V: The ADA's Collective Capacity

### Collective Bargaining Power

The one statute that does provide employees with bargaining power is the National Labor Relations Act (NLRA), which was enacted in 1935 to give workers the ability to fight for better work conditions with collective bargaining. As a result, labor unions played a vital role in speaking on behalf of workers. The workers they represented, however, were primarily white males. Unions have a long history of ignoring, or providing inadequate representation to, the nonwhite minority and women. "For much of their history, unions legally and ideologically reflected an image of a universalized worker—generally thought to be [a] white, married, male, blue collar employee, the kind of employee who constituted the actual majority of male union members," write law professors Molly McUsic and Michael Selmi.[118]

How much organized labor's checkered history can be attributed to the structure of American labor laws is open to debate. Majority rule constitutes the most fundamental operating principle underlying the American collective bargaining process. In McUsic's and Selmi's words, this process is a "form of democratic self-government by management and labor complete with legislative principles, including the principle of majority rule. Just as an individual must accept the political candidate approved by the majority of voters, the representative selected by a majority of employees was to provide the exclusive avenue through which employees would advance their interests against management. As a result, the interests of individual workers are to be reflected through the majority interests, and individual works were likewise expected to place the good of the worker community above whatever individual interests they might have."[119]

Unionization based on the majority rule principle had structural difficulties fostering difference in the workplace.[120] "To some extent it should come as little surprise that unions catered to a model worker given that labor law was originally premised on the notion that unions would operate as mini-legislatures." Nonetheless, McUsic and Selmi argue that the "unions' alignment with the interest of majority male members sometimes led to passive acceptance or even active participation in [the] sexual harassment of women workers."[121] The structural constraints of the NLRA clearly cannot account for all of its difficulties in representing women and people of color.

American unions also had difficulty recognizing different worker needs since, as Iris Marion Young describes, unions do not concentrate on the "work process itself."[122] Unlike many European unions, American unions decided against asking for concessions from management to help control the labor process. Going back to the 1920s, most union leaders took the position that management, not organized labor, controlled the labor process. Instead, American unions have fought for personnel rules such as seniority systems that do not specify how a job is completed, but rather who will fill the job. Organized labor helped management discipline the work force by depersonalizing the personnel system after World War II. Seniority systems helped in this by articulating job descriptions and then having a person fit the job according to their level of competency, training, and seniority.

This ignoble history of the American labor movement, however, is just that—a history. If the labor movement is transformed, organized labor could help women and people of color. Under the leadership of John Sweeney, the American Federation of Labor–Congress of Industrial Organizations (AFL-CIO) has been conducting a campaign to organize women and people of color. In fact, these two groups now have the highest rates of unionization, surpassing white men.

Organized labor could also help implement the ADA. While this law is a civil rights law, protecting individuals, unions could represent these individuals. This legislation has employers accommodating persons with disabilities on an individual level, but there is nothing prohibiting the collective from asking for similar treatment. Indeed, persons with disabilities could become transformative agents or *agents provocateurs*, forging their way for the collective. Unlike the provocateurs of the early twentieth century, who threw a strike into chaos, helping defeat a union, these agents would work for their colleagues, gathering information and creating precedents that could help their able-bodied colleagues as well as themselves.

## "Cripples" and Counterpower

In the early and late twentieth century, resistance takes different forms. Michel Foucault's work on control and resistance best describes the role persons with disabilities could adopt within this new type of unionism. This notion represents the very heart of his sketchy theory of liberation. Not deviating from the rest of his *oeuvre*, Foucault's theory of liberation offers no universal conception of human nature. Like power, resistance is a social construction—that is, it cannot be perceived as a freestanding category or a universal truth.[123] Both power and resistance must be embedded in specific historical contexts.

Placing a normative theory in historical context makes Foucault unusual. Most normative theories delineate a desired end—a *telos*. Foucault, however, draws no such picture of a utopia. Rather, resistance is fighting against power. It is fighting back without a recipe of what one is fighting for. While Foucault believes that political struggle is essential to free someone, he does not struggle against power to achieve justice, a term bogged down by a universal notion of truth.

Put differently, resistance means that an individual exercises counter-power.[124] Power may have formed disciplined individuals, who are rational, responsible, productive subjects; yet Foucault suggests that their action should not be confused with their nature as human beings. Being an obedient subject does not reflect one's human nature.[125] Given this space, there is a possibility for resistance wherever power is exercised.[126] To Foucault, resistance is also exercised as both an element of the functioning of power and, as Dierter Freundlieb describes it, a "source of its perpetual disorder."[127]

The key to understanding resistance is therefore by understanding how Foucault treats it in conjunction with power. Foucault insists that particular exercises of power should be understood in terms of the resistances they confront, generate, or even promote.[128] Resistance is what eludes the near hegemony of power. As a result, power seeks out resistance, its adversary. For power to minimize resistance, Foucault maintains, it must divide-and-conquer it; or as he explains it, "individualize" the forces of the institutions that it creates. Inequality constitutes an essential element of power. Resistance, by contrast, is associated with an absence of hierarchy. Foucault coins the term "counterpower" as another way to describe resistance. Resistance or counterpower, however, cannot be characterized as antimatter or a negation of power, though Foucault links resistance with horizontal conjunctions and equality. Like power, it can also be productive or affirmative. Resistance relies on strategic knowledge and represents Foucault's ideas of revolutionary action.[129] Resistance is associated with self-creation.[130]

Persons with disabilities are familiar with self-creation since, after all, they have been rejected by the majority culture. Nowhere can this rejection be seen better than in the fact that employers are reluctant to use persons with disabilities for motivational purposes. As Garland-Thomson explains, "People often respond to her [a beautiful woman using a wheelchair] as if this combination of traits were a remarkable and lamentable contradiction."[131] Similarly, Casey Martin, the golfer who greatly compromised his health if he played without a cart, was not viewed as a measure of success. An attorney representing a defendant before the Supreme Court claimed professional athletes who had the HIV virus could not be categorized as legally disabled. How could Earvin "Magic" Johnson, the famous Los Angeles Lakers star, and Greg Louganis, the Olympic diving champion, both of whom have HIV, be called "disabled"?[132] They could be professional athletes or persons with disabilities, not both. Accepting this stereotype, employers anticipate that coworkers either resent or pity workers with disabilities. Whether people sit in wheelchairs, have cancer, or are pregnant, most of them see how their condition separates them from the dominant workplace culture in the U.S.

Standing on the outside looking in, persons with disabilities have not been normalized. They do not hug the middle of the bell-shaped curve of normalcy.[133] Persons with disabilities are widely perceived as abnormal or deviant. They are what the able-bodied use as a measure of their own normalcy. "Constructed as the embodiment of corporeal insufficiency and deviance," elaborated Garland-Thomson, "the physical disabled body becomes a repository for social anxieties about such troubling concerns as vulnerability, control, and identity."[134]

From Foucault's perspective, the disabled body therefore has the capacity to become disobedient.[135] It cannot be standardized or normalized. Thus the ADA's employment provisions can turn persons with disabilities into agents of resistance. Persons with traditional disabilities, working nursing mothers, older workers, workers with a genetic predisposition to a disease, transsexuals, and intersexuals could all band together under the Three Musketeers' cry, "All for one and one for all."

## Creative Differences

The most productive type of disobedience would occur if persons with disabilities scrutinized workplace cultures, questioning the rationale underlying rules and regulations. Persons with disabilities often use alternative means to perform a job. Alternative means, being just that—alternative—call into question how something is done. By overcoming obstacles in the workplace, persons with disabilities learn about the obstacles themselves. The phonograph, for instance, was created for people with visual problems, but long before Thomas Edison invented it, people with these problems had others read to them.[136] Limited by a wide range of physical and mental conditions, persons with permanent or temporary impairments make their accommodations requests and perform their respective jobs differently than their able-bodied colleagues, giving them insight into how to complete a task the "normal" way and a different way.[137]

It is not just what tangible goods or work conditions employers provide employees with disabilities; the interactive process gives these employees the opportunity to comprehend the workings of the entire operation. If employees have the chance to view the electronic panopticon, this offers them insight into the inner workings of an entire office or plant that, if shared, many of their colleagues could benefit from. Once employees began appreciating that power may be spatially decentralized, located in a multitude of desktop computers around an office or factory when it is actually centralized, some of them might be less susceptible to shifting or losing their identity to a company. Access to this information gives employees the ammunition to battle over employee consciousness and consent, as Foucault depicts, or the employees' subjectivity, as labor process theorists describe.

The disobedience of persons with disabilities becomes most apparent by recognizing their triangular relationship with employers and the rest of the able-bodied employees. In the dominant culture, it is the employer and the able-bodied employee who closes ranks against the person with the disability. Just as they do with race, gender, and sexuality, employers often capitalize on perpetuating discrimination toward persons with disabilities.[138] Creating an atmosphere that accepts discriminatory treatment is not in the employer's interest. Rather, employers quickly discover that persons with disabilities threaten workplace normalcy and that cultivating a prejudiced environment is an effective means of undermining them.

Promoting workplace normalcy puts the employer in control. Whether it is vertical control or horizontal control makes little difference. Under vertical control, normalcy means that the workplace is hierarchal, with a long chain of supervisors monitoring their employees' performance. Many workplaces are also heavily rule-oriented with, for instance, seniority systems created by employers specified in personnel handbooks or collective bargaining agreements. Providing reasonable accommodations for disabled people undermines the authority of a supervisor. It also breaks the rules. Why should one person receive an expensive, comfortable, ergonomic office chair, and not another?

By contrast, horizontal control means that the discrimination is based on peer review rather than managerial control. Peer group scrutiny casts a negative glance at persons with disabilities. All members of the team fear that they too will become ill, injured, or infirmed one day. Aside from existential fear or anxiety, peer scrutiny can generate disgust at the perceived weakness of the person with a disability, who represents the weakest link or the person chosen last on the team. As feminists have long noted, the capitalist workplace culture is ultimately a "macho" culture in that it denies any weakness or dependence.[139] Everyone is supposed to be independent, effective, and productive. A manager who acts like a coach cheers on the strong as well as the weak, but relies only on the strong as a measure. It is the idealized or the perfect body that represents the goal.

A Foucauldian perspective about resistance in the workplace shows that the debate is not about abnormal or normal, but about control—the control of the subject. Whereas the employer refashions the rhetoric so that normal bodies become preferential to abnormal ones, it is not the labels, but the use of the labels to gain control that represents the single most vital issue. Employers prefer employees who either have the standard body or strive toward the perfect body to help them make the most profits. This is not to say that they naturally fit the standard, let alone are perfect. Rather, employers prefer that needs that must be satisfied to turn employees' bodies into the standard body be fulfilled at home, in private. As the philosopher Virginia Held explains, "The concept of [the] person selling his labor [must be rethought since it] has been constructed without adequate regard for the labor of those who have created and brought up and continue to care for this worker."[140] It is only the public body—the obedient body—that employers envision working.

From a labor process theory perspective this means that by ignoring their employees' respective needs, employers keep humanity at bay. Alienation and exploitation strip the workplace of its humanity, not because of profits per se, but because the workplace cannot sustain differences between employees. Employers try to keep humanity out by cultivating an artificial atmosphere with their workplace cultures and subcultures.

Applying literature about an ethic of care to the workplace leaves us with the same conclusion. "Feminist theory insists on reconsidering the concept of the person who is to enter into the public life of government or economic activity," Held elaborates. "There are not two or three separate entities here, a public or a working person, and a private person; there is only one person, involved in and affected by both public and private social realities."[141] Fineman also explains that human agency involves a notion of the self that is deeply situated in relationships.[142]

Employers greatly profit from the separation of the public and private spheres. Capitalism insists that the workplace is in the private sphere when it comes to regulation. Employees can act as if they are independent when, in reality, they are dependent on their families or their pocketbooks to pay for services normally rendered by a family member. Whether a spouse irons a shirt so that an employee creates a more professional appearance or the employee himself visits a dry cleaner is irrelevant. The employee's appearance may account, in part, for his or her success, but the employer only recognizes the end product or the outcome. The private American workplace is public, as all private employee concerns are left at home.[143]

## Summary Summaries

Chapter 2 offers a comprehensive definition of the mind and body. Instead of limiting disability to someone with a traditional physical or mental impairment, it throws the doors open, arguing that everybody has needs and that every individual should be viewed as having or potentially having a disability. Offering a historiography of the mind and body, this chapter concludes that Foucault, Deleuze, and Guattari present the most convincing explanation of our corporeality. It explains how Deleuze and Guattari reject the mind/body duality by referring back to the work of Benedict de Spinoza, a monist, who himself rejects René Descartes' epistemology. As a result, these two French critical theorists ask not who a person *is*, but what a mind and body *can do*.

Universalizing a definition of disability so that it embraces our corporeality or animality would create a revolutionary new labor policy, which would constitute a significant departure from both civil rights and labor laws. The employment provisions could be used to extend an ethic of care to a new location—the American workplace. It would place employers in the position of becoming caregivers.

Chapter 3 concludes that an ethic of care could be made universal if this functional definition of the mind and body, which breaks this corporeal binary, were used. An alternate conception of an ethic of care could ensure that all needs—those of men and women alike—should be taken into account. A workplace ethic of care could extend not just to a woman breastfeeding but also to a man with heart disease.

Chapters 4 and 5 present a historical overview of the American workplace to show how an expansive interpretation of the ADA would constitute a radical departure from the past. It underscores how past Taylorist, Fordist, and present neo-Fordist labor processes ignore the individuality of the worker. All three of these processes, it argues, depend on their own mind and body duality, which helps explain the reification and alienation of labor. Chapter 4 shows that American management developed scientific management, transforming the body from a whole—a mind and a body—to a standardized body that managers, being the brains behind the brawn, governed. The workplace normality and rationality that scientific managers created was based on their conception of the average body. The resulting labor process dehumanized the workplace that lives up to an ethic of rights on paper, but not in reality, let alone an ethic of care.

By the mid-1980s managers and management experts could no longer justify the Taylorist and Fordist labor processes with evidence of worker productivity and efficiency, and Neo-Fordism emerged as a result. Chapter 5 illustrates how the labor process itself changed, becoming much more individualized during the information age. Weber's notion of rationality underlying what became known as neo-Fordist labor practices, however, remained the same. Scientific management's principles of standardization created under Taylorism and Fordism have been carried on by machines under neo-Fordism. The latest incarnation of scientific management replaces managers with machines. Employers use new forms of technology that have been used to liberate as well as incarcerate the employees' minds and bodies. The information age supervises workers, turning them into self-disciplined bodies.

Chapters 6 and 7 demonstrate that the technology that allows neo-Fordism management practices to be individualized could be applied to the American workplace. It suggests that a newly conceived notion of unions—group representation with the framework of need provided by the ADA—could liberate American workers. Although employers have helped generate opposition to the ADA, the notion that persons with disabilities have too much power is empowering. Disability rights activists stand at a fork in the road of policy history. They could argue along the old lines supporting the lineage of disability policy rooted in military history—such as war veterans, the "deserving" disabled, having a right to better lives. Alternatively, they can use recent breakthroughs in medicine, science, and technology, which can help differentiate all people, and predict disease according to genes, to make the argument that all people are potentially disabled. Most activists have chosen the latter.[144]

The ADA, moreover, helps shape the legal discourse about the fluidity of our identity. Placed in context with the arguments about women, transsexuals, and the "racially mixed," the legal analogies that contest fixed categories will begin to proliferate. It is doubtful the courts, policymakers, and the public can put persons with disabilities back in restrictive identity boxes. While none of these debates should be viewed from a left/right dichotomy, all of them have critics who argue that they have given the individual too much power. Disability rights litigators advise their clients of the danger of being seen in this position. Employers view power as illegitimate. In one breathtaking step, this reaction shows how the ADA has eradicated the perception of persons with disabilities as helpless wards of the state. As the new story goes, persons with disabilities wield a significant amount of power. This book concludes that this power could be turned into counterpower or resistance, and help employees fight for justice at the workplace.

# CHAPTER 2
# The Life of the Body

The Americans with Disabilities Act's (ADA's) functional definition of disability opens many doors of opportunity for persons with disabilities without being indebted to identity politics. A functional definition of disability takes into account people—their individuality—in terms of their physicality or flesh and blood. To make a reference to the body, however, is not to say much. For the last 30 years, books have been lining library shelves about the consuming body, the flexible body, the tremulous body, the rejected body, the leaky body, the phenomenological body, and the hyper-real body. It was Michel Foucault who proposed the idea that the body could be viewed as a discursive practice.[1] As a result, medical sociologist Simon Williams writes, "A panoply of bodies now litter the field."[2]

This chapter offers its own conception of the body. It shows that disability should not be viewed as an identity, but rather as a condition that shapes how people do things. This condition, moreover, is ever-changing. Few people escape facing it sometime in their lifetime. This is inherent in our organic nature—all people are dying. Hence, the term "disabled" should not be used to characterize the unusual mind or body; it describes what habitually happens to the mind or body. It captures the *human* condition.

This chapter substitutes the term "animality" for "disability" to underscore what is distinctive about a functionalist notion of the mind and body. The term animality makes evident its kinship with the critical theorists Gilles Deleuze's and Felix Guattari's notion of "becoming animal" or "bodily becoming." For them, the critical question is "what can a body do?"

Deleuze and Guattari create a functionalist definition of bodily becoming by rejecting Cartesian dualism. Relying heavily upon the work of the monist, Benedict de Spinoza, they do not distinguish between the mind and the body. They recognize the mind and the body as one continuous substance.[3] For Deleuze and Guattari, the body is both substance and process.[4] As philosopher Eva Kit Wah Man explains, "The body is not part of passive nature ruled by an active mind but rather that the body is the inseparable terrain of human action."[5]

Deleuze's and Guattari's definition of becoming animal, moreover, is not essentialist. Insofar as the body is in process, searching for difference, it is striving. Striving, however, does not mean moving toward something. The body, they contend, has no end, no teleology. Nor is there any judge or measure of what someone *should* be striving for. Becoming animal is not limited by a standard, an average, or a median. Someone is becoming animal by composing music. Composition does not occur if someone is only playing the same notes in another song. Deleuze and Guattari suggest that composition involves putting together a different, infinite array of notes. This is to say that they base *becoming* in movement and difference.[6]

Reconciling Deleuze's and Guattari's definition of becoming animal with human need gives this book a definition of the mind and body as substance and process. To do so, however, this chapter must not only review the work of Spinoza, Deleuze, and Guattari. It also shows how feminism—both ecofeminism and radical feminism—have framed the debate in their search for a nonessentialist, dynamic conception of the mind and body. Moreover, this chapter is particularly indebted to the Australian radical feminists' interpretation of Spinoza, Deleuze, and Guattari. By disentangling the debate between feminism and critical theory, this chapter reveals that needs do not have to be characterized as ends to be fulfilled. They can be based on the individuality of each person or what makes him or her unique; needs are open-ended. Following Deleuze's and Guattari's ideas allows us to capture the "powers and capabilities" of the different mind and body.[7]

## Dueling dualisms

The mind/body relationship has been debated since antiquity. For the most part, the Greek philosophers thought the body interfered with the mind, which they associated with reason. Radical feminist theorist Elizabeth Grosz offers an apt historiography. In the *Cratylus*, Grosz explains that "Plato claim[ed] that the word body (*soma*) was introduced by Orphic priests, who believed that man was a spiritual or noncorporeal being trapped in the body" that they associated with a dungeon (*sema*).[8] Plato viewed matter itself as an "imperfect version of the *Idea*." "The body is a betrayal of, and a prison for," she elaborates, "the soul, reason, or the mind." It was evident to Plato that reason should rule over the body.[9] In a dialogue with Phaedo, Socrates scorned the body, arguing that life is training in death—"separating the soul as much as possible from the body," writes theorist Richard Shusterman "... until it is completely independent."[10]

Plato also gender-typed the body. A woman's "proper function," he argued, was to receive. Women, Plato explained in his discourse on the *hypodoche*, have no inherent shape; they are a receptacle. "The female is a non-living, shapeless non-thing," Man describes, "which cannot even be named, leading to the prohibition of the female body as a human form."[11] This is not to say that Socrates recommended that the body should be ignored or neglected. On the contrary, he suggested that the inescapable truth of human mortality was and should be humbling.[12] Women, it just so happened, were humbled more than men.

Following Plato, Aristotle accepted the duality of mind and body, including the argument that the female signified the body, whereas the male personified reason. In the *chora* in *Timaeus*, for example, he argued that a woman's womb provided shelter for an unborn child. The woman did not help produce it. Like Plato, Aristotle characterized a woman as a receptacle. It was the father who gave shape to the formless matter in the mother's womb.[13] Going one step further, he associated the female with disability, suggesting that she was nothing more than a "mutilated male."[14]

With Christianity the Greek's mind/body dichtomy turned into a discussion about form and matter. The mind and the body represent immortality and mortality, respectively. Christ was a man whose soul came from God. It was Christ's body that became the symbol of our mortality. God sacrificed his son to bring immortality or the living soul into the material world.

Christ's death also made the separation of the sacred and profane decisive. Christians did not view matter or material as sacred since they juxtaposed it with, as cultural theorist William Merrin writes, "transcendent (true) reality." Yet recognizing the world as profane did not render people powerless. The dichotomy between the sacred and the profane convinced Christians to ponder, to reflect, and to meditate. After all, Christ had died for their sins.[15]

Locking form and matter and the sacred and the profane into hierarchical binaries did not mean that Christianity split these binaries into two distinct parts. Monastic asceticism united form and matter. In the Christian tradition of Augustine and Cassian, monastic life centered on the soul's purity and chastity, which could be achieved once the body shed itself of "the evils of the flesh and other worldly vices."[16] Cassian, Benedictine's predecessor in the fourth and fifth centuries, developed a list of eight deadly sins including pride, gluttony, lust, and sloth. He went so far as to link and couple the different sins, weighing them in terms of their causality.

Over the centuries, the body became more and more marked as what theorist Pasi Falk describes as "the seat of human sin."[17] By the Middle Ages, it was thought that a disease such as leprosy was caused by greed or lust. Disease, as Grosz tells us, was "a corporeal signifier of sin."[18]

Christian doctrine, however, kept evolving, transforming the immortal/mortal and sacred/profane dichotomies.[19] One of the most significant transformations occurred when reason began to play a greater role during the Reformation, forever altering the Christian moral code. The list of deadly sins was reduced from eight to three—a lust for money, power, and sex.[20]

Then, during the Enlightenment, the mind/body relationship took on its modern secular form. Unlike the Greek philosophers, René Descartes spurned the notion that the body should inspire any type of humility. "What Descartes accomplished," elaborates Grosz, was not so much the "separation of the mind from the body, which Plato, Aristotle, and other Greek philosophers had established," but rather the separation of "soul from nature."[21] Descartes did so by envisioning two kinds of substances—a thinking substance (*res cogitans* or the mind) and an extended substance (*res extensa* or the body). Only the body could be considered part of nature, however, and therefore, writes Man, "governed by its physical laws and ontological exigencies...."[22]

What is more, the body was placed at the bottom of this hierarchy.[23] Descartes succeeded in linking the mind/body opposition to the foundations of knowledge itself, a link that placed the mind in a position of superiority. The mind, moreover, was "masculine." Like the Greeks, Descartes associated it with all that is "good," like culture, reason, and rationality, whereas he considered the body "feminine," linking it with all that is "bad," such as nature, unreason, and irrationality.[24] Descartes also compared animals to pure bodies, which is to say that they had no capacity for subjectivity. An animal, he argued, could not feel pain. A body, without a mind exercising its capacity for reason, had no agency.[25]

To Descartes, the body was an instrument or a machine at the disposal of consciousness. It was, however, a self-moving machine or a mechanical device, functioning in accordance with the laws of nature and causal laws.[26] He made a comparison between the body and clocks, ropes, church bells, and other mechanistic objects. As both identical and mechanical, this interpretation of the body helped forge a new alliance between science and social authority.

Viewing all bodies as identical opened up a vista for scientific and medical exploration, particularly in biology and anatomy. Rembrandt painted *The Anatomy Lesson of Dr. Tulp*, for instance, to illustrate the linkage between philosophy and science in the seventeenth century.[27] Descartes dominated the first half of seventeenth century by succeeding in the venture of a mathematical, mechanical science, whose first effect it was to devaluate nature by taking away its virtuality or potentiality, any immanent power, any inherent being. Cartesian mental philosophy sprang up alongside Newtonian physics. "Cartesian metaphysics," Deleuze explains, "completes the venture, because it seeks Being outside Nature, in a subject which thinks it and a God who creates it."[28]

It was not only Newtonian physics that was developed alongside Cartesian metaphysics. Empiricism also found absolute, objective truths during the Enlightenment. Empiricism located truths in experience as well as in human sensations. Inductive training, Francis Bacon argued in *Novum Organum*, "open[ed] and establish[ed] a new course for the mind from the first and actual perceptions of the senses themselves."[29]

Scientific discourse aspired to impersonality, which it equated with objectivity. By contrast, the mind, the thinking substance, the soul or consciousness, had no place in the natural world. The mind signified the soul's exclusion from nature or what one author described as an "evacuation of consciousness." While bodies are nearly identical it is "our minds," Descartes proclaimed, that "differentiate us."[30]

Armed with absolute truths, Bacon maintained that science possessed and subjugated nature. Not surprisingly, both he and Descartes exhibited great enthusiasm for exploration and colonial conquest. "Humans are lords and masters of nature," Descartes proclaimed. He linked the life of the mind, not the body, with progress; and progress emanated from human rationality. In the name of medicine and science, the body—be it the body nature or corporeality—was fodder for being scrutinized, pillaged, and plundered.[31]

In the nineteenth century, the association between the mind, the body, and progress took another turn with Charles Darwin's evolutionary theory. In *The Origins of Species*, the body acquired a new status.[32] Social Darwinists (mis)used evolutionary theory to show how a person's outward features gave other people an indication of his or her inner nature. Initially, this finding inspired criminologists, physicians, and biologists to create physiognomical typologies. Alphonse Bertillon and Cesare Lombroso, for example, used Darwin's theory of evolution to develop a phrenology that helped them classify different types of criminals on the basis of their skull measurements.[33] Criminals, they proclaimed, had small heads, whereas bright, reasonable, and law-abiding people had large heads, supposedly housing big brains.

By the early twentieth century, typologies identifying pathologies gave way to those about normality. Having so advanced their methods, doctors and scientists thought they could now assess what constituted the "normal" body type.[34] Not too small, not too big—the average person could be categorized as medium in every way. Overall, the determination that people were normal or abnormal stemmed from Darwin's vision that equated evolution (read progress) with the body, which was then extended to society. Lombroso, for instance, called criminals evolutionary throwbacks. They were "victims of atavism."[35]

Despite its significance for the twentieth century, Darwin's teleological view of progress came out of the nineteenth century. Darwin is influenced by the historian Edward Gibbon's argument about humankind's perpetual quest for improvement. In *Decline and Fall of the Roman Empire*, Gibbon writes, starting out as savages, mankind had "gradually arisen to command the animals."[36]

One of the most significant arguments integral to Darwin's theory of evolution was the idea that humans alone were conscious of the natural order. For him, "pride and its triumphs had their legitimate basis in nature." Human consciousness about the natural order stemmed from the fact that, unlike animals, people have minds. Evolutionary theory created a human-centered view of the world that also could be portrayed as a "Promethean vision of infinite possibilities." God becomes "a distant cause of causes," historian Roy Porter explains. "What counted was man acting in nature."[37] Like Descartes before him, Darwin was a secular humanist. Porter suggests he "painted a wholly optimistic, naturalistic, and thus worldly picture" of society.[38]

## Bourgeois bodies

Darwin's evolutionism, as Porter illustrates, gave the British Enlightenment's bourgeois a "clinching theory of boundless improvement."[39] Yet, bourgeois liberalism in the late nineteenth century put a different face on the Enlightenment with its notion of individualism. It relied on a humanist metaphysics that included concepts like reason, rationality, morality, truth, and human essence.[40] The dark side of human agency, which was supported by both capitalism and evolutionary theory, was that selfishness motivated the rational individual. Human beings were, by nature, self-interested.

While everybody is "in it" for themselves, this does not mean that bourgeois liberalism valued differences. "Individualism," the theorist Alexandra Winter writes, "refers to an ideological position which prioritizes the self over community, [and] assumes a common humanity to which all people should subscribe."[41] Aside from these grand pronouncements, bourgeois liberalism was little concerned with the specificity of nature. It made no suggestions about how natural causes could dictate what ought to be. It emphasized human agency independent of nature. Philosophical concerns addressed only how people represent the world to themselves.[42]

Like all earlier views, bourgeois liberalism insisted that the body was inferior to the mind. It retained the part of the Enlightenment ethos about master embodiment and nature. This type of liberalism animated the idea of making an internal/external distinction about the self.

However, instead of separating the mind from the body, the bourgeois insisted that bodily functions be hidden from public view. The middle class fostered a conception of bodily shame. "Having a lot of shame about our own bodies—and disgust, too, a shrinking from contamination that derives from a deep ambivalence about our own animality and the animal secretions that are such a prominent part of sexual experience—we seek to render our bodies less disturbing; and this frequently involves projecting our own emotions" writes the philosopher Martha Nussbaum.[43]

Put differently, cultural theorist Mary Russo argues that "the grotesque body is open, protruding, extended, secreting ... [as] opposed to the Classical body which is monumental, static, closed, and sleek, corresponding to the aspirations of bourgeois individualism."[44] Richard Twine explains that "*both* the act of compiling physiognomic codes, such as arguing that a particular shape of nose or color of skin relates to a certain personality essence, and changing one's body and general appearance according to a fear of physiognomic judgment, involve a mastering and controlled approach towards the body."[45]

As Russo explains:

> One's measure of human citizenship (for this *read* membership of Western, male, white, bourgeois-defined human identity) was measured in terms of one's ability to distance and deny such bodily functions which implied far too much commonality with the irrational sphere of nature. The disgust and shame of the body, which is unique to human beings, shows how people reject our animal kinship and even subordinate other humans arbitrarily defined as "inferior" to prove our superiority.[46]

Bourgeois liberalism socialized members of its society into believing that "the body is alien and must be cared for, and controlled by, certified agents as are electric wires by electricians, pipes by plumbers."[47] The bourgeois placed the full range of bodily functions under scrutiny. There were feelings of disgust and embarrassment around sneezing, coughing, farting, crying, spitting, menstruating, nose picking, nudity, body proximity, and body odor.

For the bourgeois, the inferiority of women stemmed from the fact that they had so many more bodily functions than men. They have menstruation, gestation, lactation, and labor. The absence of these additional bodily functions, Patricia Foster explains, is what accounts for why men feel superior. In her words, "Women are a major threat to the images of men who are made in the image of God. By her presence, she constantly reminds the male of his vaginal origin, seduction, and animal kinship. A woman conspiring with a snake represents one of our society's most vivid symbols of evil."[48]

While women may have had more bodily functions, the bourgeois defined persons with disabilities by virtue of their mind or body: they were their condition or disease. Bodies were marked by dominant *aesthetic* discourses. As Russo relays, physiognomy constitutes one of the more vital elements in these discourses. Beauty is correlated with virtue, whereas ugliness is tantamount to sinfulness.[50]

The bourgeois, however, turned the idea of the sinful mind and body into an abnormal one. Whereas for gender, the binary is masculine/feminine with masculine on top, for disability it is normal and abnormal, with normal on top. An able/disabled mind and body dualism was created.[51] This dualism can be traced back to the 1850s, when the bourgeois developed the terms "norm," "normal," "normalcy," "normality," "average," and "abnormal." Their definition of the word normal—"Constitution, conforming to, not deviating or differing from the common type or standard, regular, usual"—was used in most European languages. Earlier, normal meant that something was perpendicular or in what was called a carpenter's square. The norm did not exist as a point of comparison or as a means for conformity. The "metric" mode of thinking came about only under nineteenth century bourgeois liberalism.[52]

Before that time, people were measured against the ideal and the grotesque. Unlike the term "norm," the term "ideal" characterized an elite. The ideal was held over people as something that they could strive toward, but that few people could achieve. At the opposite end of the spectrum was the image of the grotesque, which was simply the inverse of the ideal. By the late nineteenth century, the twin notions of the ideal and the grotesque were abandoned and the norm was accepted.[53] The norm, or what Foucault called "normalizing judgments," consisted of classifications that recognized people in hierarchical terms. Unlike the ideal, the norm ordered the capacities of people not in relation to an abstraction, but in relation to one another.

Unlike the ideal or Aristotle's great chain of being, these normative judgments were inherently democratic. A society with a norm expected that the majority of the population could comply with its standards. By definition, this majority fell under what early statisticians described as the arch of a bell-shaped curve. A minority would be charted as above average on this curve and a minority as below average.

Following the Enlightenment notion of progress, the abnormal/normal binary was also turned into a wide range of medical categories as biology and medicine became more advanced in the early twentieth century.[54] From World War I until the 1970s, the medical model of a disability reigned in the U.S. and other industrialized nations.[55] This model gave physicians the discretion to diagnosis a chronic illness or a permanent injury.[56]

A medical model locates the source of disability in the individual's deficiency.[57] This model is rooted in an "undue emphasis on clinical diagnosis, the very nature of which is destined to lead to a partial and inhibiting view of the disabled individual" writes disability expert Simon Brisenden. "The only difference between us and other people is that we are viewed through spectacles that only focus on our inabilities."[58] A medical model "has portrayed disability as almost entirely a medical problem, and it has led to a situation where doctors and others are trapped in their responses by a definition of their own making."[59]

The medical model evaluated by disability studies experts was not restricted to doctors, however. Initially, it involved physicians who made breakthroughs treating chronic illnesses and injuries, which in the words of one historian later developed into a whole rehabilitation empire in the U.S.[60] In the U.S., the role that physicians played expanded as did the professions that worked closely with medicine, such as physical therapy, occupational therapy, vocational rehabilitation counseling, psychology, and social work. Persons with disabilities came under more and more scrutiny by the different "caring" professions.[61]

### An air-conditioned society or "gods with anuses"[62]

Ecofeminists use the term "biophobia" to level a vivid critique at the mind/body duality in Western humanism. This critique has great implications for the masculine/feminine, the abnormal/normal, and the able/disabled-bodied binaries. The overarching theme within biophobia is very broad in that it suggests that the Western notion of progress presents a problem. What capitalism, the Enlightenment, and Darwinism have done is create a "mass biophobia—in which whole societies distance themselves from animals, trees, landscapes, mountains and rivers. . . ."[63] Our whole species is in peril, ecofeminists claim, because we "deny, defy and defile . . . [our] animal kinship (e.g., sex, death, and digestion)."[64]

Turning the term "biophobia" into a catch-all, the ecologist David Orr explains that ecofeminists advance it to describe everything from discomfort in nature to scorn for "whatever is not man-made, managed, or air-conditioned."[65] "More than ever," he elaborates, "we dwell in and among our own creations and are increasingly uncomfortable with the nature that lies beyond our direct control." Or as Woody Allen succinctly puts it, "Nature and I are two."[66]

Man became the "imperial animal," according to ecofeminists, by harboring the illusion that he or she is "God's special creature."[67] "The deprived human is ranked near 'low animalization,' while those with resources to waste are ranked near 'high' deification–civilization."[68] Ecofeminists argue that the only means of restoring humanity, in addition to overturning all the binaries, is to link feminism with ecology. They blend the organic mind and body with its environment. Creating a new ecological ontology, Shannon Sullivan, for instance, understands bodies and environments as "dynamically co-constitutive."[69] She objects to the idea of the "anonymous body" or one that represents "nameless, impersonal aspects of bodily existence."[70]

Sullivan even suggests that feminism can reclaim evolutionary theory and the concept of nature by making ecological ontology transactional. "Combating essentialist understandings of woman that bind her to a static, fixed nature," she argues, "does not have to mean rejecting all things having to do with nature." Nature need not be spurned or cast aside. It can be redefined so that "a passive nature is not dualistically opposed to active culture ... or to active organic life."[71]

Ecofeminism reharmonizes the mind and body with mother earth. Its rejection of the mind/body dualism reaches the able/disabled-bodied and the normal/abnormal binaries as well as the gender binary. Ecofeminism helps us understand how all minds and bodies are organically moored. It also sheds light on how the medicalization of disability reflects the Enlightenment, with all its gendered subtones. Created in the name of progress in biology and medicine, the medicalized mind and body are artificial, man-made constructions that marginalize persons with disabilities from the rest of society.

## No frozen bodies

Another body of literature that criticizes ecofeminism and yet is also anti-Cartesian and addresses corporeality is radical feminism. According to Grosz, feminism should "begin with Darwin and his understanding of the thing—the dynamism of the active world of natural selection—as that which provides the obstacle, the question, the means, by which life itself grows, develops, undergoes evolution and change, becomes other than what it once was."[72] Like ecofeminism, radical feminism requires an understanding of the self that is not simply arranged around the dualisms of mind and body or the internal or external selves. It ensures that any spaces that open within the very definition of human essence or identity be filled with nondualist critiques. Redefining essence and escaping dualism are intimately tied to one another. Yet unlike ecofeminism, radical feminism is not as mired in debate about essentialism.[73]

Radical feminism advances this book's definition of the mind and body because of its deconstruction of sameness and difference. To do so, it recognizes bodies as political sites.[74] Gender, they argue, is a social construction. Yet some radical feminists such as Judith Butler use social construction as a means of throwing out the baby (or at least its body) with the bath water. As one critic purports, postmodernism dismembers women's bodies with the argument that gender is socially constructed. Instead of arguing that the self and the other are separate and oppositional, Butler, for example, suggests they are produced through a disavowal of the other. The subject is not created in "autonomous isolation." It depends on its identification with the "other."[75]

Contesting this version of social construction, another group of radical feminists—many of them Australian—have created a different type of mind/body accord. Their criticism of postmodernism in general and Butler in particular sums up the problems with social constructionism and postmodernism. Abigail Bray and Claire Colebrook, for instance, argue that it is "precisely this strict division between representation and materiality that ... sustains a Cartesian dualism in feminist theory."[76] The critique of radical constructionism and essentialism itself represents a binary that could be equated with a discursive form of essentialism.[77]

Many of these critics have correctly observed that postmodernism overstates the nature/nurture dichotomy.[78] The postmodernists assert that "any positing of the body as a brute given would lead back to biological determinism."[79] Butler exaggerates the position of the ecofeminists by arguing that they envision the body or the matter of bodies as static, or a corporeal container for the self.[80] She suggests that an identity is "congealed."[81] Meanwhile, ecofeminists maintain that postmodernists conflate "the biological with an essentialism that freezes the body, making it universal." To the ecofeminist Camilla Griggers, the biological body is "antiessentialist" since biology is neither fixed nor static.[82] Critics of ecofeminism, she submits, have miscast the body as essentialist.[83]

What both sides of the nature/nurture dichotomy downplay is that they are indebted to existentialism. The existentialist Søren Kierkegaard developed a unique way of viewing the body or embodiment. To him, the fundamental paradox about human beings is that while they are finite, they can fathom the infinite. People are corporeal and yet conscious of their corporeality. Existentialism, and later poststructuralism, make the mind and body dynamic and therefore not essentialist.

## Bodily becoming

It is the existentialism underlying the French theories of Foucault, Deleuze, and Guattari that presents us with the best means of going beyond the mind/body binary that is neither essentialist nor relativist.[84] Foucault's conception of the body and the technologies of the self has a tremendous impact on all modern theories of subjectivity. Initially, Foucault represented common ground for both the social constructionists and ecofeminists who depend on ideas about corporeality being antiessentialist and yet maintaining some notion of identity and selfhood. The human subject, members from both camps have argued, is the agent *and* the arbiter of change.

In his later work, Foucault substitutes the self as the object of study. He examines how the self is constituted through discourse. The radical feminist Rosi Braidotti describes this part of Foucault's work as "neomaterialist" because it includes the "bodily materiality of the subject."[85] Similarly, the theorist Alphonso Lingis contends that Foucault's work is ambivalent about the "notion of a natural or biological body." In his studies on biopower and its inscription on bodies, Foucault himself observes that the body is "the inscribed surface of events" or the "locus of a disassociated self." The body is "in perpetual disintegration."[86]

Foucault further undermines the mind/body duality by rejecting the humanist interpretation of the self that views the soul as "contained within the body." As Winter writes, "The soul is a salient marker for humanist constructs of identity . . . that lies in the (illusory) depths of the individual." By contrast, "Foucault uses the term 'soul' to refer to 'psyche, subjectivity, personality, [and] consciousness.' "[87]

Deleuze shadows Foucault by adopting his analysis of subjectivity, which challenges what it is to be human. For Deleuze, the human being is "virtual, potential, unstable."[88] In radical feminist theorist Mariam Fraser's words, Deleuze purports that the person has "no essence, no independent form or content."[89] Deleuze concurs with Foucault that power and knowledge bring the person—the subject—into existence. The body is the site where power and knowledge are conjoined, integrating subjectivity, identity, and corporeality. "You will be organized, you will be an organism," write Deleuze and Guattari, "you will articulate your body."[90] For them, this is the way that one can create an "alternative" formation of subjectivity. What Deleuze does with existentialism and Foucault's work is set the mind and body into motion.

## Identities, Spinoza, and all that

To fully comprehend how radical feminists as well as Deleuze and Guattari reunite the mind and the body in a way that elucidates the body, we must examine their interpretation of the work of Spinoza, René Descartes' rival. Spinoza was a monist, not a dualist like Descartes. Instead of dividing the mind and the body, he viewed them as one substance.[91] Monism sees the two parts as merging from, and belonging to, the same substance. "[The] mind is constituted by the affirmation of the actual existence of the body," philosopher Eva Kit Wah Man writes, "which enables the activity of reason." "Activity," Man elaborates, "should be understood as one's participation in one's situation which, instead of being dominated by the mind, depends on the body's character, manner, and context."[92]

The body is a *process*. As Man adds, "The body's meaning and capabilities will vary according to its context, and its limits and possibilities can be revealed only by its ongoing interactions with its environment."[93] The radical feminist Moira Gatens suggests that unlike the essentialist position, Spinoza's monism has a nonmechanical and nondichotomized view of nature and culture. His definition of monism cannot be applied to the pure social constructionists such as Butler, however, since he believes the mind and body constitute a substance.[94]

Spinoza sees the mind and body as reciprocal. According to Gatens, he develops a "dynamic theory of the capacity to be affected (the power of acting and suffering); and in the last instance to the theory of the particular essences that express themselves in the variations of this power of action and passion."[95] Spinoza views the body, she elaborates, by "breaking it down or dissembling it in order to appraise its ability to act [which] makes it impossible to maintain the domination and authority of single primary identities."[96]

Spinoza's ideas about the reciprocal nature of the mind and body become more concrete if one adopts his vocabulary. To him, the mind and body are composed of attributes. These attributes cannot be considered alone, however; they have modes. For instance, Spinoza refers to the mind as a mode of thought and matter as a mode of extension. An existing mode is affected in a great number of ways. The operative word here is "affected." A mode has affections by virtue of a certain capacity of being affected. Affectivity refers to Spinoza's method of defining a body by its power to affect and be affected.[97] Spinoza proceeds from the parts to their affections, and from these affections to the affections of the existing mode as a whole. Extensive parts do not belong to a given mode except in certain relations.

A mode thus has two sorts of affections. First, a mode is described as states of a body or ideas that indicate these states. The term is plural since modes are infinite just as attributes are. Second, changes in the body or ideas indicating these changes produce another mode. The changes in the body are tied to the states of a body, and change with them. The two sorts of modes can never be conceived of separately since they overlap. As Deleuze explains, "One senses how, beginning with an initial affection, our feelings become linked with our ideas in such a way that our whole capacity to be affected is exercised at each moment."[98]

On a concrete level, two kinds of affects exist. First, there are the modifications or changes made through the encounter with another body. Second, actions where a body is its own cause of action generated from internal affects and passions, where a body is acted upon by external bodies and where actions or affects are produced through the relations between bodies. "A horse, a fish, a man, or even two men compared one with the other, do not have the same capacity to be affected:" writes Deleuze, "they are not affected by the same things, or not affected by the same things in the same way."[99]

One way of making Spinoza's ideas more concrete is to realize that passions are the most common kind of affect. They rise through parallel mind's and body's inadequate knowledge and are also comprised of two kinds—sad and joyful. When relations with another body increase our powers of acting, Spinoza calls this joyful. By contrast, when we encounter a body that decomposes us or diminishes our power of acting, Spinoza refers to this passion as sad. As Deleuze describes it, "Power is added or subtracted according to what kind of affect exists."

But all this turns, ultimately, on certain characteristics of modes. The first idea is that people have passive affections, inadequate ideas or imaginings. To Deleuze, Spinoza believes that "an inadequate idea is an idea of which we are not the cause (it is not formally explained by our power of understanding); this inadequate idea is itself the (material and efficient) cause of a feeling; we cannot then be the adequate cause of this feeling; but a feeling of which we are not the adequate cause is necessarily a passion. Our capacity to be affected is thus exercised, from the beginning of our existence, by inadequate ideas and passive feelings."[100] One cannot see how a finite mode, especially at the beginning of its existence, could have any inadequate ideas; and one cannot, consequently, see how it could experience anything but passive feelings.

An equally profound link may be found between ideas that are adequate, and active feelings. An idea we have that is adequate may be formally defined as an idea of which we are the cause; were it then the material and efficient cause of a feeling we would be the adequate cause of that feeling itself; but a feeling of which we are the adequate cause is an action. According to feminist theorist Claire Colebrook, Spinoza suggests that "insofar as our mind has adequate ideas, it necessarily does certain things, and insofar as it has inadequate ideas, it necessarily undergoes other things. . . . The actions of the mind arise from adequate ideas alone; the passions depend on inadequate ideas alone."[101]

Spinoza's conception of the body is never static. To him, the body is not a materiality that is then rendered meaningful. Our being is about becoming. The body is therefore becoming meaningful.[102] Theorist Genevieve Lloyd writes, "Spinoza's attributes are mirrors, each expressing in its own way the essence of substance. But what is 'expressed' is also enveloped in the expression, like the tree in the seed. This is no passive reflection, but an active, dynamic articulation."[103]

Spinoza's ontology suggests that being is never in itself but is always becoming of specific qualities. His ethics of joy, for instance, view the expression of identity as an activity of a particular being's becoming. The body is open materiality as a set of possibly infinite tendencies and potentialities that may be developed.[104] For Spinoza, Deleuze states, "Being is not an inert presence that is passively doubled in images. Life itself is an infinite becoming of images, with one particular image, the body, taking itself as the center of all images."[105]

## Deleuze's functionalism

Deleuze takes Spinoza's idea that the mind and body are all part of one process to inform his own ideas of functionalism.[106] In Deleuze's own words, Spinoza's fundamental questions are: "What is the structure (fabrica) of a body? And: What can a body do?"[107] He states that Spinoza is "not amazed at having a body, but by what the body can do. Bodies are not defined by their genus or species, but their organs and functions." Instead, Deleuze elaborates, bodies are defined "by what they can do, by the affects of which they are capable."[108]

Providing a functionalist definition of the body, Deleuze starts by drawing upon what Spinoza calls "infinite attributes." For Deleuze, there is no standard individual, person, or self that could be the object of study. He conceptualizes both difference and becoming, though this difference and becoming cannot be associated with the becoming *of* some being.[109] Deleuze is not concerned here with carving out a singular identity with something like full rights, because his agenda does not directly address the status of individuals as citizens. He opposes any form of identity politics since it demands "territorializing" or staking out one's turf in the social hierarchy.[110]

This emphasis on citizens without identities is best explained in *Difference and Repetition*, where Deleuze demonstrates in Colebrook's words that "the minute we feel we have grasped what thinking and difference *are*, then we have lost the power of difference."[111] "Repetition is not the reoccurrence of the same old thing over and over again", she elaborates, "to repeat something is to begin again, to renew, to question, and to refuse remaining the same."[112] For instance, people actualize sound waves by hearing music. Alternatively, "a bat," Colebrook explains, "actualizes sound waves by seeing and navigating."[113]

Deleuze thinks "life begins with pure difference or becoming, or tendencies to differ, such as the differential waves of sound and light. . . ."[114] Difference, as Deleuze argues, is not difference *from*. Difference is not a question of negation. The body has infinite connections and variations.

Deleuze articulates that "a body's structure is the composition of its relation. What a body can do corresponds to the nature and limits of its capacity to be affected."[115] To Deleuze, Spinoza's actions and passions are suited to politics of the social body.[116] A body can be anything—it can be an animal, a body of sounds, a mind. . . . The body is best understood as an "assemblage of forces or affects disturbed on a plane of immanence."[117]

A more graphic way of understanding the body according to Deleuze and Guattari stems from the term "becoming animal." The first half of this term is "becoming" because they spurn any notion of essentialism; whereas the second half is "animal" to illustrate the departure from the traditional conception of the human that has the mind that reflects reason. An individual has the power to transform oneself in perceiving difference.[118]

Becoming animal is not attaining the state of what the animal means (the supposed strength or innocence of animals); nor is it becoming what the animal is. Becoming animal is a feel for the animal's movements, perceptions, and becomings: imagine seeing the world as if one were a dog, a beetle, or a mole. Herman Melville and Franz Kafka write literature that embodies Deleuze's and Guattari's notion of becoming animal. They recognize "the power to perceive differently," explains Colebrook, "by tearing perception from its human home." As Melville's novel *Moby Dick* progresses, Ahab acts not for any external reason or end. According to Colebrook, "The whale is perceived in its singularity." Deleuze and Guattari do not view it as a symbol or a metaphor for life. Neither the becoming of man (Ahab) nor the becoming of nature (where the whale would represent life in general) are singular. There are two distinct becomings.[119]

## Ethology

Deleuze and Guattari integrate Spinoza's monism into what they call an ethology of humankind. Unlike an epistemological perspective, an ethological one examines how a body has the power and capacity to affect other bodies and to be affected itself. This term is used by biologists and naturalists to study animal behavior.[120] According to Deleuze, an ethological appraisal of any given being will attend to the materiality of existence—the physics of bodies discussed earlier. An ethological appraisal will reveal what a given body seeks out and what it avoids.[121] It provides a sketch of that which aids and that which harms a particular being's characteristic relations with its surroundings, along with a description of its desires and aversions.

An ethology has no conception of what is universally good or bad, virtuous or wicked.[122] It envisions each individual within a wider totality of all other individuals and ultimately nature itself. The powers and capacities of an individual cannot simply be deduced from knowledge concerning the species or genus to which it belongs.[123]

Spinoza and Deleuze are no more sentimental than Frederich Nietzsche about the general conditions of life. Spinoza, for instance, does not dispute that animals have minds and feelings. This information, however, does not mean that people should stop killing and eating animals.[124] The death of one body is used to sustain another.[125]

A Deleuzian ethology helps resolve some of Spinoza's practical dilemmas. First, how does one cultivate joyful passions and freedom when our place in nature seems to condemn us to bad encounters and sadness? Second, how are adequate ideas formed when our natural condition seems to condemn us to having only inadequate ideas of our body, of our mind, and of other things? Third, how does one become conscious of oneself, of God, and nature when our consciousness seems inseparable from illusions? It is here that the ethological approach to Spinoza's ethical and political theory proves useful. By understanding human endeavor across time as a process of experimentation, ethology offers a map that indicates what encounters and combinations reliably lead to human thriving, what encounters do not, and why they do, or do not.

For Deleuze the question is not answered by asking if someone *is* ethical. Instead, the question is if he or she is "active." To be active means that this person has developed "adequate ideas," which are not false, biased, or prejudiced.[126]

Deleuze illustrates the best way of becoming active with graphic examples. Active people strive toward edges. They design and swim their own stroke. This aspect of Deleuze's ethology is what radical feminism underscores and finds so appealing in his work. "If I learn to swim by mechanically copying the instructor's movements as they are demonstrated out of the water," Colebrook explains, "then I will never learn the art of swimming." The swimmer must have a creative response for the instructor. "I do not repeat his arm movements; I repeat the sense of the water or feel for the waves that produces his arm movements. My arms need to feel the water and become in the way a swimmer's arms become. Because my body is different—female—this might mean that a *faithful repetition* of his swimming might require slightly different arm movements. I have to feel what good swimming *does*, not what it *is*." The swimmer must feel how to act and not copy the movements of other swimmers. In abstract terms, Deleuze's ethology means that becoming "is not bounded by what has already become or is actualised, but it is spurred on by perceiving the virtual powers that are expressed in actions."[127]

Deleuze, however, realizes that an ethology based on difference is problematic because so many communities scapegoat difference. Offering an explanation that is similar to Theodor Adorno's and Max Horkheimer's notion of *idiosyncrasy,* Deleuze recognizes that many people are uneasy and even revolted by difference. Adorno and Horkeimer believe that transgressions against rules disturb us because they break the spell of consciousness.[128] Similarly, the sociologist Harold Garfinkel notes that breaking rules not only foregrounds the existence of the rule, but it can bring out powerful responses like disgust, anger, and revulsion.[129] For instance, great art may be appreciated for its transgressive effects and loathed simultaneously. Some people look at art and do not know whether to feel attracted or repelled by a piece.[130]

## Deleuze and disability

The notion of animality outlined in this book suggests that a perpetual connection between the mind and the body exists. The mind informs the body and the body informs the mind in a perpetually reciprocal relationship. Every body experiences this reciprocal relationship between substance and process that ecofeminism, radical feminism, Spinoza, Deleuze, and Guattari outline.

While every body (or everybody) experiences this, persons with disabilities may be more conscious of the connection between the two. Further, persons with physical disabilities embody Deleuze's notion of repetition and difference or that the body is always in flux or in process. They must live life on the edge. Daily tasks must be approached with creativity since the physical and social environment that surrounds persons with disabilities excludes them. The staircase designer has had little thought about the person who uses a wheelchair. On the most basic level, persons with disabilities must navigate around all sorts of environmental obstacles, making them aware of their minds, their bodies, and the relationship between the two.

This is not to say that persons with disabilities are mired in what Grosz describes as "essentialist accounts of the body."[131] The body is not opposed to culture—it is itself "a cultural, *the* cultural product."[132] The staircase is a product of culture—the idea that climbing up steps is preferable to rolling up a ramp only exists because it is a product of culture.[133] Persons with disabilities view environmental obstacles as socially and culturally derived.

In this way, disability can be transformed from a *lack of* to *difference* as Deleuze and Guattari describe. A physical or mental impairment underscores the uniqueness of humankind because it embodies difference. It shows the infinite connections and variations of the body. Each disease takes its own course or journey, and every condition, whether permanent or temporary, has a different trajectory. The body is by nature as individual as each person's fingerprints or DNA.

Recognizing a physical or mental impairment as the norm means that there is no measure or yardstick. Persons with disabilities are not compared to people without them. A Deleuzian perspective of persons with disabilities suggests that normalizing judgments should not be attempted, let alone sustained. The normal/abnormal binary itself is artificial. Persons with disabilities perpetually strive toward no end.

A Deleuzian mind and body can also be viewed as dynamic rather than static. The mind and body are viewed in time, which is to say that change must be addressed. Deleuze's notion of functionalism and bodily becoming or animality underscores corporeality. By so doing, it travels between or above the normal/abnormal binary with the argument that all bodies are different and permanently dying whether or not the individuals housed in these bodies are conscious of it. Furthermore, it looks at the different bodies to create the way for the more standard body.[134]

What Deleuze and Guattari mean by the proper outlet is *not* championing persons with disabilities or turning their situation into a personal triumph story. A personal triumph is a moral tale that imposes values on persons with disabilities. These tales are not about difference, but similarity. Scrooge gives Tiny Tim the financial means for the operation so that he can be like everyone else in his family and the rest of the population. He will no longer be separated by his difference. Deleuze's notion of difference or bodily becoming or becoming animal is just the opposite. It is difference, which may be more visible or functionally visible with persons with disabilities, that reveals our humanity.

The moral philosopher Alisdair MacIntyre, who has also linked having a physical or mental impairment with being animal, demonstrates the difference between a metaphysical conception of disability and one rooted in French critical theory. MacIntyre asks what difference moral philosophy makes if it treats the facts of vulnerability and affliction as central to the human condition. "In philosophy where one begins generally makes a difference to the outcome of one's enquiries." He argues that "the facts of disability and dependence presuppose either a failure or a refusal to acknowledge adequately the bodily dimensions of our existence.... [So] we conceive of ourselves ... as other than animal, as exempt from the hazardous condition of 'mere' animality."[135]

MacIntyre states first that human beings never separate themselves from their animality. He purports not just that people have animal bodies, but that this type of body makes them identify with each other. Second, being animal underscores one of the problems with modern moral philosophy. It places too great an emphasis on autonomy. The virtues of independent rational agency, McIntyre contends, must be accompanied by dependence. "A failure to understand this is apt to obscure some features of rational agency."[136]

MacIntyre, however, is a moral philosopher, not a critical theorist. He believes in humanism. He views humankind as moving toward a *telos*—an end. MacIntyre is also an essentialist. His conception of animality still creates morality tales or stories of personal triumph like Dickens's Tiny Tim. What is so striking about Deleuze and Guattari is their notion of difference or capability is a functionalist definition—to be affected and to affect. They break down the striving toward difference into functions. Becoming animal is not about being—but rather living, experiencing, or doing. It imposes no limitations or constraints.

Persons with disabilities reflect human existence. They cannot be defined by the essence of their conditions or diseases. Nor does having a condition or disease make them the exception to the rule—that we all live in a society composed of healthy, normal human beings. They are not busted or broken human beings. Persons with disabilities are the rule. They understand their mortality. They are aware of their animality—that they are flesh and blood. And persons with disabilities envision life as doing. The doing is about becoming(s).

The idea that the notion, perfect, or model human being is not dependent upon his or her mind or body and those others with minds and bodies is an illusion. This illusion is not beneficial to these so-called model human beings, let alone to persons with disabilities. They do not live on the edge, but rather in unprofitable packs and herds constrained by their anthropocentrism.

## What's in a definition?

Numerous authors of disability studies have made some connections between disability and postmodernism and poststructuralism.[137] Most notably, Irving Zola, an avant garde poststructuralist, locates the body in the postmodern world. He first examines individual/societal relations rather than focusing on the individual *or* society.[138]

Theorizing disability as fluid and continuous instead of permanent and dichotomous, he argues, makes politics and the academy more open. This definition also accepts the near universality of disability. Zola orchestrates a diverse chorus of voices, demonstrating that disability affects everyone. Zola hopes to link the material, social, and cultural dimensions of disability.[139]

What Zola and other poststructuralists and Foucauldian scholars have done is find new ways to examine the "impaired" body without losing the social model's political edge.[140] Marian Corker, Susan Wendell, and Jenny Morris have a postmodernist perspective of disability studies.[141] Corker, for instance, argues that poststructuralist discourse on disability can liberate persons with disabilities.[142]

Aside from these theorists, however, many members of the disability rights movement are stuck in their own binary. Beginning in the mid-1960s, the disability rights community insisted that they not longer be seen as "non-people with non-abilities."[143] Disability studies swung entirely to the other side, arguing that disability results from society's failure to adapt.[144] "The disablement lies in the construction of society," suggests disability studies expert Simon Brisenden, "not in the physical condition of the individual."[145] The disabling aspect of living with a physical or mental impairment, disability studies experts and activists argued, is totally environmental. It is not personal. Disability has nothing to do with the body. The disability rights movement creates models based on their own medical/societal binary.

## No more rights, please

This environmental model of disability has created a political corollary—the social model of disability. Associating with other persons with physical and mental impairments, disability is a new form of minority politics.[146] Mathew Diller argues that the Americans with Disabilities Act is based on "an implicit analogy between the problems facing people with disabilities and those faced by women and racial minorities."[147] But as social scientists Pam Brandwein and Richard Scotch rightly argue, the analogy is problematic.[148]

A physical or mental impairment should not guarantee rights to persons based on their identities. If disability is viewed as a condition and not an identity, there is no longer merely the choice between politically conservative biological reductionism or idealist or dualist anthropocentrism. Making disability conditional on the individual and the society underscores the modern biological breakthroughs that reveal just how fluid identities actually are.[149]

As Oliver Sacks argues, identities are "organically moored." He suggests that society take into account "our embodiment" or our fleshy all too human selves.[150] But this is not to say that Sacks believes in identity politics. To him, identity should be equated with the individuality of our minds and bodies.[151] The British disabilities studies expert Michael Oliver explains that impairment is "nothing less than a description of the physical body."[152] Persons with disabilities have needs. Their needs are more observable than those of the rest of the population. At the same time, the lack of societal accommodation is more pronounced. So persons with disabilities have wants. But this is not because of who *they* are but because of who *we* are—human beings.

Recognizing the fluidity of this definition then shows how the ADA should be read as ideology. It is not a rights-based law, but a needs-based one. The next chapter shows how a functionalist interpretation of the mind and body reveals just how revolutionary the ADA is in terms of how it breaks free of the strictures of special treatment and equal protection.

In the next chapter, this conception of the body is used to place the ADA within the context of a Deleuzian ethic of care. Conceiving of disability as an almost universal construction makes a critical care ethic applicable to everyone. It turns needs from something negative into a difference. Physical and mental impairments are transformed from a lack of perfection into a human condition.

This notion of mind and body no longer makes a care ethic indebted to ontology. Instead of examining care in terms of human essence (read being), a care ethic can be based on human experience and activities (read doing). It also rejects the distinction between the caregiver and the care-receiver, arguing that receiving care is universal. We all need to be cared for. The next chapter shows that the caregiver offers help not because of some benevolent impulse as some feminists have argued, but to promote our survival.

# CHAPTER 3
# An Alternative Ethic of Care

Defining disability as a condition that shapes how people do things instead of an identity that characterizes who they are, transforms it into an ever-evolving, nonessential, social construction that is nearly universal. This definition captures our animality and underscores how every mind and body is in some state of change. Identities are fluid, and cannot be bound to static categories like race or gender. As the French critical theorists Gilles Deleuze and Felix Guattari observe, we are "bodily becoming."

Building a care ethic on Deleuze's and Guattari's definition of animality would mean that this morality could reject the gender binary altogether. It would take into account the individuality of both the caregiver and care-receiver rather than replacing a masculinist notion of rights with a feminist account of ethics. Deleuze's and Guttari's "universal" conception, however, should not be confused with universals based on humanist metaphysics. Given their indebtedness to structuralism, poststructuralism, and existentialism, there is no white Western male privilege associated with this universal. Deleuze and Guattari present ethics based on critical theory that disputes the idea that truth and identity exist. Just as the activists seeking justice for transsexuals, intersexuals, and political race avoid identities based on binaries, this conception of a care ethic could be grounded not in *being*, but in *doing*.

Finally, an ethic of care based on Deleuze and Guattari reflects the influence of Benedict de Spinoza. Spinoza, who some believe is the first critical theorist, offers a relational rather than an oppositionary view of the individual and the community. He spurns the liberal notion of the autonomous individual and rejects the idea that the individual's interest must be subsumed by the collective. Spinoza believes that people pursue their self-interest by depending upon one another. Mounting a care ethic on Deleuze's, Guattari's, and other radical feminist theorists' interpretations of Spinoza gives it a critical edge. A critical care ethic could successfully span the liberal/communitarian divide, widening its capacity to critique liberalism and capitalism and offer an alternative.

## Myths of autonomy

The Americans with Disabilities Act (ADA) is the first civil rights law that embodies an ethic of care. A care ethic tries to counterbalance the problem with rights. Rights are rigid. "An ethic of rights," law professors Francis and Jennifer Carleton write, "is an individualistic, competitive and hierarchical concept that focuses on the preservation of one's autonomy. . . . [It] downplay[s] the communal aspects of human society, and leaves out in the cold those who do not have the economic or social power, or perhaps even the inclination, to wield their rights against the claims of others."[1] Rights-based antidiscrimination protection provides only two avenues for recourse—equal treatment or special protection.

Feminist theorists and disability studies experts have long shared the concern that legislation based upon either equal treatment or special protection is flawed. On the one hand, antidiscrimination laws premised upon the equal treatment approach strive to treat women the same as men, regarding persons with disabilities as no different than "normal" people. This approach advanced by liberal feminists overlooks the problem that the very standard from which rights are derived—men or able-bodied persons—is inherently biased.

On the other hand, legislation that gives women and persons with disabilities special protection, as propounded by radical feminists, is bogged down by a different set of problems. Protective legislation accentuates difference, which separates women, people of color, or persons with disabilities from the mainstream. Relegated to the margins, they are considered deviant by other members of society.

Some feminist legal theorists, such as Catherine MacKinnon, Robin West, and Judith Baer, try to solve this dilemma by calling into question the constitutional foundation underlying the equal treatment and special protection approaches to antidiscrimination legislation.[2] To them, the equal protection clause of the Constitution has helped men more than women. They offer a critique of liberal constitutionalism and new notions of constitutionalism.

MacKinnon's theory of dominance focuses on how power underlying the Constitution manifests itself. She argues that the American system of law is captured by a gendered hierarchy in which men claim that the system is neutral, when in fact it has been carefully crafted to maintain their dominance. Hence the whole hierarchy must be overturned.[3]

West also declares that all modern legal theory is masculine, including critical legal studies.[4] Rejecting both liberal or conservative legalism, she creates an instrumental jurisprudence or progressive constitutionalism that tries to transcend the idea of care and justice by arguing that legal and political institutions have failed "to protect and nurture the connections that sustain and enlarge us" and "to intervene in those private and intimate 'connections' that damage and injure us."[5] West offers an internal critique of an ethic of care and the ideas of autonomy (the capacity to form and act on a conception of the good), self-respect, integrity, and the equal moral worth of people.

Finally, Baer develops a notion of feminist postliberalism that injects needs into the traditional language of liberal theory. She suggests that "the right to the means of meeting human needs, at the very least, must join the traditional rights of liberal theory."[6] She departs from the traditional feminist critique, however, by arguing that a notion of personal responsibility can be placed within an individualistic framework. To Baer, personal responsibility helps balance out the problems associated with individual freedom, making law more accountable for men and women.

Each one of these feminist legal theorists expands upon the care ethic that Carol Gilligan first introduced in *In a Different Voice*.[7] In that book, Gilligan differentiates between an ethic of justice or rights and an ethic of care. The former depends on contractual relationships between autonomous individuals, whereas the latter is based on the moral reasoning of women that is grounded in providing care, preventing harm, and maintaining relationships.[8]

## Defining morals

Gilligan's discussion about an ethic of care or a feminist morality reinvigorated the discussion about theory, morality, and politics in the 1980s. According to the ethicist Dorothy Emmet, morality is about the "considerations" we make and "what one thinks is important to do and in what ways; how to conduct one's relations with other people; and being aware and prepared to be critical of one's basic approvals or disapprovals."[9] When morality is interposed into politics, however, the pressing question becomes which comes first—morality or politics?

While many care ethics advocates initially dodged this question, political theorist Joan Tronto tackles it head on. She adopts Aristotle's position that moral values should only be introduced into politics in relation to other political concerns. But because this is Niccolo Machiavelli's position, Tronto realizes that the flexibility inherent within this argument makes many an ethicist uneasy. Still, she concludes that an ethic of care does not put people in this dilemma.

Tronto suggests that "care can serve as both a moral value and as a basis for the political achievement of a good society."[10] An ethic of care refers to a situation where people reach beyond themselves. They must take action, however. A care ethic, Tronto explains, does not mean that these people care (read sympathize or empathize) for the world's hungry. It means that they take care of the hungry. It is not an emotion or a sentiment, but rather an "on-going practice."[11]

While scholars in a wide range of fields have seized upon Gilligan's notion of an ethic of care, her work and that of the first wave of feminists following her is criticized for being essentialist.[12] That is, Gilligan argues that moral reasoning is based on a perspective that only women possessed. Many feminists balk at this part of Gilligan's argument, suggesting that she is privileging women. Some, such as Sara Ruddick, draw a clear distinction between sex and gender.[13] Although more women care for small children, it is their *gendered experience* rather than their nature, Ruddick submits, that gives them insight about oppression and the capacity to follow a care ethic. Because gender traits are learned behaviors, she argues, both women *and* men could live under an ethic of care.

Social constructionists carry this distinction between sex and gender further, discarding the very idea that men or women could be identified by any of their inherent traits or natures. These feminists contribute to a third wave of literature that started deconstructing the opposition between difference and sameness.[14] Sheila Greeve Davaney, for instance, criticizes white feminists for implying that "there is *a* perspective from which we can perceive the way things really are."[15] Women, she argues, have no special essence or nature that gives them insight into the realm of emotions. Instead, she says, all experience is "a social product and hence is relative, ambiguous, and challengeable."[16]

Feminist theorists rely on Michel Foucault and argue that individuals are socially constructed and that male domination is an integral part of their construction. "... laws, customs, and social rules that come from men," Hirschmann purports, "... are imposed on women to restrict their opportunities, choices, actions, and behaviors."[17] Social construction allows feminists to explore the heart of why an individual makes the choices that he or she does. It exposes why, how, and where masculine gender privilege still exists.[18]

In the late 1990s and onward, most studies exploring a care ethic had moved away from women and the sex/gender debate, relying on some form of social construction. Law professor Kathryn Abrams observes that an ethic of care now recognizes law as a "complex set of practices that are structured, supported and incentivized by a range of institutional decisions and social norms, and that differentiate and position women in relation to each other."[19] As feminist legal theorist Martha Fineman illustrates so well, care does not revolve around a dyadic between mother and child. Family law should rid itself of what she calls "the sexual family," which recognizes the sexual relationship of men and women. Marriage, divorce, and child custody should be reoriented around who cares for the children without making any reference to gender identities.

Social constructionism, however, does not escape the dilemma associated with essentialism. Social constructionists, the philosopher Manuel De Landa relays, declare themselves "antiessentialist." Yet he notes that they "share with essentialism a view of matter as inert." To the social constructionist this matter is acceptable since it does not come "from a Platonic heaven or from the mind of God, but from the minds of humans (or from cultural conventions expressed linguistically)." [20] For De Landa, this distinction is not enough. Social construction must take one further step, making matter dynamic rather than inert or static.

## Four pillars

While theorists offer different versions of a care ethic depending on their position on essentialism, they share four interrelated principles. The first is that all relationships are political.[21] Human agency involves a notion of the self that is deeply situated in relationships. Theorists developing a care ethic criticize what Fineman calls "the myth of independence."[22] "We are 'autonomous' in the sense that we have powers and abilities as well as desires, wants, and needs, but these are 'relational;'" explains Hirschmann, "they come from, exist in the context of, and have meaning only in relation to others."[23]

Second, an ethic of care makes no distinction between the public and private spheres. Having so long neglected the private sphere, political theorists and philosophers, the feminist theorists insist, take into account only relationships between equals that emphasize rights. Relationships between unequals are ignored. However, by neglecting them, mainstream theorists have overlooked how care and nurturing affect civil society. Children, for instance, may have no right to the love of a parent, yet this love is considered vital in a civil society. It also assumes that care, like that given by a parent, is benevolent.[24]

Third, given its concern for the vulnerable, an ethic of care underscores the value of difference. Wary of rights and duties, this ethic questions deductive reasoning. A set of logically consistent principles cannot lead to maxims of action that will be appropriate for everyone. One size does not fit all. If everyone is alike, in other words, how can they all be distinctive individuals? A theory of difference, radical feminist theorists claim, should not explain away difference by describing who should be characterized as a *typical* or *normal* community member.[25] A care ethic abandons formal consistency and respects difference, thereby giving people dignity.[26]

Finally, an ethic of care is discursive. Steering clear of universals that inherently claim their impartiality all the while disguising their partiality, it takes into account particular peoples with their own specific histories. "[T]he only level that really matters," according to Davaney, is "the level of concrete and practical consequences."[27] At the same time, some female ethicists such as the existentialists who preceded them, believe in reform. A caring world, they contend, can be born out by acts of caring. Hence, a care ethic is a normative plan of action.

## Critiquing care

Some proponents of an ethic of care have gone further than others with the argument about social construction, that it should not be considered a feminist morality. It must cover women and men who are both caregivers and care-receivers. Tronto, for instance, asks if care must be limited to something that can only be done for others. "To presume that the carer is an active agent and the receiver a dependent continues to perpetuate ... some of the worst aspects of the 'man' moral agency model ... we are trying, in part, to dislodge." Circumventing the problem with positive liberty, Tronto suggests that feminists should "think about care from the standpoint of the vulnerable recipient of care."[28]

Tronto insists that theorists should stop talking about women's morality and start discussing "a care ethic that includes the values traditionally associated with women."[29] Furthermore, she believes that such a morality should be placed in a political context. Tronto thinks politics is in "the realm in which resources are allocated, public order is maintained, and disputes about how these activities should occur are resolved."[30] The world, she adds, should be viewed differently so that "the activities that legitimate the accretion of power to the existing powerful are less valued." A care ethic could help "legitimate a sharing of power with outsiders."[31]

Daryl Koehn also rejects the female morality underlying an ethic of care.[32] She offers a dialogical ethic, which is to say that she tries finding a way of being an individual in a community of individuals. She advances the relational self rather than the individual self. At the same time, she maintains that a benevolent concern for the vulnerable makes little of the difference between the public and the private sphere. Koehn values difference and imaginative discourse, all with the hope of changing the world.

To do this, Koehn creates what she calls a "dialogic ethic of care." Simply put, she argues that a dialogue should take place between the caregiver and the care-receiver. She urges that care should be thought of as a conversation. To her, the positive notion of liberty is easily manipulated.[33] "Conversation," by contrast, "requires that one or more of the parties to the spoken exchange is persuadable by what is said in the exchange. In order for persuasion to be a possibility," Koehn purports, "participants must commit to certain principles, principles that are not derived transcendentally but that are articulated and consented to in the course of conversation itself." She questions the assumption that a feminist morality is benevolent by nature. Accordingly, she relies on conversation to create "a *critical* openness."[34] Most importantly, she insists that the duality of caregiver and care-receiver should be cast aside to ensure that feminists with a care ethic are not stifled by their own metaphysical dichotomy.

## A different standard or a standard of difference?

What those who look at feminism from a universal and yet socially constructed way do is extend the notion of being female. This is particularly important to ensure that an ethic of care should not be taken literally. A care ethic involves not just the caregiver and the care-receiver, but it renders a critique of liberalism and capitalism.

Few works, however, have used an ethic of care to critique more than the notion of rights in specific statutes and public policies. One notable exception is how Hirschmann and Zillah Eisenstein use relational justice or a care ethic to critique liberalism and capitalism. They argue that relational justice should cast aside the positive notion of liberty and rely on a negative conception.[35]

Negative liberty—the absence of external restraint—is rights-oriented and based on the individual. People remain forever unconnected and separate from one another. Each person is autonomous. The concept of negative liberty recognizes a dichotomy between internal and external constraints, whereas positive liberty does not. As Isaiah Berlin describes it, negative liberty embodies the idea of being free *from* external constraints.[36] One person is prohibited from harming another person. It reflects John Locke's famous notion of a night watchman, who ensures that no one person hinders or harms another.

By contrast, positive liberty is best characterized as the freedom *to* do something. The night watchman does not just prohibit, he helps people by providing them with goods and services. A person cannot be free, for instance, unless he or she is healthy. Therefore, the state must provide health care. The need for universal health care rests on a positive conception of liberty.

A positive conception of liberty also means that a person should be unhindered by his or her internal constraints. It focuses on internal barriers such as fears and addictions that can inhibit freedom. One must have the will to be free.[37]

Eliminating external constraints does not, however, penetrate the state and society as deeply as eradicating internal constraints does. One of the greatest ironies about individualism is that pursuing freedom from external constraints accentuates the similarities rather than the differences among people. Negative liberty does not foster difference. Women who succeed, do so, for instance, on male terms. They must act like white men since it is men who set the norms and standards that cannot be violated. Lifting the barriers so that women can enter the workplace does not mean that they will feminize it by changing its culture if all it means is being freed from external constraints.

By contrast, alleviating internal barriers or constraints is more invasive. How can a woman be free in a male-dominated workplace that perpetuates masculine norms and values that individuals must embrace and even internalize to guarantee their success? The dilemma associated with positive liberty is that it depends on what Hirschmann describes as a Rousseauian trap or "second guessing."[38] Who determines the appropriate balance of male and female values that governs the workplace?

To avoid the problem associated with second-guessing, Eisenstein and Hirschmann argue that relational justice should change the fundamental standard for assessing equality. In this way, the standard itself would no longer promote sameness as Berlin's notion of negative liberty does. To do so, they suggest that the pregnant woman should represent the standard for equal treatment in the workplace, potentially "decentering the phallus."[39]

Pregnancy is viewed as "a problem" within a liberal democratic state, Eisenstein argues, because men cannot get pregnant. As a result, the unique capacity of the female body is viewed as a liability rather than an asset in the workplace. In accordance with this logic, legislation recognizes pregnancy as special or in need of protection. That is, it takes into account the difference and provides whatever benefits are necessary for the birth on this basis alone.[40] However, because stigma is often associated with a difference, many legal theorists regard protectionism as paternalistic.[41] After all, naming such legislation protectionist requires a presumption of weakness.[42]

Feminists have called for legislation that recognizes the specificity of pregnancy and calls for equality, not protectionism. Once the female rather than the male body becomes the starting point, the standard of neutrality is altered. As Eisenstein contends, if the female instead of the male takes into account the pregnant female body, then being pregnant becomes the norm. It is no longer a condition that deviates from the norm. The association between pregnancy and protectionism is broken.

Changing the standard, Eisenstein submits, circumvents the most basic problem underlying antidiscrimination legislation. The new standard can account for difference and still be inclusive of both sexes without facing the Rousseauian problem of forcing people to be free. If a door is constructed to accommodate a pregnant woman, few men would have a problem fitting through it as well. It does not penalize women and men who undergo no such change or who need fewer accommodations.

Eisenstein spreads a universal net wider than a negative conception of liberty, which treats men and women as different and yet not unequal.

The key element here is difference. An ethic of care should anticipate what people need, recognizing differences among them. Otherwise differences are transformed into an identity problem. If someone bases differences on a concrete category such as race, ethnicity, or gender, it becomes an inferior identity. It leads to stereotyping or typecasting. To be different is to be less than others. Alternatively, taking advantage of a difference because of a rigid category can be seen as corrupt. The difference might not be associated with a need—it is the rigidity of identities and categories that makes recognizing difference problematic. This is how critics of affirmative action prevail.

By casting this net in terms of gender and not the mind and body, however, Eisenstein misses an opportunity to cast it even wider. The pregnant body is only one type of body that could represent the standard. One of the least rigid and most inclusive standards would be the *different mind or body*—the mind or body that society perceives as different from the norm—the body of the person who has or is regarded as having a physical or mental impairment. Since pregnancy and other physical and mental conditions associated with maternity constitute a departure from the norm (albeit temporarily), this physical change could be subsumed under the definition of a disability. This is where an ethic of care could be bolstered by Spinoza and French critical theory.

## Doing, not being: a different ethic

Two theorists who create universal ethics that takes into account difference are Gilles Deleuze and Felix Guattari. Many radical feminists like Elizabeth Grosz, Moria Gatens, Claire Colebrook, and Genevieve Lloyd have embraced the thought of these French critical theorists since it is universal without being phallocentric. However, unlike Eisenstein and some other radical feminist theorists, Deleuze and Guattari cast aside the idea that a singular identity with something like full rights should ever be carved out. They oppose developing any form of identity politics, even if it is a pregnant woman who embodies the standard bearer.

To Deleuze and Guattari identity politics demands "territorializing." Identity politics stakes out one's turf in a social hierarchy or it creates a new social hierarchy. Deleuze argues that identity fosters a "struggle for territory or centrality of position ... [or] a pride of place."[43] For him, no standard individual or self can be an object of study. Deleuze sought to conceptualize both difference and becoming without relying on subjectivity. This difference and becoming should not be interpreted as "the becoming *of* some being."[44]

Basing an ethic of care on Deleuze's notion of difference is not tainted by inferiority. To be different is not to be second best. Difference for

Deleuze is an essential part of acting human. He identifies difference with creativity and individuality. Injecting Deleuze's notion of difference into an ethic of care would mean that people would be seen for who they are—not their essence, but in their becoming, or more specifically, in their doing.

It could be said that Deleuze and Guattari create existential ethics.[45] At first glance, this term contains an oxymoron. How can existentialism produce ethics? Existentialism examines how we behave, not who we are. By contrast, ethics advise people that by behaving ethically and morally, they will be ethical and moral. By contrast, Deleuze and Guattari establish ethics by advocating that people become more active beings. They should *do* more.

Deleuze and Guattari base their ethics on Benedict de Spinoza's work. Spinoza develops ethics himself because he insists that truth and knowledge must be associated with real world history and politics.[46] Indeed, Spinoza is considered the founder of critical theory because he anticipates what the theorist Christopher Norris considers the most vital issue among French theorists like Foucault, Jacques Derrida, and Deleuze. Spinoza is the first to "articulate self-understanding of critical philosophy as a discourse that was obliged *both* to take account of its own historical conditions of emergence *and* to subject those same conditions to a form of rigorous immanent critique."[47]

Spinoza believes that thinking is never carried on in "an abstract heaven of pure ideas." He does not ignore the pragmatist reduction of truth to what is "good in the way of belief," of knowledge despite power/ knowledge. The theorist David Bidney succinctly summarizes Spinoza's ethics, placing them in historical context by stating: "Plato had said: All virtue is knowledge. Francis Bacon added: All knowledge is power. Spinoza concluded: Therefore all virtue is power." Spinoza accepts the Platonic doctrine, Bidney maintains, "that virtue is knowledge but interprets knowledge in the Baconian sense of efficient power." Truth and knowledge are affected by "knowledge-constitutive interests."[48]

Spinoza uses critical thinking for ethics that cross the liberal/ communitarian divide. On one hand, Spinoza rejects the individualism underlying liberal political theory.[49] Spinoza counters the grim Hobbesian maxim, man is a wolf to man (*homo homini lupus est*) with man is a God to man (*homo homini deus est*).[50] It is not that Hobbes is wrong. Spinoza recognizes that a human being can be "wolf-like." Instead, Spinoza argues that Hobbes's account of human nature is incomplete. Some individuals will act like wolves, whereas other individuals will act like Gods or saviors, helping others. "There is nothing more useful to a man," writes Spinoza, "than a man." [51]

Spinoza maintains that one person will help another depending on the relationship between them. He insists that the individual and community should be distinguished in reciprocal and relational terms rather than oppositional ones. He departs from the work of Hobbes and other liberal theorists by rejecting the belief that the abstract individual is autonomous.

Using the same logic, Spinoza also condemns the communitarians for placing the individual and the community in opposition. Communitarians take the exact opposite position of liberal theorists by having the community or the collective subsume individual values and norms. The individual is sacrificed as the self dissolves into the community. They believe that social and political goods are shared and public in nature.[52]

Furthermore, the communitarians have no theory of power.[53] This is an omission Spinoza considers romantic and naïve. To him, politics is all about power.[54] The power dynamic, however, is framed in terms of relations between individuals rather than privileging either the individual or the community.[55] It is the relationship between the two that matters.[56] "Once we conceive of politics as power," philosopher Warren Montag explains in his interpretation of Spinoza, "the individual ceases to be a meaningful unit of analysis. For the power of the individual as individual—that is, as separate and autonomous, is so minimal as to be theoretically negligible." The key for Spinoza, Montag argues, is that "individuals alone do not possess sufficient power to preserve themselves and thus of necessity unite with others to survive."[57] In other words, Spinoza rejects the idea that social relations are between the individual and the state as the liberal social contract theorists like Locke and Hobbes propounded. For Spinoza, the fundamental relationship is between the state and the multitude—or in Montag's words, the state and the masses and their movements.[58]

In changing the fundamental relationship, Spinoza then must prove that individuals can and will unite—that they are not autonomous individuals. To do so, he explains that human beings, like other animals, have appetites. As such beings, they are determined to seek out what enhances, and avoid what depletes, their capacity to satisfy their appetites. What separates human beings from animals is that the former are conscious of their appetites. People remember how they satisfied their appetites earlier. Spinoza contends that they can also imagine their appetites, helping them figure out how to satisfy them in the future. He argues that human beings want their appetites and their future appetites to be judged "good" by the community at large, whereas they hope that the things that they dislike—their aversions—will be considered "bad."[59]

Spinoza concludes that people form desires to repeat those encounters that past experience has judged to be good. They are experiences, in other words, that produced joyful passions.[60] If one person experiences joyful encounters with another person, this shows that the two people struck an agreement.

Spinoza's relational approach is best illustrated in what he calls "common notions."[61] This term represents the hinge that connects the imagination and joyful passions to reason and adequate knowledge. Common notions arise when one individual encounters another with whom it is compatible. He or she therefore experiences joy. "To man, then, there is nothing more useful than man. Man, I say, can wish for nothing more helpful to the preservation of his being than that all should so agree in all things that the Minds and Bodies of all would compose, as it were, one Mind and one Body; that all should strive together, as far as they can, to preserve their being; and that all, together, should seek for themselves the common advantage of all."[62] Recognizing a community as a multitude of bodies in motion, Spinoza argues that when two individuals of entirely the same nature are joined to one another, they compose an individual twice as powerful as each one.

Common notions are essentially what Spinoza calls "adequate ideas." If an idea is adequate this means it will produce other adequate (read good) ideas.[63] These ideas, however, are not cognitive. They are embodied rather than epistemological. Spinoza believes that a theory of knowledge and a physics of bodies are interconnected, creating ethics.[64]

Spinoza recognizes, in other words, what the individual and the community have in common. To him, the individual cannot be viewed alone. The individual body is all about motion. This means that an individual is a "union of parts" that are communicating and communicating with motion. Each body exists in relations of interdependence with other bodies and these relations form a "world" in which individuals of all kinds exchange their constitutive parts. This notion of sociability, which cannot be separated from his understanding of individuality, leads to the enrichment of some individuals and the demise of others. Eating, for instance, involves the destruction of one body at the same time as it involves another's enhancement. Hence each individual body exerts a causal force, and each is in turn constantly being impinged upon by others.[65]

Spinoza's relational view of power means that people preserve themselves by forming associations. Members join these associations and organizations because they agree with other members.[66] The associations, as Gatens and Lloyd describe, "congeal into institutional forms, such as juridical norms, through which the inevitable disagreements between individuals (as members, subjects, or citizens of a complex body) will be settled. Initially, however, the formation of viable associations will depend mostly upon the passions of hope and fear and will create common causes for these passions. . . . The simplest means for securing agreement within a collective is by creating common causes of hope of reward and fear of punishment. Such associations draw their force from Spinoza's notion of passion and imagination, rather than reason."[67]

Harmony occurs when the individual person's power is aligned with that of the collective. There must be unity. The individual and the collective, in other words, are mutually reinforcing. According to Gatens and Lloyd, "The political problem (how do we form associations) is analogous to the epistemological problem (how do we come to form adequate ideas)?"[68] These forms become mutually reinforcing. Together, they form a well-functioning unity.

All people must seek harmony to enhance their power.[69] A community, therefore, revolves around the principle that the more virtuous people are, the more power they have. The most desirable community, moreover, is one where this type of power has spawned peace or harmony.[70]

## A critical conception of care

An ethic of care based upon Spinoza's view of common notions and Deleuze's interrelated conception of difference offers us a morality that could humanize capitalism. Unlike the social constructionists' work on an ethic of care, this ethic would not be based on humanist metaphysics. Care would not stem from benevolence or the kindness of family members and strangers, something that makes some ethicists wary. Grounding a care ethic on critical theory means that it would be founded upon a different conception of what it is to be human.

Nonetheless, this critical care ethic still retains the four pillars of the old one. First, the idea that human beings are relational is interwoven into the very fabric of a critical conception of care. Spinoza's idea that people depend upon each other is not derived from the fact that we are "good" people. Neither Spinoza, Deleuze, nor Guattari rely on altruism. To them, Man is God to Man and Woman. People depend upon each other not because it makes them feel better, but because they realize that it is in their own self-interest. The abstract notion of an individual that drives capitalism and liberalism is not independent, as Hobbes and Locke argue, but rather interdependent, as Spinoza points out. This critical morality makes needs, not care, the operative term.

Needs should be taken into account not because of benevolence or because women are more caring than men. Benevolence smacks of paternalism. The problem is that others impose their will. Hirschmann and Eisenstein are properly cautious about second guessing. A care ethic should not mean that independent people (read caregivers) are dictating what dependent people (care-receivers) should do. Both the independent and the dependent should be free. This freedom stems from the realization that all human beings are interdependent. We depend upon each other to survive. The theoretical myth of autonomy that liberalism, and capitalism perpetuate must be broken.

An ethic of care should recognize needs *and* individuality as part of the human condition. This condition is based on doing rather than being. The state and society should have no preconceived notion of norms or identities. Rather, an ethic of care should start with "you need this to do that." It should be based on a positive conception of liberty that is not burdened by the Rousseauian dilemma of second-guessing because everyone is involved in determining needs.

Integrating such a care ethic into the workplace would introduce sociability—no worker would stand alone. A harmonious workplace is one that promotes the capacities and powers of its workers, not for their sake alone but for the sake of the entire workplace. The needs of the individual and the collective are mutually reinforcing. To be sure, the doing of the individual must be juxtaposed with the doing of the collective. The individual pursuing his difference would not be trampled if a system of proportional representation, not winner take all, is instituted. If a man stays home with the children, then he will have certain needs that emerge not from his identity as a man, but as a person interested in painting. An ethic of care based on individuality acknowledges both the mind and the body and its infinite possibilities.

A Spinozian ethic of care retains the second pillar of the feminist morality. It too makes no distinction between the public and the private spheres, as do capitalism and liberalism, which are governed by an ethic of rights. The public is simply an extension of the private. For Spinoza, how two people get along is multiplied and extended to all of the state and society. The personal is the political. Spinoza, Deleuze, and Guattari argue that the body is a microcosm of society and the state. Beginning with a body, they extend their idea to all bodies—the individual can be extended to the multitude. As explained earlier, Spinoza coins the term common notions to illustrate how everyone should be regarded as interdependent and that there is no distinction between personal and public spaces.

The third pillar of an ethic of care—difference—is exhibited in its critical incarnation. A critical conception of a care ethic begins with the notion of difference. Spinoza, Deleuze, and Guattari, however, perceive of difference not in terms of identity or being, but in terms of doing. They agree with the ethicists that difference is not second best. Their notion of difference and becoming helps create an ethic of care based on needs that are not static or rigid. Needs can be universal and yet not phallocentric as long as the Cartesian dualism is replaced with Spinoza's monism.

The final, fourth pillar that an ethic of care is discursive is also an integral part of the new conception of care. A critical ethic of care rests on the idea that there are no universals. Spinoza, Deleuze, and Guattari reject universals from the point of Cartesian epistemology. They all question knowledge. These critical theorists go further than the traditional ethic in that they reject the duality of the mind and body. Examining our corporeality transcends the categories of sex, gender, race, and sexuality.

## Location, location, location

Creating an ethic of care in the workplace could also put bodies in revolt. Difference can be transformed into resistance. Critics of Foucault insist that his work is so pessimistic that it offers no chance for reform.[71] If Foucault argues that power is everywhere, then is there any room for resistance?[72] Jurgen Habermas sums up Foucault's paradox simply as "why fight?"[73] Foucault's critics, however, overlook his argument that power relations can be unmasked in local areas. Casting aside universals, Foucault claimed that power and resistance exist in specific locations, like a prison or a workplace.[74]

Foucault treats power and resistance as analytical conditions of each other by deconstructing dualisms like power and powerlessness or the individual and society. To Foucault, resistance, like power, is a socially constructed category. It cannot be perceived as "out there" or as a free-standing category.[75] Resistance is both an element of the functioning of power and, as Dierter Freundlieb describes it, a source of its perpetual disorder.[76] Resistance is associated with self-creation.[77] Hence, there is a possibility for resistance wherever power is exercised.[78]

Furthermore, Foucault insists that particular exercises of power should be understood in terms of the resistances they confront, generate, or even promote.[79] Resistance is what eludes power. As a result, power seeks out resistance—its adversary. For power to minimize resistance, Foucault maintains, it must divide-and-conquer, or as he explains it, "individualize" the forces of the institutions that it creates. Inequality constitutes an essential element of power, whereas resistance must be associated with an absence of hierarchy in what Foucault calls "counterpower." Resistance or counterpower, however, cannot be characterized as antimatter or a negation of power, though Foucault links resistance with horizontal conjunctions and equality. Like power, it can also be productive or affirmative. Resistance relies on strategic knowledge and represents Foucault's ideas of revolutionary action.[80]

To liberate someone, Foucault agrees that political struggle is essential. But one does not struggle against power to achieve justice, a term bogged down by a universal notion of truth, but rather to take power or to exercise counterpower.[81] Power may have formed disciplined individuals, who are rational, responsible, productive subjects, yet Foucault suggests that their action should not be confused with their nature as human beings. Being an obedient subject does not reflect one's human nature.[82]

Jessica Kulynych, a political scientist, maintains that Foucault's notion of resistance is best portrayed "performatively" or in terms of performative action. Unlike representative action, performative action has no antecedent referent. There is no precursor or forerunner. As Kulynych explains: "The character to which the action refers, as the theatrical portrayal of a character, only comes into being through the action itself."[83] Impairment is not tantamount to weakness. There is "an unchallenged dogma that the possession of an impairment leads to social vulnerability," says disability studies expert Vic Finkelstein. "This is despite the fact that history teaches us precisely the opposite: that the natural vulnerability of human beings has significantly shaped the development of all the machinery of modern life."[84] "Able-bodied people have deposited their own natural 'vulnerability,' and genuine social dependency," he adds, "into us as if this was unique to being disabled."[85]

Where can persons with disabilities practice resistance? One obvious location is in the American workplace. The next chapter reviews the hierarchical nature of the workplace. It describes how this workplace became rationalized, standardized, and formalized in the late nineteenth and early twentieth centuries. This historical overview will then help us understand how persons with disabilities—not those without them—can liberate their fellow workers by undermining Max Weber's notion of rationality in modernity.

# CHAPTER 4

# The Body at Work

When industrial capitalism emerged in the U.S., the idea that a care ethic might govern the workplace could not have been further from the mind of most employers. Most employees were not governed by an ethic of rights that had any political or legal grounding. The market dictated work conditions. By selling their labor rather than the goods they made with it, wage laborers accepted a hierarchical form of managerial power and authority that is antithetical to a Spinozian care ethic based on sociability. It was not employee differences but their similarities that employers hoped to capitalize upon.

Indeed, industrial capitalism constituted its own mind/body duality. The worker represented the body—not the unique body of the craft worker, but the standardized body of the factory line worker. It was the owner, the manager, and the scientific management expert who embodied the workers' minds, giving them detailed instructions about how to work on the factory line. Armed with stopwatches, scientific management experts conducting time–motion studies advanced this mind/body duality by studying a worker's performance to identify the one "right" way to accomplish a specific task. These experts then presented this information to the factory owners and managers who aggregated and processed it, enabling them to run efficient factories and offices that produced goods and provided services.

Industrial capitalism and later mass industrial capitalism built work forces upon the Enlightenment principle that bodies are identical. Bodies are considered interchangeable parts on the factory line. The notion behind workplace standardization rests on the assumption that the human form is machine-like. René Descartes viewed the body as mechanistic, with hundreds of interrelated pieces working in harmony like a clock.[1]

While the body represented the machine that worked toward efficiency (read profitability), it was the scientific management expert who tinkered with it. The expert designed, configured, and reconfigured the "body machine." One of the key elements of this expert design was that scientific management worked with a new perspective about time.

Before industrialization, time was task-oriented. "The working-day lengthens or contracts," E. P. Thompson insists, in accordance "to the task."[2] Time was elastic, changing as each person took different amounts of it to fulfill a day's tasks. The completion of tasks and duties was dependent on the individual.

With the emergence of wage labor, time takes on a different meaning. Time becomes money—"the employer's money." The worker "clocks in" as employers buy their labor on the basis of time. It is no coincidence, as Thompson observes, that Henry Ford, whose theories both he and Max Weber view as the apogee of rationalizing and standardizing labor, started his career repairing watches.[3] "If any social upheaval can ever be attributed to one man," Daniel Bell elaborates, "the logic of efficacy as a mode of life is due to [Frederick Winslow] Taylor. . . . We pass the old rough computations of the division of labor, and move into the division of time itself."[4]

The new conception of time prevented capitalists from addressing individual needs in the workplace. Fulfilling a worker's needs would undercut the industrialized notion of time. It would also undermine the very idea of the standardized workplace, built not for the individual worker, but the *average* worker. Industrialization little recognized a worker's needs, taking into account his or her individuality.

Individuality should not be confused with individualism, however. As explained in the last chapter, individualism rests on humanist metaphysics, which in turn relies on truth, rationality, and a firm belief in human essence. It "refers to an ideological position which prioritizes the self over community," writes cultural theorist Philip Hancock, "and assumes a common humanity to which all people subscribe."[5] While every individual may be "in it" for himself or herself, individualism places little value on difference. It awards each individual an identity, whereas individuality spurns the idea that people have one. Each person is distinct, separate, and unique.

Capitalism rejects needs as well by questioning the idea of human agency. The notion of need makes human beings products of their environment rather than its masters. Needs undermine the dualistic ontology created during the Enlightenment that both separated and hierarchically ordered subjective and objective reality. Human beings were seen as what Hancock characterizes as "the rightful masters of the material environment, controlling and transforming it with the help of reason and science."[6] While some human beings literally are masters, such as factory and business owners, managers, and scientific experts, others (namely the workers) implement their masters' vision. Despite this division, all parties are supposed to work together advancing history or the *telos*.[7]

Recognizing worker needs therefore defies the Enlightenment notion of reason. To show need is to reveal fragility and vulnerability. Human beings are victims of natural circumstances. Whether the needs are those of men, women, children, or persons with disabilities makes little difference. It is the notion of need, which supposedly diminishes human agency, that is antithetical to the capitalist workplace.

## "Needs are dangerous"[8]

Since the nineteenth century, market behavior followed a utilitarian or laissez-faire mindset. That is, the market revolved around material incentives. Everyday life centered on a materialistic morality and only one day of leisure was reserved for an idealistic morality.[9] On Sundays people devoted themselves to spirituality and contemplation.

Adam Smith went so far as to create a theory of moral sentiment based on the separation of the material and the ideal. Part of Smith's perspective depended on a camera theory of knowledge, or what he called spectatorship. This theory maintains that under a material spectatorship objects can be accurately represented, thereby making natural laws understandable. Smith, however, relied on a different type of spectatorship to understand moral sentiments. These sentiments, he contended, could be distinguished from material ones because they belong to the internal, as opposed to the external, world. Smith construed moral sentiments as the passions, affections, and feelings that we all have within our individual internal world.

Separating the material from the ideal, Smith suggested that the two different spectatorships contained different motives, both of which he attributed to nature. These motives were both eternal and immutable, like economic laws. It was only through the camera lenses of both spectatorships that people had the capacity to observe human behavior. Conclusions about human behavior could be made first because of observation, and second, he said, by relying on empirical data.[10] Smith observed behavior with one lens while pondering what moral principles had guided this behavior with the other.

To understand society as a whole, Smith examined the interplay between the natural efforts of each individual for making his or her own condition better. This should be taken into account along with the impact of moral sentiments through the constancy of human nature.[11] The public interest was "best served by permitting each one to pursue his own interest in his own way."[12] Smith summed up the economic determinism of his notion of the invisible hand with the term "the rational pursuit of self-interest."

Needs, however, do not fit within Smith's conception of a rational society. They cannot be classified as either observed behavior or moral sentiments. They are neither rational nor ideal.[13] Indeed, neoclassical economists who closely follow Smith's footsteps argue that there is no such thing as needs. "What do you mean by a need?" some economists ask. "Is a need just something you want but aren't prepared to pay for?" These economists are simply converting needs into preferences and demands.[14]

Unlike needs, preferences and demands fit well into the utilitarianism of orthodox economic theory. Utilitarianism places value in individual utility. Preferences and demands have utility—they can explain how something is used—whereas needs do not. Put differently, preferences and demands cannot be defined in terms of a mental characteristic such as pleasure, happiness, or desire. Instead they are defined in terms of the achievements derived from this characteristic.[15] As the heterodox economist Amartya Sen explains, utilitarianism "treats preferences, choices or tastes as private, individual, unconditional, unconditioned and arbitrary. Even abstract preferences such as the desire for security or freedom are considered to be formed inside each individual."[16] Needs, by contrast, can explain someone's preferences, but they have no utility.

By making abstract principles personal or internal, utilitarianism is suggesting that society cannot (and should not), anticipate peoples' needs. Each individual must be left alone to choose what he or she needs and what he or she should spend. "What humans do and do not need," heterodox economists Len Doyal and Ian Gough expound, "is something that can only be determined by themselves."[17] In fact, utilitarianism derives its moral power from this fundamental principle. Whether people decide to live in poverty or wealth is a personal choice. Neither society nor the economic nor political system makes these choices.[18]

The libertarians Friedrich Hayek and Robert Nozick further claim that when policymakers try to gauge needs they fall short. Needs are such rigid tools, Hayek and Nozick argue, that they lead to tremendous policy-making failures. Supposedly, urban blight can be attributed to policy-makers with a needs orientation. It is the rigid housing codes that led to planned communities, which turned into "ghettos."[19] Hayek and Nozick also claim that the policymakers developing such needs-oriented programs have bypassed economics altogether. Instead of abiding by the rules of a capitalist economic system, they are making an "end run" toward equality and social justice.[20]

For Hayek and Nozick, the needs of any one individual or group of individuals cannot be satisfied by capitalism. A policy that fulfills needs, such as welfare, can be justified as charity. Charities, however, are not part of the economic system. They are extraneous. Fulfilling needs therefore cannot be integrated into the economic system.

## Needs at work

Examining the role needs play within the workplace reveals similar lines. Utilitarians as well as other orthodox economists think needs are unnecessary because they undermine the wage–labor relationship. This relationship is founded on wage earners selling their labor for a financial reward. Employers buy their time. Wage earners exercise their agency not by helping set work conditions, but by their power not to enter or to exit a particular workplace.

Beginning with Karl Marx, critics of capitalism have long objected to the selling of labor. They argue that it is "against the principles of 'democracy' for human bodies to be bought outright like objects" but that "they are nonetheless given a numerical value, called a wage."[21] This explains why Marx described the capitalist wage system as "wage slavery."[22] Or as critical theorist Brian Massumi explains, Gilles Deleuze and Felix Guattari believe that: "Bodies that collect surplus value and control money as means of investment are capitalists; bodies with only enough money to use it as a means of investment are capitalists; bodies with only enough money to use it as a means of payment are workers. Workers are human bodies that have been converted into commodities for purchase by capitalists."[23]

The heterodox economist Robert Heilbroner views the wage–labor relationship similarly. He highlights the legal system that provides for human agency, arguing that this helps account for capitalism's success. Wage earners maintain their agency since they can "enter" or "leave" the work relationship as it suits them. "Under a wage labor system," Heilbroner says, "workers are entirely free to enter or leave the work relationship as they wish." They have the "contractual right of refusal" not to work for a firm or factory. It is this right that "gives the mainstream economists the moral justification for this system."[24] Ensuring that the worker has the right to choose protects both the employee and the employer from the coercive use of property.

When capitalists buy wage earners' time they are buying the right to be the master of it. The wage–labor relationship is hierarchical. It has no pretension of being democratic. "The factory offered the ancient as well as the modern world an organization," Frederick Engels contended, "conducive to strict supervision."[25]

"The wage relationship itself," Heilbroner elaborates, "becomes a manner in which the domination of one class over another is invisibly introduced into the workings of the system."[26] Yet, was it a foregone conclusion who would dominate whom? Classical and neoclassical economists insist that capitalism is a free-floating concept. It is governed by theory, not shaped by history. Critics of capitalism like Marx, Engels, and Heilbroner, however, disagree.

By contrast, feminists exploring patriarchy give capitalism a historical dimension. Capitalism is a relative latecomer, they argue, only being introduced in the late eighteenth century, whereas patriarchy was not. On a theoretical level, the emergence of capitalism threatened patriarchal control. It destroyed many old institutions and created new ones, such as a "free" market in labor. Yet if capitalism eliminated differences of status among laborers, why did women remain in an inferior position in the "free" labor market? The feminist theorist Heidi Hartmann answers this question by developing the dual systems theory—that is, men used capitalism's penchant for hierarchical organization and control to extend the traditional division of labor between the sexes. Capitalism and sexism operated hand in hand.

Hartmann defines patriarchy as "a set of social relations, which has a material base and in which there are hierarchical relations, and solidarity among men that enable[s] them to dominate women."[27] Before capitalism, a patriarchal system existed where men controlled the labor of their wives and children. It was this system, she argues, that taught men "the techniques of hierarchical organization and control."[28] Once industrialization occurred, these men refused to relinquish their control over the labor power of women.

What did change was how patriarchy shaped the workplace. The direct personal system of control created by patriarchy was transformed into an indirect, impersonal system of control, mediated by society-wide institutions. Sexual stratification occurred alongside increasing productiveness and specialization in the work force.[29] "Patriarchy, far from being vanquished by capitalism," Hartmann argues, "is still very virile...."[30] It helps direct and form and shape modern capitalism. At the same time, capitalism helps change traditional patriarchal institutions.

### A classic pyramid scheme

The hierarchical relationship among workers, managers, and owners is critical to capitalism because it separates labor from the direction of production. In precapitalist society, a guild worker had no intermediary between himself and the market. This stemmed from the fact that he sold goods and products, not his labor.[31]

What is more, the master–journeyman–apprentice relationship was organized along linear lines. The apprentice could become a master. Capitalism, by contrast, facilitates no such upward mobility. In what heterodox economists like Stephen Marglin describe as a pyramidal hierarchical structure, workers are limited since their wages can never generate the capital necessary to become a capitalist.[32] The capitalist sits on top of a pyramid of control that no worker can scale without winning the lottery.

Finally, the capitalists themselves have little to do with producing the goods. They amass capital and mediate the entire production process without having much to do with the actual product. Given blinders by the division of labor, the worker not only lacks capital but also has little working knowledge about the different levels of production. Having both capital and information, it is the capitalist who achieves his success as a "middle man." "If the organizer became a producer himself," writes Marglin, "he would have had to settle for a producer's wage. ... Not much wit was required to see that their prosperity, as well as their survival as mediators, depended on this system."[33]

Marglin also argues that creating a strict hierarchy in the workplace is vital to capitalism not because of technical efficiency, but because of accumulation. The capitalist stands between producers and consumers. Adam Smith's pin manufacturer succeeded not because of technological superiority, but because he created an essential role for himself. The capitalist integrates the separate efforts of different workers into a marketable product, controlling the labor process, including how much is produced.[34] Workers agree to sell their labor, Marglin observes, because of their preference for goods and leisure. Deciding whether to work or not gave them little control over the labor process.[35]

### Gilded cages

In the early stages of capitalism, hierarchical control was established in harsh and cruel ways. Charles Dickens gave life to the harsh conditions in England with his fiction, but the U.S was no exception. It was not until after the Civil War that owners and managers paid much attention to work conditions. Then, between 1870 and 1900, a movement sprang up for "industrial betterment."[36]

Some employers, like the railroad magnet Cornelius Vanderbilt, joined the industrial betterment movement because they thought their employees were often "drunk and unreliable."[37] To "better" their workers, they established the Young Men's Christian Association (YMCA), which offered them recreational facilities, classes, and social clubs as a means of diverting their attention from alcohol and other "unsavory" activities.[38] Vanderbilt, however, was an exception. Most of the industrial betterment movement members were clergy, journalists, novelists, and academics.[39]

The industrial betterment movement collapsed by 1900 after the economy had undergone significant structural changes such as the emergence of mass production and corporate consolidation. Firms lost control of their work force not just because of poor work conditions, but because of badly trained managers. In fact, factory owners realized that workplace administration "had become increasingly chaotic, confused, and wasteful."[40] Part of this confusion stemmed from the fact that few managers knew their employees well any more.[41] At the same time, workers started demanding better treatment. Not only did some workers start participating in strikes and lockouts, hoping to force their employers' hands, but labor groups like the Industrial Workers of the World (IWW) and Eugene Debs's Socialist Party began talking about sweeping political and economic reform.[42]

## A revolution in management, not labor

The technological revolution that accompanied corporate consolidation irrevocably changed the relationship between employers and workers.[43] Relying on Protestant rhetoric, owners and managers decided it was no longer their duty to "better" employees. "No self-respecting workman," Frederick Winslow Taylor proclaimed, "wants to be given things, every man wants to earn things."[44]

Taylor developed a new managerial style—scientific management— aimed at giving employers rational control over the workplace. With this type of control, managers could maintain "harmony, not discord." Scientific management, or Taylorism, was designed to help each worker achieve his or her greatest efficiency and prosperity."[45] In return for this efficiency, some employers such as Henry Ford offered their work force a larger financial reward than ever before.[46]

Scientific management, however, created a system of control that was just as hierarchical as the form of simple control used by the industrial betterment movement. It was based on the day's principles about science and engineering. These principles could be described as impressionist, like the movements in science and art.[47] In the seventeenth century, nature and reality had been viewed like clockwork. This mechanistic view changed with the discovery of cells, molecules, germs, and electrons, all of which made it feasible for scientists, physicians, and artists to break down complex wholes into component parts.[48] Similarly, Taylor maintained that economic performance could be improved by breaking down the component parts of the labor process.[49]

Taylorism reflected the Enlightenment epistemology, which suggests that human behavior can be both observed and controlled. "Employees were to be studied, categorized, and understood in terms of what objectively definable needs must be met to overcome the negative effects of alienation," writes Hancock, "and ensure maximum motivation and commitment to their everyday activities." Scientific managers did not strive for this information to promote humanity. Rather they wanted to "ensure maximum motivation and commitment to their everyday activities" at the workplace.[50]

Taylor based action on thorough knowledge of the situation and on the application of empirical scientific or engineering principles. He observed discrete units of production, conducted time–motion studies and absorbed the workers' knowledge about how to perform specific job tasks.[51] The addition of new technology, the introduction of new work rules, the change in wage formulas, and the level of direct supervision happened because of management's recurring effort to control the physical and mental efforts of their employees in the early twentieth century.

The fundamental principle underlying Taylorism involved disassociating a worker's skill from his knowledge by dissolving the unity of the conception and the execution of a job task. As labor-management expert Harry Braverman describes, the difference between managers and workers was that some people conceptualized production, whereas others executed it.[52] According to management expert Peter Drucker, Taylor's belief that the "key to productivity was knowledge not sweat" proved to be the most effective idea of the twentieth century.[53]

The management style of Taylor depended on "science," which was grounded in "full-blooded empiricism" rather than the "rule of thumb."[54] Taylor himself expressed an "unshakeable belief in utility and morality of scientific reasoning."[55] The rational methods scientific management used were cost accounting systems, production, and wage payment plans. Taylor, however, retained the classical economic axiom that most people are self-interested. It was through their mutual self-interests that employees and employers could work together on an economic, as opposed to a human, endeavor.

To ensure the best means of executing a job task, Taylor also focused on how the body functioned physiologically.[56] What could the average body accomplish? Scientific management set goals for the average member on a factory line. It developed standards based on what his or her capacity could be.[57] Managers scientifically selected, trained, taught, and developed workers to make sure they performed at full capacity, whereas in the past these workers chose their own work and trained themselves as best they could.

Taylor developed an almost equal division of work. Ultimately, the task idea meant that "the work of every workman is planned out by the management at least one day in advance, and each man receives in most cases complete written instructions, describing in detail the task which he is to accomplish, as well as the means to be used in doing the work."[58] Taylor helped redefine the industrial revolution with an emphasis on division of labor that increased productivity by analyzing and then standardizing each step of the production process.[59] Management was responsible for quality and productivity.[60]

Taylor, however, did not believe that laborers should be paid according to their productivity. He rejected profit-sharing and was very patronizing about the work force. If the "class of labor" is paid "more than about 60 percent" of what they produce, he proclaimed, "they become less thrifty."[61] Condemning Taylor for this practice, the populist muckraker Upton Sinclair remarked, "I shall not soon forget the picture he gave us of the poor old laborer who was trying to build his pitiful little home. . . . [He] was induced to give 362 percent more service for 61 percent more pay."[62]

Workers were not supposed to be involved in determining the labor process. It was managers who performed the organization's brainwork. Scientific management therefore propagated the mind/body duality. Taylor triggered a revolution by getting managers to change the way they thought about themselves. Becoming the mind of the workers, management became a profession. Engaged in this new profession, managers started developing concepts, research methods, and specialized techniques that could help their colleagues and eventually became a course of studies.[63]

Initially laying out his philosophy when he appeared before the American Society for Mechanical Engineers in 1895, by 1911 Taylor's ideas had become so popular that his book, *The Principles of Scientific Management*, was a national best-seller.[64] Progressivism in the 1910s and 1920s further extended the reach of scientific management, endorsing its emphasis on science, empiricism, rationality, efficiency, competence, and moral integrity.[65]

### First the cages

For Max Weber, scientific management in the U.S. marked the apex of the application of formal rationality. This management technique, he argued, fully rationalized the human being, essentially turning each individual employee into a tool or a machine. This whole epoch of scientific management revealed the centralization of the means of control and the mechanization of production. Most important, the individual employee had his or her behavior standardized—that is, each machine was designed to accommodate the average person. Output was based on what this average person could produce. As the process for rationalization became more complete, individual workers became more adapted to the machines. Those who lagged behind were either terminated or left the workplace voluntarily.

As scientific management became the dominant management technique, the relentless growth of rationalization became the hallmark of the American workplace.[66] Capitalism, however, was only part of the larger quest for the rationalization of the American state and society. As the theorist Martin Albrow explains, "Whenever the doctor prescribes a medicine, the accountant draws up a balance sheet, the electrician makes a circuit, the airline pilot checks his altitude, or the school pupil does an exercise in arithmetic, they all make use of a set of principles of enormous extent, intricately related, codified in textbooks, learnt by painstaking application, being constantly developed and providing the basis for rational action."[67] Formal rationality made practical affairs effective. Activities could be ordered methodologically with rules, regulations, and routines. Sophisticated routines could be established for government and for business.

Formal rationality was only one of the three types of rationality that Weber distinguished as having the capacity to give purpose to human action. Practical rationality complemented formal rationality. This latter type of rationality involved selecting the easiest and the most efficient means available to achieve a desired end. Like formal rationality, practical rationality did not help someone make value judgments about politics. Both formal and practical rationality were devoid of these judgments.

The type of rationality that did render such judgments was substantive rationality. Substantive rationality was laden with values, with people postulating beliefs that imposed order on the world. Unlike practical rationality, substantive rationality made the world conform to the deeply held values of those subscribing to it. Substantive rationality is also relative to points of view. Ultimately, however, it indicates that someone is making choices about which values to pursue.

When Weber laments rationality, he is speaking of the first two types—practical and formal—not substantive. To him, the modern world, with its huge, well-reasoned bureaucratic governments and companies, fostered formal rationality and that formalism propagated superficiality. Finding the key to understanding superficiality was the key to understanding modernity.

Weber recognized that most individuals embraced formal and practical rationality for many reasons. Some supported the theory underlying formalism, while others just thought it was easier to subscribe to it and follow formal rules. Few individuals pursued substantive rationality, rethinking their values and their value structure as times changed. Rationalization, a term Weber coined to describe the advancement of formal and practical rationality, gained ground in the twentieth century in such a way that most people either accepted the new rules and regulations or at least adapted themselves to them. The new routine could be as simple as using a multiplication table or as complex as having judges and jurists understand the techniques of modern law.[68]

Weber thought that reason, which had once helped human beings control the world, yet now led to alienation and disenchantment.[69] He associated reason with control and domination instead of freedom. This explains why Weber was so pessimistic about modern society and how it limited the freedom of individuals.

It was the bureaucracy, however, that represented the purest example of formal rationality. Staffed by officials who provided sober, rational, impersonal service, the bureaucracy, whether it generated knowledge and information that could be wielded by the government or a workplace, followed strict rules and regulations.[70] Up against the bureaucracy, the ordinary citizen or the individual employee hardly stood a chance of exercising his or her own will. It was not just the rules and regulations, but the bureaucrats' actual expertise these individuals could not match when wielding their own discretion.[71] And once a bureaucracy gained authority because of its association with the rules, its domination was more complete. To be sure, Weber does not argue that the bureaucrats had agency. The bureaucrats themselves exercised little control or discretion.[72] Rather, the rationality underlying the bureaucracy was systemic.

For Weber, modernity meant that formal rationality had vastly increased its hold over the state and society and that people could claim less and less mastery over their lives.[73] Beginning with the monastery and the military, formal rationality established a type of control that spread to the hospital, the home, and the factory.[74]

In the American factory, scientific management came to be an almost perfect expression of Weber's notion of formal rationality. Employers created standards without giving much thought to an individual's particular circumstances. It is the employee who complies with the standard, not the reverse. A rationalized workplace means, in other words, that employees have had their behavior standardized.[75]

The primary ramification of establishing the explicit and formal rules under American scientific management was the disempowering of labor through the transfer of working knowledge from labor to capital and management.[76] These mechanisms included not only the formal rules orientation of bureaucracy, but also the specialization of task, division of labor, separation of task conception from execution, strict hierarchy, and differential reward according to level found in this organizational form, with the emergence of bureaucracy in the mechanisms of the organizational structure channel behavior.

Nothing could be further from the rationalization of the American workplace in the early twentieth century than an ethic of care. Workers themselves were not viewed as individuals. Suggesting that employers should look into the faces of these individuals to discover their needs would have been considered outlandish. Workers entrusted their bodies to owners, managers, and scientific experts, who decided what to do with them. Their minds and bodies would be studied and transformed to increase productivity and profits. The owners, managers, and scientific experts shared some of the profits without relinquishing any control over the labor process. Scientific management entrenched the division between the mind (owners, managers, and experts) and the body (workers), making it an integral part of modernity.

### Management's human touch?

By the 1920s, the fundamental techniques of scientific management—piece rate and time–motion studies—were commonplace.[77] Not all experts, however, remained enthusiastic about scientific management's emphasis on science, engineering, and rationality. Lillian Gilbreth and Henry Gantt turned to psychology, sociology, and political science as a means of giving more attention to the human aspect of the labor process. Most notably, Gilbreth turned this human aspect into a new field of personnel management.[78] She created what became known as the human relations scientific management approach where productivity *and* social harmony, she claimed, should be fostered as a means of ensuring management legitimacy and success.

The optimistic twist Gilbreth gave this new management technique came from the psychologist Abraham Maslow's ideas about self-actualization.[79] Maslow's hierarchy of needs offered personnel managers a standardized model for understanding human behavior. Self-actualization represented the pinnacle of human development, describing people who could be "reconciled with their ontological destiny."[80]

Underlying the preoccupation with the social-psychological aspects of work, as management expert Reinhart Bendix illustrated, was the idea that managers could better secure compliance by shaping workers' attitudes.[81] "Personnel managers," writes Hancock, were the new "front-line troops" who make every effort to combat the negative effects of employee alienation in the workplace....[82]

By the 1940s, the human relations school of scientific management had spawned a new area within management—personnel.[83] Personnel departments supplied managers and supervisors with behavioral technologies. They conducted tests gauging the aptitude, personality, job preference, and manual dexterity of their employees, all based on the law of human averages. With the creation of these departments, managers became aware of themselves as members of a distinct class set apart from the rest of the work forces.[84]

As managers, they tried to be more effective at regulating their workers, attending not only to their behavior but their thoughts and emotions. Control was more subtly exercised under scientific management than ever before. It was no longer the expert with a stopwatch. By the late 1940s it was a bureaucrat armed with formal rules and procedures who controlled the workplace.[85] Management expert Charles Perrow observes that the whole workplace structure, including the belief system and the vocabulary of all the employees, came under a new form of unconscious and therefore unobtrusive control.[86]

While the hierarchy between the employer and the employee was now manifested by bureaucratic rules and regulations, this did not mean that employees required any less supervision. One of the first management experts in the academy, Chester Barnard, insisted that workplace design create an organizational geometry that would give employees only a very narrow space to operate in. The hierarchy got taller as the bureaucratic form of management created many levels of authority.[87] Barnard developed what could be characterized as an organic theory of control, with managers making organizational decisions based primarily on an economic notion of efficiency.[88]

## Group discipline

Initially, scientific management experts had been hostile toward organized labor. Workers had no need for representation under this type of management. After World War II, some experts started rethinking this position. They thought unions could help discipline workers. Given organized labor's emphasis on seniority and setting wages to job descriptions, rather than the individuals who fill them, unions, particularly industrial unions during the postwar economic boom, have helped promote and maintain this discipline.[89]

Morris L. Cooke, for instance, embraced collective bargaining.[90] Cooke believed that American unions could help play a role in scientific management in large part because they could help discipline the work force, and yet they were not involved in the labor process.[91] After World War II, it became clear that unions, which had few labor leaders who were attentive to the labor process, would remain uninvolved. American unions, labor historian Howell Harris explains, gave employers "the right to manage."[92]

With many employers realizing that organized labor would not disturb their power and authority, some actually decided that unions could help them ensure group discipline. Many management experts contended that to further strengthen managerial prerogative power, an efficient organization should strive toward maintaining group discipline. "Not only are affirmative incentives lacking," says the economist and management expert Oliver Williamson, "but there are disincentives, of group disciplinary and promotion ladder types, which augur against resistance to authority on matters that come within the range customarily covered by the authority relation."[93]

Industrial relations legal experts like Archibald Cox saw the saliency of group discipline immediately. He argued that the collective bargaining agreement "should be understood as an instrument of government as well as an instrument of exchange."[94] He said that "the collective agreement governs complex, many-sided relations between large numbers of people in a going concern for very substantial periods of time."[95]

## "Do it and shut up!"

The next incarnation of scientific management—internal labor market literature and transaction cost theory—had its roots in the industrial relations economics literature of the 1950s and 1960s.[96] By 1975, Williamson introduced transaction cost theory, which transformed what mainstream economists previously had considered a management problem into an economic one.[97] Williamson and other members of transaction cost economics contend that vertical integration is necessary to maintain efficiency.

To Williamson, the entire employment contract depends on a hierarchy in the workplace. An employment contract between an employer and an employee only exists when "W agrees to accept the authority of B in return for which B agrees to pay W a stated wage."[98] To maintain the integrity of this type of relationship, Williamson insists that a firm should deindividualize employment relations.[99] "The internal labor market achieves a fundamental transformation," Williamson suggests, "by shifting to a system where wage rates are attached mainly to jobs rather than to workers."[100]

Williamson makes two assumptions about assessing the nature of contracts: first, the ability of economic actors to achieve rationality and efficiency in their transactions is bounded. Second, actors are opportunistic.[101] "Although it is in the interest of each worker, bargaining individually or as a part of a small team, to acquire and exploit monopoly positions," he concedes, "it is plainly not in the interest of the *system*."[102] Labeling individual bargaining "opportunistic" because it gives workers opportunities they would not otherwise have, Williamson claims that this type of bargaining not only wastes resources, but it possibly delays management from making efficient adaptations in the workplace.

Williamson argues that the employment relationship should be transformed. Bargaining costs should be lower; internal wage structure must be rationalized in terms of objective task characteristics; and consummate rather than perfunctory cooperation could be encouraged so that investments of idiosyncratic types, which constitute a potential source of monopoly, are undertaken without risk of exploitation.[103]

An employee consents "to tell and be told."[104] "The power of fiat ultimately resides in the fact than an employee within a certain 'zone of acceptance' is indifferent to the exact content of the work to which he or she will be assigned. In turn, this indifference is based on the fact that an employee has contracted for a fixed salary and therefore faces what Williamson calls weak incentives."[105] Control systems need to be designed so as to elicit an employee's consent and commitment to the interests of the firm, thus avoiding agency problems.[106]

The control systems vary from simple, personal control systems to highly bureaucratized and formalized systems with much explicit contracting. The particular control system used depends mainly on sociopolitical factors such as the extent of labor mobilization and other indicators of the relational strengths of employers and employees; technical efficiency considerations are assumed to be less important determinations of the kind of control system used.[107]

## Braverman's bodies

The above description shows that managerial prerogatives, or the employer's absolute right to govern, represents the vital component of all forms of scientific management. Not all economists, however, agreed with Williamson's supposition that a hierarchical organization promotes economic efficiency, particularly as the century wore on. By the mid-1980s, Robert Hayes and Steven Wheelwright, from the Harvard and Stanford Business Schools, respectively, found that "the larger the work force, the more supervisors, coordinators and managers are required ... communication and coordination becomes more difficult, so additional support personnel are required. For example, whereas a 200-person work force would normally have at most three organizational levels above the workers, a 2000-person work force typically has four or five levels."[108]

Criticism by Hayes and Wheelwright as well as other management experts led to a reevaluation of hierarchical control and helped transform management practices in Fordism and neo-Fordism. David Gordon shows that in 1994, 17.3 million supervisory jobs existed in the U.S. This figure, he underscored, was between three to six times higher than in any country in Western Europe and Japan.[109] "If a labor-management system relies on hierarchical principles for managing and supervising its front-line employees on the shop and office floors—as does that in the United States," Gordon maintains, "then it needs more than just the front-line supervisors who directly oversee these production and nonsupervisory workers. ..." The question then becomes 'Who keeps the supervisors honest?' In such a hierarchy, you need supervisors to supervise the supervisors." As one worker succinctly described this emphasis on managerial prerogative power—his supervisor often said: "Do it and shut up!"[110]

Management always controlled the labor process as scientific management underwent different incarnations from Taylorism, human relations, and bounded rationality, to transaction cost theory. It could be argued that the entire twentieth century was dominated by management following the fundamental principles under scientific management. Human relations tried to humanize it and bounded rationality used another element of rationality emphasized by social science, but the idea of separating the method of work from its execution remained constant.

In the groundbreaking book, *Labor and Monopoly Power*, Harry Braverman renders the most significant critique of scientific management and its different incarnations throughout the twentieth century.[111] Given its significance, a whole school of labor-management experts began to ponder the issues Braverman introduced in the 1970s.

Braverman's critique could be viewed from the perspective of the critical care ethic laid out in chapters 2 and 3. What Taylor does is separate the worker's mind from his body. In a Descartian twist, Braverman suggests owners, managers, and scientific experts embody the worker's mind. They instruct and direct the workers. Scientific management experts supply the owners and managers with the data. These experts, however, derive the data from watching the workers themselves.

Under scientific management the workers are therefore recognized solely for their brawn or their bodies. Taylor treats them like machines, going so far as to study physiology to ensure how best to make use of the human body. Increasingly subdividing jobs into smaller and smaller fragments, Braverman argues, degraded the labor process without the workers fully realizing it.[112]

To Braverman, Taylorism therefore violated the most important aspect of work—that it is purposive action. Moreover, by placing work in a political-economic context of the capitalist employment relationship, Braverman shows that this relationship was not established at will. Employers hire employees to "expand their capital base, while employees seek employment because they have no viable alternative by which to sustain their lives and those of their families."[113] The employer/employee relationship was interdependent yet asymmetrical, with the former having more flexibility. They decided who they would hire, whereas most employees accepted a job to support themselves and their families and were fortunate to be given any choices.[114]

Braverman's critique fits in well with that of an ethic of care. Employers buy their time, using this time to make profits. The employee's idea that an employer should become a caregiver, anticipating and taking care of an employee's needs is antithetical to this core principle within capitalism.

With the history of American management intertwined with scientific management, relying on employee needs rather than profits would also upset employers. Management has become so successful because it adopted different incarnations and yet retained some of the key principles underlying Taylorism. While the human relations approach and its different incarnations claimed that they took into account human relations, they did so without looking at the individual. The individuality of the worker, let alone his or her needs, was ignored. The new scientific management experts worked with the law of averages and other actuarial terms to take into account what the average worker would and should do in the workplace. This positivistic approach dehumanized labor no less than Taylor had.

More importantly, the human relations approach saw the mind as part of the body, a part that should be captured. Management introduced Maslow's notion of self-actualization and other psychological theories not for the workers' benefit, but as a means to increase productivity and profits. As explained earlier, they became so successful that organized labor even participated in building the rules and regulations that helped discipline workers. Seniority systems and all the rules and regulations in the collective bargaining agreement also dehumanized the worker. It was not the individual worker who filled a job, but that the job description was filled by an individual worker. This did not make the human relations approach or the transactions cost theory any less hollow than Taylorism. Positivistic assumptions about human behavior can be found behind all the incarnations of scientific management.

At bottom, what the different theories of scientific management share still can be attributed to Taylor himself. He tried to directly influence efforts of workers while maintaining control over the intended purpose of their activities. Scientific management was transformed from command and control to control and inspire, and then as Gordon describes, back to command and control.[115] Hence, the main element in the scientific management equation is in Braverman's words, "managerial control."

Ultimately, Taylor's model led to what today is called "management by objectives."[116] A manager spotted his or her goals and then tried to reach these objectives with his or her work force. The objective, not the process, was the most important aspect of the job. The worker gets sacrificed to the objective. By the mid-1980s, all this began to change as the notion of vertical control, whether manifested by supervisors looking over workers' shoulders or through bureaucrats imposing extensive rules and regulations, was no longer seen as efficient. Worker productivity dropped tremendously. As a result, the very lynchpin of scientific management—vertical control—was questioned by management experts.

Changing managerial control could have been very liberating. In the mid-1980s, capitalists decided that vertical control was no longer productive and that forms of horizontal control and cooperation should be adopted. Most important, these capitalists had information technology that allowed them to forego another key principle of scientific management—that the manager and the expert constituted the brain-power of a factory or an office.[117]

The calls for reform from management itself spoke of reuniting the mind and the body of the factory worker or the office employee. Quite simply, they wanted employees to think for themselves. The old duality, in which workers were viewed as bodies and managers and experts were seen as minds, was fundamentally altered. Employees were engaged in thought, though not without the help of their new taskmasters—the computer and the robot.

The significance of this transformation cannot be overstated. Aided by high technology, the workplace could be tailored for each individual. With machines quickly sorting and absorbing data, there is no need to work on the basis of the average worker. Computers can assess the output of every individual every hour, let alone every day. Each employee could fit into the workplace like a piece of a continually changing jigsaw puzzle. Standards and the law of averages could be suspended.

American management, however, did not individualize the workplace, giving employees more discretion. The next chapter will show that rather than using this capacity for individualizing the workplace for the greater good, new techniques in management stop trying to command the employee's body, opting for shaping his or her mind. Neo-Fordism, the new managerial system, takes a Foucauldian turn as managers try to make their workers self-disciplined. They try to capture the subjectivity of their employees, hoping that the employees will make their individual needs tantamount to those of the office or the factory. This phenomenon, *Fortune* magazine reported, has consultants turning businesses and corporations into "corporate culture vultures."[118]

# CHAPTER 5

# Unmasking Control

If employers take into account human needs, they could profit from the individuality of their employees. To be sure, they would be pushing against the tide of twentieth-century history, challenging the forces of rationalization in modernity that Max Weber described.[1] Yet from the mid-1980s, robots and computers have given employers the capacity to benefit from the singular strengthen of each employee. However, instead of liberating their work forces, employers have wielded new technology to create ever more effective ways of supervising them.

Most importantly, information age technology has induced owners and managers to re-evaluate the worth of vertical or hierarchical control of their work forces. Many management experts observed that this type of control was no longer effective in the mid-1980s. A movement for horizontal or peer control emerged, heavily aided by technology. Computers and robots could gather most data needed to monitor and supervise a work force. The irony of post-Fordism is not that employee supervision has diminished, but that the number of supervisors themselves has been reduced. Machines have replaced the manager and scientific management experts—the supposed brainpower behind the mind/body duality of the work force that existed under Taylorism and Fordism.

In hindsight, the U.S.'s transformation to the information age in combination with its sinking fortunes in terms of productivity in the 1980s had been long coming. Once the postwar boom ended in the 1970s, the consumer market became saturated. The U.S., like many First World nation-states, became vulnerable to charges that the economy was no longer well managed. The libertarian Friedrich Hayek proclaimed that it was Keynesian economics that had caused massive inflation and what later became known as stagflation.[2] Hayek, moreover, was not alone. Critics from all sides leveled the charge that the effort to achieve full employment had failed and that the Fordist production system was obsolete.

Out of this economic crisis rose the postindustrial information age. What made this age distinctive was the dwindling number of blue-collar workers, the increasing number of white- and pink-collar workers, and the emphasis on gathering information and producing services instead of manufacturing traditional goods and products. The production process also changed, becoming marked by flexible specialization. A shift away from Keynesian economic management to neoliberal laissez-faire management occurred that spurned state involvement. Neoclassical economists, members of the business community, and many politicians argued that a new "permanently unemployed underclass was unavoidable."[3] A new term—the "working poor"—was coined.

Postindustrial and later global capitalism have created a new culture that has not only affected the new underclass, but also the middle, upper-middle, and wealthy classes in the United States. Weber's era of capitalism, which had been an expression of bourgeois society, ended as there was a shift away from a restrictive Protestant work ethic toward consumption.[4] Capitalism moved from the production of "useful" goods and services to the generation of semiotic codes and images. In *The Mirror of Production*, Jean Baudrillard shows how the role of the consumer, rather than the producer, increased.[5] Today, global capitalism must produce goods and produce consumers to ensure demand.

Generating consumption, however, is a much more expansive task than producing goods. "Rather than production/exchange operating as the regulating principle of social relations," explains managerial expert Philip Hancock, "the new technologies of information gathering and mass media has led to a situation whereby the codified signs produced through and by these technologies has emerged as the controlling determinations of everyday life."[6]

As part of the production of demand, Baudrillard suggests that the forms and substance of society itself are manufactured to sustain consumption. Every dimension of social existence is essentially a complex simulation of reality, designed to sustain the fragile cycles of political, economic, and cultural reproduction. The new organization of power invites individuals to behave as "collaborators" who fulfill their needs and desires by completing the outlines of constrained personal choices left partially unfinished, Baudrillard adds, in the codes of commodification. Commodity fetishism has become the new focus.

Once the idea took hold that the owners of capital must produce demand, critical theorists like Baudrillard, Gilles Deleuze, and Felix

Guattari contend that capitalism no longer really needed to justify itself.[7] Consumer capitalism is an economic system that is now stronger than the ideologies that helped produce and reproduce it. "The men who personify it—the Donald Trumps and the Michael Milkens of the world—do not represent capitalist ideology," explains cultural theorist Brian Massumi. Instead, Deleuze and Guattari purport, they personify a mode of irrationality.[8] Capital is an unmediated desire, or abstract machine. In theorist Nick Land's words, "Political cultures—traditions and subjectivities are dissolved as a result of consumer capitalism, which is defined by that fact that everything (even life itself) can be bought."[9] Or, as Massumi says, "Everybody must buy. . . . We all stand naked and alone before the capitalist relation that has come to encompass existence."[10]

Employees have been integrated into the economic system in terms of being both commodities on the job market and consumers under Fordism and post-Fordism, while an increasingly large number of employees cannot gain steady employment.[11] For those working, the battle is not over class but subjectivity. According to Massumi, Deleuze and Guattari aptly observe that "the new American right, for all its apparent archaism, has been more attuned than the traditional left to the forces of actual lines in late capitalist society." The new right perceives that the most volatile pressure points—"lifestyle" or "cultural" questions—"have shifted from class conflicts to subjectivity battles."[12]

Employers and managers have been well trained about how to battle for their employees' very souls. Management theories present many strategies and techniques to capture worker subjectivity. One of the most innovative techniques is establishing horizontal rather than vertical or hierarchical managerial control—that is, workers supervise each other and themselves. Horizontal control, however, only became possible because of technological advancements such as the computer. This type of control, combined with a spatially decentralized but highly centralized computer supervision system suits the new knowledge economy. Also, it is still effective in the old sector of the economy—manufacturing—where companies used robotics and complex computer systems.

Requiring brains rather than brawn, horizontal coordination in the workplace undermines traditional vertical control.[13] Theorist Manuel Castells uses the term "informationalism" to describe this phenomenon.[14] The informational work process, he explains, calls for cooperation, teamwork, workers' autonomy, and responsibility. Managers must therefore pay more attention to cultivating a cooperative and productive workplace culture.

Giving more autonomy and responsibility to the worker initially seemed as if management had created a "kinder, gentler" system. However, this system does not weaken the control managers exercise over their work force, or even lessen their prerogative power. Teams now give workers no more autonomy or better work conditions, or less of a hierarchical structure than the old system of vertical control. With information technologies such as the computer increasing the scope and reach of workplace surveillance and techniques for normalization, employers and managers simply mask their control.

Reviewing the scholarship of Foucauldian management experts William Sewell and Shoshanna Zuboff, this chapter will show how the combination of horizontal and vertical control affect the subjectivity of individual workers, making them increasingly self-disciplined and self-controlled. The irony here is that this type of labor process is more accommodating than either the vertical or horizontal one alone. The control, however, is more insidious and pervasive than the old system of scientific management and is not always detected by workers.

This crisis for employees who have managers inducing them into a self-disciplined work force has also created a significant chance for reform. Under the protection of the Americans with Disabilities Act (ADA), persons with disabilities could become agents of resistance as Michel Foucault imagines. Less susceptible to subjective control by the dominant culture, persons with disabilities can enlighten their colleagues about the human cost of surveillance. What is more, the control exerted by technology is not necessarily reflective of the mind/body duality of the old work force governed by scientific management and its different incarnations. Technology offers ways for employers to take into account individuality as never before, yet employers are not going to relinquish control without a fight. Half the battle for control over the workers' subjectivity would be lost if the employees knew precisely how employers orchestrate their activities.[15]

## Capturing employee hearts

The idea that businesses prosper, in Hancock's words, only when they learn "to extract maximum levels of task-orientated motivation and commitment from their employees, is nothing particularly new."[16] It was Taylor's initial idea. As another management expert elaborates, Taylor's scientific management is more than a set of technical processes and procedures, it is an "embryonic attempt at a project of cultural management, which seeks to combine instrumental and substantive values into a coherent cultural technology."[17]

Taylor saw nothing insincere or devious about cultural management. To him, scientific management rested on "the firm conviction that the true interests of the two [managers and employees] are one and the same."[18] They both want prosperity, which the employer gains in profits and the laborer receives in higher wages.

Gaining employee cooperation has taken a slightly different form in the global age." Managers reconstitute their employee's subjectivity by cultivating an environment that gives them the illusion of autonomy.[19] The defining factors of organizational life no longer exist within the economic or technological realm, but rather within the culture- and value-laden domain, which Hancock defines as component elements of "the organizational ideological superstructure." He partially attributes this "shift to the emergence of a range of innovative managerial discourses; most notably those of enterprise, flexibility, quality, and human resource management."[20]

## Going global

In 1970, only 3 percent of the work force used computers. By 1991 this figure increased dramatically with well over one-third of all employees becoming managers, supervisors, professionals, or technical workers, who relied on computers in addition to other forms of information technology.[21] It is now difficult to find a workplace without a computer.

At the same time, the number of professional and technical jobs has increased over 300 percent since 1950.[22] Traditional production, such as assembly work, data entry, fast food, and other types of direct labor, has decreased precipitously. In some high-tech firms, for instance, this type of work constitutes as little as 2 to 3 percent of the work force. As industrial relations expert Robert Reich notes, "it is the symbolic analyst—the administrative and technical specialist who manipulates ideas or data rather than things—not the factory line worker, who now represents the 'typical' worker."[23]

The demographics of the work force also underwent tremendous change. While in 1960, 61 percent of all households had a woman who remained at home, 30 years later only 25 percent did. The number of households in which both partners worked outside the home had increased from 28 to 54 percent by 1990. Also, the number of women in managerial executive positions grew from 20 to 40 percent and professionals increased from 44 to 51 percent.[24]

In the mid-1980s, management practices, still influenced by Fordism, started reflecting these changes. Management experts questioned the effectiveness of hierarchical or vertical control over the labor process. Some experts sought what became known as horizontal managerial control. They promoted teamwork under the theory of "total quality management" (TQM). Other management experts suggested that supervisors depend more on technological control—namely the computer. By the end of the 1980s, it was estimated that private enterprise had spent a trillion dollars on computers, robots, and other automated equipment.[25] With terminals placed everywhere—in offices and on shop floors—the computer constituted a spatially decentralized tool that offered supervisors a highly centralized system of social control. Managers could supervise their entire work force with the help of these machines.

By the 1990s, neo-Fordist labor practices displaced the Fordist ones. Neo-Fordism extended the central principles underlying Taylorism and Fordism by continuing to identify discrete manufacturing activities and reunifiy them into an integrated production system. It centralized control by transferring workers' knowledge to managers, and incorporating workers' "know how" into production machinery. The key management technique is called "reengineering." Replacing managers with computer surveillance and other labor-saving devices, this technique helps managers "do more for less." As labor-management expert James Rinehart explains, reengineering is a "polite" term for downsizing.[26]

While the primary distinction between Taylorism and Fordism stems from the latter applying scientific management techniques to a more sophisticated assembly line, neo-Fordism also broadens Taylorism by introducing centralized computer information flows that run throughout a business organization. Centralized computer centers give employers the leeway to eliminate layers of middle management. As labor-management expert Francis Wilson explains, "The advent of the lap top or hand held computer network and advanced digital telecommunications has changed the way information is collected, analyzed and stored."[27]

This technology supervises workers, not the managers. Whereas Taylorism and Fordism relied heavily on supervisors, neo-Fordism diminishes the decision-making authority of lower and middle managers with computers replacing them.[28] John Micklethwait and Adrian Wooldridge demonstrate that reengineering is the "first management theory to use computers as a starting [point] rather than a neat addition."[29] Both of the principles underlying Fordism and neo-Fordism, moreover, apply not just to assembly lines but also to white-collar employees working in offices[30]

Computer-based management does not replace the technologies of vertical control underlying scientific management and Fordism. Instead, this type of management offers employers a more insidious form of control.[31] "Computer-based information and communication technologies (ICT)," Wilson says, "coupled with quality management (QM) methodologies provide enhanced control over work force activities and provide management with improved surveillance and disciplinary efficacy."[32] Overall, information technology now gives employers irresistible opportunities for surveillance. As far back as 1994, one expert reported that of 300 companies, 70 percent admitted using electronic methods of covert employee monitoring.[33] For more than ten years, some employers have been using computer programs that secretly watch employees through video screens.[34]

Managers can monitor almost every type of worker all over the world with what labor-management expert Philip Kraft calls "continuous feedback."[35] Computer operators, for instance, can have their keystrokes per minute counted and the quality of their data entry monitored as they work, while telephone sales people have the number of "closing" statements they make scrutinized and the amount of time they take to complete a transaction recorded throughout a working day.[36]

Other companies use an electronic badge system. Employees wear small plastic badges that send infrared signals indicating their location. With the badges sending and receiving messages simultaneously, supervisors have the capacity to monitor their employees' work performance on a video screen, representing a modern day version of Bentham's panopticion.[37]

Whether it's by counting keystrokes or having employees wear badges, workplace surveillance is done 7 days a week, 24 hours a day at little cost. For service employees, the irony is that surveillance is touted as a means to better serve the customer rather than to control them.[38] For employers, the irony is that surveillance is countereffective with some, though not all, employees. One study, for instance, shows that employees who were watched closely were less productive than those who were not.[39] Another study reveals that employees who knew they were under close surveillance were more likely to leave their jobs than others.[40] As one New York lawyer's labor relations committee reports: "There simply is no credible evidence or factual or statistical proof that electronic monitoring and surveillance have achieved any positive results for employers."[41]

## To have, to own, or to exercise

Meanwhile, many labor-management studies show that the combination of horizontal control and a highly centralized computer system that monitors employees has been effective and can affect their subjectivity.[42] To be sure, employees have become increasingly self-disciplined and self-controlled. They internalize the rules and regulations that govern the workplace. While owners and managers might well profit from self-discipline themselves, middle managers and other employees clearly do not, causing many critics of capitalism to wonder why any employees participate in their own subjugation.

Explaining workplace alienation in nineteenth-century terms, Karl Marx characterized the mode of production as shaping the labor process from the top down. Private property produced the power that led to the proletariat's exploitation. To sustain this exploitation, the capitalists propagated an ideology that gave the proletariat "false" consciousness.[43]

Labor reform in the early and mid-twentieth century in Britain and Europe, not to mention the U.S., indicated that Marx's idea of false consciousness had served little purpose. While social scientists kept arguing after World War I, World War II, and during the 1960s that the proletariat knew that its consciousness was "false," few signs of revolt were in sight. Most postwar orthodox Marxists and neo-Marxists realized that the proletariat would need to lose more than their "chains." For some scholars, it was first Harry Braverman with his classic book, *Labor and Monopoly Capitalism,* and later Foucault, who have provided the most apt explanation of the "false" consciousness dilemma. Both Braverman's and Foucault's work explains employee subjectivity.[44]

Unlike Marx, Braverman no longer thinks management extracted the surplus value out of labor in the production process. Instead, he argues that exploitation resulted from an unequal market exchange between workers and capitalists. The market, not class conflict, creates exploitation.[45]

Most importantly, Braverman contests the *a priori* assumption underlying Marx's theory of class conflict that capital and labor have a zero-sum relationship. To him, this assumption ignores the twofold character of the capital/labor relationship. Marx downplayed worker agency. He could not have anticipated how much management would rely on the initiative, creativity, and motivation of their work force in the twentieth and twenty-first centuries.

After Braverman's untimely death, a school of thought called labor process theory emerged. Labor process theory further explores the *relationship* between capital and labor, focusing on employee subjectivity. Examining why employees give their tacit consent under mass industrial capitalism, and later global capitalism, becomes a central concentration of study.[46] Michael Burawoy, for instance, maintains that employees create their own workplace subcultures, which gives them a modicum of control over the labor process.[47] Employee's subjectivity, he argues, constitutes a source of consent as well as resistance.

In fact, understanding the value of gaining their employees' consent, large and small businesses alike initiated new tactics and approaches for supervising their work forces, starting in the mid-1980s, such as participatory schemes that involved giving everyone from the janitor to the chief-executive officer stock options, as Amazon did. Fordism began relying less on coercive means of managerial control than ever before. The new approaches work best when employers gained their workers' nominal consent. If employees think they share their employers' interests they are more compliant. According to Burawoy, management has initiated "unobtrusive modes of control" with the hope of gaining and maintaining workplace peace, harmony, and productivity.[48]

As labor process theory increasingly began emphasizing employee subjectivity, some scholars drew directly on Foucault's work.[49] Although Foucault never analyzes the workplace and contributed little to economics, his notion of the subject and disciplinary power gives these scholars insight about the employee's subjectivity. To him, it is the ruling class ideology that leads to false consciousness *and* consent, not (as Marx put it) class consciousness and a proletarian revolution.

According to Foucault, the precondition for consent is the technology of power. He therefore presents a strategic concept of power that resembles Niccolo Machiavelli's "strategic concerns" or Antonio Gramsci's notion of the hegemony as a "war of maneuver."[50] Examining the malleable, ever-changing subject, Foucault is concerned with how power is *exercised*, not what power *is*.[51]

Unlike Marx, Foucault locates exploitation and alienation not in terms of the economy, but in the creation of obedient bodies.[52] Capillaries of power reach "into the very grain of individuals, a synaptic regime of power, a regime of exercise within the social body, rather than from above it."[53] Power is not imposed from the top down or from the state or the economy onto society. It is not wielded by a judge who sentences a criminal. Rather, it is diffused or spun like a web throughout society, being exercised in local centers like the courtroom.[54] "Discipline may be identified neither with an institution nor with an apparatus," Foucault writes, "it is a type of power, a modality for its exercise, comprising a whole set of instruments, techniques, procedures, levels of application, targets; it is a 'physics' or an 'anatomy' of power, a technology."[55] As labor-management expert Ron Sakolosky puts it, power is *omnipresent*, rather than omnipotent.[56]

Realizing that power is a web of relations offers more insight into why it cannot be described as purely negative or repressive. Foucault envisions power as a positive and enabling force.[57] The individual who is subjugated does have some agency. Like knowledge, which Foucault characterizes as repressive *and* true, power is repressive *and* productive. It is both an outcome *and* a cause. Whereas Marx, being a child of the Enlightenment, was guided by the categories of truth and falsehood, Foucault spurns such terms, arguing that power and knowledge are simultaneously true and false, which is to say neither. Foucault, in other words, avoids universals.

Foucault's postmodern position does not preclude him from taking a normative direction, as some of his critics contend—he does condemn certain practices.[58] Disciplinary power and its negative consequences, however, can be only understood in terms of particular socio-historical settings.[59] Rather than arguing that ideological hegemony leads to class consciousness, Foucault might well have suggested that capitalist institutions have used disciplinary power for their own gain. These institutions have relied on normalizing instruments and surveillance to achieve their goals in specific locations.

## Corporate culture vultures

Few pieces of rhetoric fit Foucault's ideas about normalization better than TQM, the defining managerial strategy of the 1980s regarding workplace culture. William Ouchi's *Theory Z* and Terrence Deal's and Allan Kennedy's *Corporate Cultures* are good examples.[60] Ouchi, Deal, and Kennedy analyze how organizations transform managers and professionals into disciplined and disciplining members who identify with the corporations they work for. Creating a corporate culture, these professionals have internalized the language and the lifestyle associated with their work.[61] Most importantly, managers impart this culture to the employees they supervise. "The impact of strong culture on productivity is amazing," write Deal and Kennedy. "We estimate that a company can gain as much as one or two hours of productive work per employee per day."[62]

The overall argument underlying TQM is best expressed by the old adage that it costs less to make a good product than a bad one. Poor workmanship makes a product expensive. First, there is the cost of inspections and repairs. Second, not striving for good quality demoralizes employees, making them less productive. Finally, shoddily-made products turn customers away, reducing profits.[63]

To promote better workmanship, TQM instructs managers to cultivate an atmosphere that is based on making "continuous improvements."[64] If employees care about their work, as the story goes, they will work harder, develop a strong sense of loyalty toward their employers and the company itself, and be more likely to produce quality goods.[65] Therefore managers no longer measure and monitor the employee's behavior by looking over his or her shoulder. Instead, they find ways of predicting and controlling outcomes with what is called *ideational control*.[66]

Ideational control centers on a manager appealing to an individual employee's consciousness or subjectivity. Management experts often refer to ideational control as a postbureaucratic form of control because it no longer has an explicit rules orientation.[67] Rather than reprimanding employees for violating rules, supervisors convince their employees to internalize management's goals.[68] This type of control turns managers into coaches, who increase the productivity of their units by cheering them on.[69] Although TQM is a system based on rewards and sanctions, most of them are morale-boosting ones, not tangible ones like increased pay or bonuses.

By the end of the 1980s, the notions of culture, commitment, and continuous improvement became explicitly intertwined with management's efforts to revitalize the economy. TQM became so influential that it was considered a social movement rather than a management style. Public bureaucracies, health care organizations, nonprofit and even educational institutions adopted this style.[70]

After a decade TQM was no longer seen as sufficient in the highly competitive global business environment and it was transformed into reengineering. Its principles are considered too bureaucratic. Advocates of reengineering, by contrast, develop cross-functional approaches to the design and delivery of goods and services. In *Business Process Reengineering* the authors argue that "a company should be rebuilt as a process-oriented business ... where everyone regards working in cross-functional terms as the norm ... [and] knows that the key goal is to produce a service or product that the market perceived to be best."[71]

A greater emphasis has been placed upon customer service and on changes emphasizing teamwork and continuous, rapid improvement of processes or *kaizen*. "*Kaizen* asserts that while perfection is not reachable," explain Peter Webb and Harold Bryant, "it should be a goal."[72] *Kaizen* therefore constitutes a departure from the traditional American management perspective, which claims that progress stems from technological breakthroughs. Focusing on these breakthroughs, critics maintain, has meant that American employers rarely concentrate on making small quality improvements, which *kaizen* proponents insist has a tremendous impact on a product's quality.[73] Lester Thurow, a well known economist, attributes the low productivity rate in the United States to the fact that managers did not adopt innovative "process technologies" like *kaizen*.

As further evidence of this, Thurow writes that, unlike their European and Japanese counterparts, most American managers have little technological training. Yet, both TQM and *kaizen* have technological components that would be appreciated by people with this type of background. These managerial styles rely on statistical process control as well as statistics for quality improvement.[76]

Reengineering makes managers take a close look at the production process. It can be defined as a "radical redesign of a company's processes, organization, and culture to achieve a quantum leap in performance."[77] It has also been called simply "starting over." Only when executives are liberated from the shackles of company tradition or methodology do they focus on bringing about the radical changes inherent in reengineering.

Reengineering combines formerly distinct jobs with specific tasks. It reverses the fragmentation of Taylorism and Fordism. A generalist or "case worker" performs the whole labor process from one end to another with a team of cross-functionally trained workers. Ostensibly, individual employees are given more power and authority since whole layers of bureaucratic control are eliminated.[78] With less need for direct supervision, reengineered companies can vertically compress their organizations, reducing the bureaucratic overhead they can ill afford in a highly competitive global economy.[79]

Finally, reengineering includes the term "benchmarking," which describes the "continuous process of measuring products, services and practices against the toughest competitors or those companies recognized as industry leaders."[80] Team working constitutes the means of creating a "better" environment, emphasizing that a vertical control over the labor process is ineffective. The three main areas of success are: first, customer satisfaction; second, a labor process package of striving for quality, teamwork, and flexibility; and third, that local staff manage the labor process, creating a work force in which the employees "care about the company."[81]

To many critics of global capitalism, TQM and *kaizen* are just as repressive as scientific management or Taylorism in the early twentieth century. Labor-management experts Graham Sewell and Frank Webster, for instance, argue that managers established TQM so that employees could be controlled in the most efficient manner with a minimum of supervision.[82] TQM and other similar management styles such as reengineering, they argue, only gave the illusion of being less coercive than Taylorism. In reality, these styles strengthen management's disciplinary power. To Sewell and Webster, TQM is simultaneously repressive and productive, as Foucault describes.[83]

TQM, and particularly reengineering, has been aided by arguably one of the most important tools in the postindustrial and the global workplace—the computer. In the new computerized office, employees sit at individual workstations, often in cubicles, where they become "visibly accountable and responsible workers."[84] As individualizing tools, computers give managers the capacity to create a self-disciplining work force. That is, the computer makes each individual employee responsible for completing specific tasks. The individual controls his or her own output without being dependent on coworkers.

However, the fact that this individual controls output does not hinder a manager's ability to judge this individual's work performance. Employers conduct minute-by-minute time-study analyses about each person. This information is then correlated, aggregated, and used to place the individual in context with the entire work force.[85] How many items does each person sell who answers the phone for a catalogue? How long does it take him or her to make these sales? Specially designed computer programs give managers the capacity to untangle a mass of tasks—the average person sells $x$ number of red sweaters in 8 hours as opposed to blue ones.

Computers allow managers to customize the workplace, taking into account each individual without losing control over all units of production. They provide an illusion of decentralized control, which is further maintained by their flexible configurations. A password, for instance, gives managers access to information and power networks, yet the system of "logging on" provides this manager as well as the workers he or she supervises with an illusion of privacy. The perception of centralized control is therefore obscured.[86]

Other companies have instituted "hot desking" or "hotelling." What this means is that employees no longer have personal workspace. They share desks, with some employees working from home rather than an office. Whole offices have been set up around the concept of the virtual organization, where employees use computer networks for communication, diminishing the importance of an office.[87]

Computer technology produces a modern-day form of what Jean-Paul Sartre called "serialization." Each employee relates to his or her colleagues through statistics. He or she is judged, using the most productive employee as the measure, and his or her performance is assessed perpetually. While serialization empowers some employees, particularly those who become the measure or have been shifted, the close monitoring of everyone's performance constitutes a "big brother" type of control.[88] To avoid being alerted about a poor work performance record, many employees will try to be more productive throughout the day. A self-disciplining work force is the result.

Some employees do so well in this type of a self-disciplining workplace, either ignoring the surveillance or accepting it as a natural part of their job, that management experts have coined the term "shifting" for this type of identification. By individualizing their employees' respective workloads, management *shifts* its loyalty from itself to the company. The self-disciplined employee ignores his or her own self-interest and internalizes the company's goals and values.[89]

Mrs. Field's Cookies represents a good example of how corporations rely on centralized information systems. From the beginning, this company has had very few people from its central office monitor some 635 outlets and over 5,700 employees.[90] Mrs. Field's Cookies uses information technology that reaches from the bottom to the top of a hierarchy, facilitating the centralization of control through standardization of information. Over time, record keeping has become more complete and information is processed faster than ever. Even the number of cookies an employee eats is calculated and assessed as acceptable "sneaking" or alternatively a pilfering problem that would lead to his or her termination. The computer, not the employee at the outlet, makes all the decisions about baked goods, labor scheduling, and hourly quotas on the sale of the cookies. There is little or no discretion given to the local work force, which has little need for human supervisors.

## "A panopticon without walls"[91]

It was the theorist Jean-Paul de Gaudemar who initially drew the analogy between electronic surveillance and Foucault's panopticon.[92] In Jeremy Bentham's prison, inmates, Foucault describes, remained under the perpetual gaze of an unverifiable observer—their wardens—in a panopticon tower. The panopticon or the all-seeing tower was a physical source of surveillance. Yet it was the invisibility of the wardens that made it work. The prisoners never knew when they were being watched. The inmates became self-disciplining subjects as an illusion of continuous surveillance gave a small number of prison guards a tremendous amount of control.[93] When the inmates thought they could not violate the rules without getting caught, they began disciplining themselves.

For Foucault, the panopticon represents an ingenious method of social control. It directs behavior by imposing a "totalizing and instrumental rationalism."[94] Applying this type of social control to the high-tech workplace, Zuboff writes that "the counterpart of the central tower is the video screen."[95] It is workplace surveillance as an "information panopticon," erected as a byproduct of "informating" work, in which integrated manufacturing control systems shape work tasks and provide the determinants of skill.[96] Domination, the theorist Mark Poster elaborates, is "electronically wrapped."[97] Building on Foucault, Poster calls the emerging network of scrutiny in the workplace the "super-panopticon."[98]

Like the prison wardens, the visibility of electronic surveillance is so faint that it can, and often does, go unnoticed. New unobtrusive, electronic forms of surveillance, such as electronic badges, are intertwined with cultural bonds are created between employees as a means of gaining their consent.[99] Not only does information technology incorporate the data gleaned from the production process, but the technology gives management the ability to judge how well each individual operates within this process.[100]

Generally, two types of surveillance exist in the workplace. A broad but unsystematic type of surveillance gathers and accumulates surveillance data in the hope that the sheer bulk of it will help management make "better" decisions.[101] Second, management undertakes highly focused surveillance that helps it supervise employees by minutely monitoring their workplace performance.[102]

Surveillance's import stems not just from the actual information gathered, but rather from what Foucault calls its self-disciplinary effect. Employees anticipate the surveillance and, in anticipation of potential consequences, they try to accommodate it. Similarly, workplace surveillance can be both repressive and productive. It provides a company or an office with information about employees who fall short of production targets as well as those who exceed them. Surveillance becomes productive, for instance, as the company publicly rewards an "employee of the month," the week, or the day. This reward benefits not just this worker, but it is publicly showing how much a company "cares" about the workplace.[103]

Surveillance has also transformed the nature of teamwork, redefining the very notion of autonomy. A team can now provide a context in which each employee retains autonomy over his or her own work, and yet the information about each employee can be used to influence the work of his or her teammates. Labeled horizontal, as opposed to vertical, surveillance or peer group scrutiny, teamwork involves what one management expert labeled "concertive" control.[104] Although this is a direct form of surveillance, it is not panoptic. Everyone's peers, rather than their superiors or the wardens in Bentham's tower, make horizontal surveillance operational. If it were not for the high-speed, sophisticated, information-gathering computer programs, this type of scrutiny would be associated with the traditional role of a supervisor.[105]

Given these new forms of surveillance, a number of studies have shown that teamwork is not "the edifying and empowering experience" described by management experts such as Ouchi, Deal, and Kennedy.[106] As one author said, "Life in teams can be stressful," because teammates must "conform to intense peer pressure." Another management expert suggested that teams practice "unpleasant bullying tactics."[107]

Peer pressure, moreover, takes on a life of its own as it is turned into values and norms. Each team adopts its own set of norms, evaluating each other's performance. The whole team recognizes who is a "good" or "bad" employee, and doles out rewards or sanctions accordingly.

Work performance is not based on the subjective judgment of each team member, however. It is not a popularity contest since the company supplies the team with the empirical information gathered by surveillance. With the surveillance technology recording the smallest deviation from a team's performance norms, employees become self-disciplining subjects who work toward creating self-disciplining teams.

Kay Electronics, an overseas plant of a Japanese-owned manufacturer of consumer electronics, which deployed teams with 12 to 40 members who assembled printed circuit boards (PCBs) by manually inserting components, serves as a vivid example of concertive control. The plant used surveillance to gain information about how well and how fast each individual employee assembled the PCBs.[108] At the beginning of every shift, team members had the previous days' quality performance information displayed above their work stations in the form of "traffic lights." Green, amber, and red cards signified whether the PCB's constructed by a team member had exceeded, landed in the cautionary zone of acceptable quality limits, or had fallen into the unacceptable zone. Each employee's performance record went back 20 days.[109]

Identifying the above-average, the average, and the below-average team members had a tremendous disciplinary effect on the whole workplace. Not only did vertical surveillance label the poor workers, but a persistent green card also alerted everyone—management and the employee's peers alike. The person standing under it deserved attention since she or he had probably made an innovation in the work process that had given her or him this edge.

While Kay Electronics was based on sanctions and rewards, the company gave the team itself a great deal of discretion to make the determinations. When one member of a team was absent, the whole team had to cover for him or her. And to achieve minimum targets, the team would have to reorganize itself. The combination of everyone being aware of each person's performance rating and other factors like absenteeism allowed each team to identify which members "weren't up to it." With few externally derived rules to moderate this intersubjective behavior, the forces of normalization could take on any form the team considered necessary to ensure an acceptable level of compliance. "OK, so no one likes to have a red card hanging above his head," said one employee, "but it's when you see other people with red cards when yours is green that it really gets to you."[110] What caused such offense was not that an individual's performance might drop below expectation on a few occasions but that others were seen to fail the team continually. Peer group scrutiny became all the more intense as team members tried influencing each other's behavior, since management expected team members to improve their individual performance as a condition of employment.[111]

## Performing resistance

Foucault's critics characterize his ideas about disciplinary power as so all-encompassing and pessimistic that they preclude any possibility of change.[112] However, Foucault leaves room for resistance.[113] Power relations can be revealed or unmasked in specific locales or areas such as a school or a workplace.[114]

To Foucault, power and resistance are both social constructions and analytical conditions of each other.[115] Wherever there is power, there is resistance. What is more, power and resistance are associated with self-creation.[116] Particular exercises of power, Foucault demonstrates, can be viewed in terms of the resistances they generate and confront.[117]

The only means of minimizing resistance according to Foucault is to divide-and-conquer the forces that an institution has created. He describes resistance as an absence of hierarchy, calling it "counter-power."[118] By contrast, inequality is a fundamental element of power. This said, resistance should not be portrayed as a negation of power. Like power, its analytical partner, it can also be affirmative. Resistance depends upon strategic knowledge. It constitutes Foucault's ideas of revolutionary action.[119]

However, resistance is best understood in performative terms. Unlike representative action, performative action has no precursor. It is pure action based on experience rather than essence, or a universal notion of human nature.[120]

Put differently, resistance resembles sabotage. Foucault's image of a saboteur, however, is not similar to the mythical image of someone who is an isolated, irrational misfit or malcontent.[121] Instead he characterizes the saboteur as one who exercises complex behavior that is symbolic, social, contained, and yet conspirational.[122]

## Cracks in concertive control

What happened at Kay Electronics, as recounted above, can also expose the limitations associated with the double bind of discretion and panoptic forms of discipline, as Foucault illuminates. Surveillance at Kay Electronics did not necessarily make individual employees pursue "continuous improvements."[123] If team members realize that in disciplining themselves, they are intensifying their own work practices, they may challenge the normative hegemony of teamwork as a "good" thing. Instead of being concerned with how they are perceived by their peers, team members can start to redefine the limits to empowerment in the workplace from the shop floor upward. As one worker explains, management "give[s] the impression we work together when it suits them, but when it gets rough, we're the ones who get it."[124] But, "the totalizing portrayals of new managerial controls," argue management experts Peter Fleming and Graham Sewell, "where employees are simply programmed automatons," does not capture every employee's consciousness.[125] Not all employees are as subservient and naive as some labor process theory scholars contend.[126]

Some labor process theory scholars suggest that too bleak a picture has been drawn of the workplace and the subservience of the average worker, who surrenders his or her subjectivity without a fight.[126] These scholars reveal that workplace resistance has undergone a fundamental change from a Newtonian perspective of large bodies moving in classic physics in picketing and strikes to a relativist perspective that captures a more nuanced approach to transgressions such as sabotage.[127]

Supplementing Foucault's ideas with those of the political theorist James Scott, some workplace studies demonstrate that resistance is tantamount to foot dragging, false compliance, feigned ignorance, dissimulation, and petty complaints, among other things.[128] Under a sheer cloak of legitimacy, people perform acts of resistance. This cloak makes their resistance no less threatening than a picket or a strike.[129]

Studies have documented different forms of employee resistance. First, employees may "resist through distance" by not "buying into" the workplace culture.[130] That is, they refuse any kind of involvement or interest in key organizational processes, punching in and out of their jobs. This happens not only when the factory line worker refuses to join the management club that will provide him or her with small bonuses, but also with the computer consultants who will not attend the company holiday party.

Second, "resistance through persistence" occurs when employees seek out as much information and knowledge as possible about their employers so they can develop criticism of the internal employment practices.[131] As one management expert illustrates, this role suits shop stewards, many of whom came from the rank and file of factory workers, so well that they have been called the "detectives."[132] Similarly, some women who face sexual discrimination, like being denied promotion after returning from maternity leave, might resist by helping other pregnant women challenge the company rules about this practice or related ones. Finally, whistleblowers also practice this type of resistance.[133]

Sabotage represents a third form of resistance.[134] An employee with the technical skill to perform a task in 2 minutes when the computer system grants 12 minutes, might use the extra time for other activities.[135] "If we let the computer run, we look bad, so we manipulate the computer," said one factory employee. "We are not trying to cheat anybody or steal. We are trying to deal with the human element involved."[136]

This practice of accumulating output, making time, or what is called "fiddles" gives employees some control over their production level and is called a kitty, a stash, or a bank.[137] Having this stash represents a source of pride and self-validation. It confirms that workers used their technical skills, knowledge, and experience to beat the system.[138] This type of resistance also helps employees prohibit employers from intensifying the labor process. As one study shows, a group of auto employees, who worked at a fast clip in the morning, took turns in the afternoon going on long trips to the bathroom, which was the only room not under surveillance.[139]

"Scrimshanking" or shirking one's duty constitutes another form of resistance.[140] Employers find this form of resistance insidious since it means that the employee is fragrantly subverting what the company frames as its common good.[141] Shirking one's duty, moreover, affects others in that the person practicing this invites his or her peers to observe with the hope that they will follow suit. Employers are then locked out of the performance or the dialogue with little hope of changing the environment without giving in to some of the resistant employee's demands.[142]

The most tangible sign of resistance is found in business losses. Management experts insist that violence against employers is increasing.[143] What is more, management often prefers not to attribute this loss to sabotage since this shows how vulnerable it is. At one white-collar workplace, an unnamed employee flooded a basement filled with electronic equipment, yet management refused to call this act sabotage. The company preferred to label the flood an "accident." However, this did not stop the employees from championing the person who had caused the accident.[144] Management, moreover, succumbed to the employee's demands, which had caused him or her to flood the basement in the first place.[145]

The idea that it is only the factory worker—the saboteur—who stops the assembly line by throwing his *sabot* or shoe into the machines is misleading. Labor-management experts Danny LaNuez and John Jermier show that both blue-collar and white-collar workers who feel frustrated by how little control they wield over their work practice small acts of sabotage. One study about a health maintenance organization (HMO) with 168 employees is particularly revealing. Here, employees resisted company practices by interrupting training sessions with questions about the impact the new computers might have on their health. Working for an HMO, they asked about the likelihood of contracting carpal tunnel syndrome or the risk they were exposing unborn fetuses to if they were pregnant, as well as the toll on their vision.[146] According to this study, the resistant employees posed these questions to assert their awareness of computers and their affects on society just to keep management on their toes.

Another form of white-collar resistance practiced is submitting "proxy grievances." These grievances let managers know about an office's shortcomings not so much to correct it as to provide space for more of their concerns to be heard. Some of the employees will even "talk like management," as one study describes, to ensure that their ideas get heard by their supervisors.[147]

Finally, other employees in this HMO resisted by refusing to convert from the old manual system to the new totally computerized system of filing insurance claims and processing other paperwork. Upon questioning, the expert conducting the study discovered that these employees would not comply as a means of asserting their autonomy rather than their ability to work the new system. Subsequently, once they became accustomed to the new system, some of these same employees would document the flaws in the computerized system. Management went so far as to call this activity "software bitching."[148]

### Information as power

Persons with disabilities are ideally suited to become agents of resistance. Living outside mainstream society and culture means that employers are less likely to have captured their subjectivity. They are liminal, as Victor Turner described in his classic essay, "Betwixt and Between."[149] Persons with disabilities are in that transitional phase from isolation to emergence into full "personhood" or citizenship. They exist in that type of social limbo—having lost their old identity as ill or infirm, but having no new identity.

Given the strength of the disability rights movement and the passage of the ADA, the indeterminacy of persons with disabilities could not be resolved by re-segregating them. Now, more than any other time in American history, the citizenry of the U.S. are poised on the edge of "denaturalizing disability's assumed inferiority," as disability studies expert Rosemarie Garland-Thomson argues could be cast "as difference rather than lack."[150] This is all the more true because of genetic testing.

With tests showing what illnesses many people will face long before they manifest themselves, there is no better time to emphasize human corporeality.

The liminality of persons with disabilities, moreover, has its advantages. Few employers will have induced disabled persons into thinking that a company's or a corporation's interest is tantamount to their interest. Setting standards in terms of work conditions apply to few of them since their different minds and bodies cannot be considered standard. Persons with disabilities, moreover, do not have the luxury of taking their work conditions for granted. No one need remind persons with disabilities about how they stand outside the law of standards, averages, and medians.

However, disabled persons must be recognized as part of Gilles Deleuze's swim team or composers, not as second-class citizens or deviants. As explained in chapters 2 and 3, becoming animal or bodily becoming captures the life of persons with disabilities who are always striving. The philosopher Benedict de Spinoza, Deleuze, and Felix Guattari argue that an individual mind and body must be viewed as one continuous substance and process that strives with no end. This striving is what their existence is all about. It also means that someone is not playing a tired old song, but actually composing music. They are swimming not as their instructor tells them too, but how it suits their own minds and bodies. The water must be tailored to the mind and body, and vice versa. The workplace should be no different.

Most importantly, the ADA puts persons with disabilities in a unique position to negotiate with their employers. Reasonable accommodations requests could undercut managerial prerogative power, a power that does not foster a happy, productive, and efficient workplace. Persons with disabilities make these requests by engaging with their employers in what the ADA refers to as the interactive process. As explained in chapter 1, this means that employees or potential employees can negotiate with employers or prospective employers about what are the essential and nonessential tasks of a position to determine accommodations.

Assessing what are essential and nonessential duties is an infinitely complex process. It involves not just the person seeking employment or the person working but the details of the office or company. The assessment process under the ADA mandates that an employee must perform the essential tasks of a specific job. The employee, in other words, must have the qualifications to perform all these tasks. This same employee, however, can be released from performing the nonessential tasks. What makes this complex is that there is no fixed rule about the difference between the two. There is no rule, for instance, that the job category of administrative assistant means that he or she must answer telephones. An essential duty can only be determined after locating one particular employee in a specific setting. If an administrative assistant with a severe neck injury works with three other assistants in an office, answering the telephones would not be essential. The other three assistants could do this. The employer could award the accommodation. By contrast, if there were no other staff members working with the administrative assistant, the employer would not be required to accommodate him or her.[151]

Persons with disabilities could be in a position to scrutinize business operations by examining the essential and nonessential duties of the position they are seeking. They could be portrayed as the auditors of workplace conditions. Furthermore, disabled persons gain insight about workplace rules and regulations that are applicable to everyone, not just themselves. Requests for accommodations provide persons with disabilities the capacity to observe management's logic. This logic could be gained about the operations of an entire workplace. Hence, disabled persons challenge what their employers and employees without disabilities perceive as the "normal" workplace.

Half the battle over gaining an employee's subjectivity involves keeping workplace operations ambiguous. Many studies show that horizontal control works precisely because employees do not fully comprehend the extent to which they are being supervised by electronic machinery. At the same time, these employees do not fully comprehend the consequences of this surveillance. The supervisor who stood over their shoulders under the old Taylorist and Fordist system may be gone, but the supervision is not. Indeed, horizontal control involves supervision that is more invasive and insidious than ever before. Global capitalism has managers monitoring their employees very carefully by using the centralizing flow of information gathered by computers. If employees with disabilities understand how invasive supervision is by knowing, for instance, what type of information is gathered, the fact that this supervision is electronic and despatialized may no longer make it seem less oppressive than it is.

By making requests for reasonable accommodations, moreover, persons with disabilities could gain access to the floor of the information-gathering rooms, so to speak. This information would be invaluable for exposing how management tries to capture the subjectivity of its employees. Nothing prohibits a worker with a disability from sharing this information. The employer enjoys no rights to privacy about how he or she is monitoring a work force.

## Resistant cultures

Turning persons with disabilities into agents of resistance would alter the workplace culture. These agents would expose managerial control as power. Providing information to the rest of the work force, they could disabuse employees who surrender their subjectivity, believing that they share their employers' interests. It would also create a sense of entitlement that the Occupational Health and Safety Act (OHSA) has little provided. Equally important, these agents taking need into account would foster a workplace that promoted the individuality of its workers. Employees might well feel less alienated, thus increasing productivity and reducing workplace resistance and sabotage.

Resistance creates a different culture at the workplace. In the mid-1980s, Louise Lamphere and Salli Westwood conducted pioneering studies about the feminization of the workplace.[152] First, explaining that work culture involves a complex set of relationships between cultural meanings on one hand and behavioral strategies of management on the other, both Lamphere and Westwood demonstrate that women have had a great influence on their workplaces.[153] They show how women used their common identities as wives, sisters, and mothers in a way that promoted communication. Cultivating this common identity then helped women bridge large, cultural, ethnic, and age divisions within their work force, often making them more united against management than their male counterparts.

Westwood, for instance, argues that women's work culture offered a context of resistance to management. The irony of this resistance was that it took the form of holding celebrations that confirmed a traditional vision of femininity (which is essentially patriarchal and assumes subordination of women). Celebrations like birthdays, baby and wedding showers, and potlucks and retirement parties feminized the workplace, albeit by cultivating a traditional view of women as giving and nurturing.

Similarly, Karen Sacks examined what women brought into the workplace, arguing that it is precisely the set of values and social connections forged in working class families that made it possible for a group of female black hospital workers to stage an effective walkout and begin a union drive in a southern city.[154] As a result, she shows that women workers built ties among Hispanic, Anglo, African-American, and Asian working women.[155] These ties helped them mitigate their differing ages, marital status, and ethnic backgrounds. She shows how, in 1979, these ties helped the women pull off a successful wildcat strike in a sewing plant.[156]

Workers with disabilities could forge bonds on the basis of our corporeal needs. The key for reform, however, involves having the definition of a disability transformed into the more comprehensive notion of animality, ensuring that more persons with disabilities become agents of resistance and saboteurs. Women returning back to work and in need of a private station for breast pumping could gain insight about how the company operates its maternity leave or bathroom policies. They could acquire a more comprehensive understanding about how a company or factory allocates private space for the different activities of other employees as well as management. Or if someone with hypertension requests a later start time in the morning than other employees, this request could expose how willing and effective certain corporations are about making the schedules of different individuals idiosyncratic. Finally, if an employee with cancer or other serious illness is regarded as having a disability, they can inform other employees about the limits of the health care benefits and leave policies. At present, employers benefit from the employees' fragmentation.

Supervision and limits imposed on work conditions should be presented to employees up front so that they can make informed decisions about the employment they seek. Some attempts have been made to pass legislation protecting an employee's right to privacy from the incessant monitoring and supervision that includes, for instance, posting how long each employee spends in the bathroom each day.[157] Both the state and federal courts, however, ruled supervisory tactics like this were not an invasion of an employee's privacy.[158] The judiciary has long made it clear that an employer's right to manage trumps an employee's right to privacy.[159]

The pertinent question is: does supervision work? Do employers protect themselves from employee theft and create a more efficient workplace? Or would it be better to promote the development of employees by better utilizing technology to individualize the workplace? The electronic machinery used to supervise workers could be retailored and refashioned to suit many employees.

If the term animality is used to make persons with disabilities a more all-encompassing term, the American work force might become more efficient. Persons with disabilities and those who comprehend that they are disabled should be out on the edge, leading other employees. A significant number of technical inventions, including the typewriter, the scanner, the telephone, and the phonograph, have been made to suit not the similarities that people share, but their differences. However, employers have not made the workplace cater to the individual needs of a business or office precisely because management prefers to leave this process muddled.

An expansive definition of what constitutes a disability would give persons with traditional disabilities and those with untraditional ones the chance to build a base of solidarity among employees. Just as Lani Guinier and Gerald Torres suggest that the white working class should identify with people of color rather than the white middle or upper-middle class, so too should persons without disabilities support those with disabilities.[160] Few people, after all, escape a serious illness or injury over the course of their lifetime. It is therefore not in the long-term self-interest of an employee without a disability to join sides with employers instead of with their colleagues with disabilities.

Our bodies could unite us, creating a very expansive concept if the myth of independence is abandoned. "The disabled body exposes the illusion of autonomy, self-government, and self-determination," Garland-

Thomson contends, "that underpins the fantasy of absolute able-bodiness."[161] At the same time, she levels a chilling critique of women's studies. The feminist theorist Jane Flax, Garland-Thomson observes, asserts that women are 'mutilated and deformed' by sexist ideology and practices."[162] Yet Flax seems unaware that the association between deformity and sexism is offensive to persons with disabilities.[163]

If able-bodied workers could either overcome misconceptions they have about disability or the resentment they harbor against employees who receive accommodations, they could join forces with persons with disabilities. The ADA's employment provisions could give disabled persons a more universal notion of the organic mind and body. These provisions could help American workers, giving them protections where the civil rights and labor laws have fallen short.

The workplace should become individualized. It could be modeled after Spinoza's conception of common notions and this author's critical ethic of care laid out in chapters 2 and 3. Neither this conception nor a critical ethic recognizes the individual alone. Each person is a "union of parts" and each group of persons composes an even bigger union. Similarly, employees in an office or a factory can act as a union of parts, complementing one another. They would recognize how each of their individual bodies affects their colleagues.[164] To maintain such a relational perspective of a workplace, worker solidarity is essential. Persons with disabilities, even if a more expansive definition of who that includes is rendered, cannot stand alone before an employer. This would make them deviant and they would undoubtedly be defeated.

This solidarity cannot sacrifice the individual needs for the collective, however. It must take into account individuality as Spinoza defines it. To Spinoza, if two individuals with similar natures join one another, they compose what in effect is similar to another individual twice as powerful as the first two as individuals. This perspective embraces Spinoza's maxim that "to man, there is nothing more useful than man."[165] The workplace should be no exception, particularly since it is aided by information-age technology that makes it more efficient.

The next chapter shows how persons with disabilities could be associated with the one collective voice in the workplace—organized labor. The ADA is a tool that could bridge the individual and collective rights divide. This vision could not be implemented with any one union, but rather with one that relies on cosmopolitan unionism that champions the differences of employees rather than their similarities.

# CHAPTER 6
# Unions: Bridging the Divide

To divide, separate, or portion workers into categories, groups, and classes has long been one of business's most effective strategies against labor whenever it tried to organize for better work conditions or higher pay. "I can hire one-half of the working class," boasted robber baron Jay Gould, "to kill the other half."[1] It was employers who benefited when white working-class men fought former slaves, British Protestants would not work with Irish Catholics, and men protested the increasing numbers of women in the work force. Now able-bodied employees question the reasonable accommodations employees with disabilities receive. Whether it is ethnicity, race, gender, or disability that separates these groups makes little difference. Nor does it matter much whether these divisions are based on malice, prejudice, or a subtle bias. What matters most is that when employers perceive workers as a threat they often use the divide-and-conquer strategy that usually puts them on top.

The employment provisions of the Americans with Disabilities Act (ADA) offer labor a way out of this dilemma. If employees did not view reasonable accommodations made for their coworkers with disabilities as a threat to their own work conditions, they could recognize that these accommodations could help benefit all employees. When an employer accommodates one employee, this accommodation represents a precedent that another employee might profit from in the future. The ADA's employment provisions present employees with a powerful means of gaining better work conditions.

Most employees could be defined as having a substantial life impairment that should be accommodated at some time in their lives.

117

The ADA, as discussed earlier, presents an expansive definition of a disability because it is functional. It is about what people do, not who they are. Reasonable accommodations can be construed as workplace needs. This means that employers would no longer rely solely on an employee's actual or potential for making profits. Instead, they would view work conditions on the basis of need.

Yet if a lone employee faces employers with these requests, he or she might well be rebuffed. The power differential between an employee and many employers is large. This chapter shows that this differential could be mitigated by collective bargaining. Quite simply, labor union leaders could help workers with disabilities engage in the interactive process that helps determine what reasonable accommodations they should receive. By representing persons with disabilities during this process, unions would infiltrate the information panopticon described in the last chapter. Unions could empower disabled workers, giving them the strength and the solidarity that they need to maximize their capacity for receiving accommodations.

The interactive process would also give organized labor the possibility of playing a larger role in determining workplace conditions. To most workers' chagrin, labor leaders have been much less involved in setting work conditions than their European counterparts. They have honored American businesses' "right to manage."[2] Under globalism this control is heightened for two interrelated reasons. First, the new economy serves individuals under what is called the "California ideology." This reflects how management views labor as "radically individualized" rather than as a collective body. As one labor-management expert Christopher May describes, labor is seen "as a fragmented and amorphous group of individual contractors."[3]

Second, this new emphasis on individuals makes the new economy and globalism particularly hostile to organized labor. As a result, some advocates for organized labor have gone so far as to suggest that "the focus, then, for the new unions must be on individual workers and individual company performance."[4] These unions should help employees gain more flexibility at the workplace. The ADA could help organized labor carve out such a niche for itself. Organized labor's involvement would diminish managerial prerogative power in the workplace.

The reasonable accommodations model created by the ADA could become a very effective means of helping workers receive affirmative rights. Reasonable accommodations are substantive or tangible work conditions that employees receive on a case-by-case basis. What is essential for the accommodations model to work, however, is that the outspoken prejudice, the conscious *and* the unconscious biases, and the well-meaning paternalism of employees without disabilities be overcome.

Benedict de Spinoza's conception of common notions must be practiced in the workplace. That is, workers should recognize their common interests and unite with other workers. Two individuals are stronger than one. The fundamental relationship for Spinoza is not between the individual and the state, but individuals and the state. Recognizing that all politics is power, one individual alone can do little to nothing, whereas a mass of individuals can bring about significant reform and change.

Applying Spinoza's logic to the workplace, this means that individual employees must stand united against their state, which is their employer. Individual workers should realize that to protect their self-interests, they must suspend their passions—in this case their prejudice against persons with disabilities—which will only pull them apart, benefiting their employers. "Men, in so far as they are assailed by emotions which are passions, can be contrary one to the other," Spinoza wrote.[5]

The divide-and-conquer strategy can only work if employees harbor biases and prejudices or what Spinoza described as negative passions. When an employer thinks labor is threatening his or her interests and resorts to using this tactic, it is utterly dependent upon the employees having these emotions. To be sure, employers have a better chance of provoking this response if they frighten workers into believing that furnishing accommodations creates a zero-sum situation that disadvantages them. But Spinoza's point is that these emotions create an atmosphere that becomes self-defeating, not to the employers, but to the collective of employees. Employers reap the profits if a mêlée, with individual employee battling individual employee, breaks out.

The fundamental assumption underlying this interpretation of workplace politics is that employers and employees are locked into a zero-sum situation. No where is this better illustrated than with employers providing accommodations. The real question is: who loses? Who do these accommodations disadvantage? Is it able-bodied employees or employers? To answer this question without arousing the able-bodied employees' prejudice or biases, they must know how much the average accommodation costs. In fact, studies have shown that most accommodations are well within the budget of an office or a firm.[6] Yet what these studies do not reveal is how much awarding accommodations undermines managerial prerogative power. Accommodations therefore threaten the interests of employers not only because of financial loss, but because of a managerial loss of control over their workplace. In making the zero-sum calculation, it is therefore vital for employees to know whether employers are more concerned with the dollar and cents cost of accommodations *or* with maintaining tight control over the entire workplace.

This book argues that it is in the interest of all employees to stand together. Based on the philosophy of Spinoza, it concludes that what benefits one helps all. Disability rights and the accommodations model are unique in that they can benefit both an individual employee and the collective simultaneously. As agents of resistance, employees with disabilities can undermine normalcy in a way that would help their colleagues gain more control over their workplace. Hence, the ADA—an individual employment law—has the capacity to bridge the individual rights–collective bargaining divide.

## Law has its privileges

Both statutes and common law play a vital role in constructing and shaping the identity of the "privileged" in American society. As law professors Marion Crain and Ken Matheny describe, "whiteness and maleness" conferred a legal status on white men that gave them property rights. Similarly, the law constructs other racial and gender identities.[7] In the 1990s, cultural studies scholars started focusing on whiteness, arguing that it had a great impact on the history of the American labor movement as well.[8]

As the story goes, American labor, which helped construct unions and shaped the labor movement, privileged white men. The hostility that unions harbored toward nonwhites and women in their long history of exclusionary and discriminatory practices has been well documented.[9] "From slavery days to the present," suggests law professor Stephen Plass, "white working-class consciousness and ideology have been molded to separate black and white workers, and to accommodate practices designed to subjugate black workers."[10]

Beginning with industrialization in the 1870s, African-American leaders like Frederick Douglass recognized the potential danger black workers posed to white-dominated unions. Yet it was not until the *fin de siécle* that organized labor represented "a grave economic threat to black workers."[11] Even then, most African-Americans lived in rural areas untouched by unionization. Few unions had had any success organizing black or white workers in the South. Nonetheless, African-American leaders from a range of different political perspectives denounced organized labor. Booker T. Washington, Douglass's successor as the nation's leading African-American spokesperson, for instance, castigated organized labor for its discriminatory practices. J.E. Bruce, a regular contributor to the *Colored American* also articulated some of this sentiment by characterizing organized labor as "a greedy, grasping, ruthless, intolerant, overbearing, dictatorial combination of half-educated white men . . . I am against them," he added, "because they are against the Negro."[12]

With African-Americans still under the grip of Jim Crow laws, the demise of laissez-faire jurisprudence of the Lochner era that led to the modern labor movement in the late 1930s and early 1940s came at an inopportune time.[13] "The free black worker encountered legislative indifference," writes Plass, "during the most vibrant regulatory years in the early twentieth century." Federal labor law became the "domain" of white men.[14] "The codification of white worker interests and attitudes," he elaborates, "helped to perpetuate existing racial tensions and workplace disunity."[15]

Knowing that the American Federation of Labor (AFL) and the Railroad Brotherhoods either excluded African-Americans or created segregated Jim Crow locals, the federal law "reinforced white working-class consciousness." Plass adds that the Railway Labor Act of 1926 and the National Labor Relations Act (NLRA) of 1935 improved "white worker status through unionism ... permitting unions to wield their statutory powers as a sword against black workers, thereby perpetuating the racial division of workers."[16] In part, the AFL did so by adopting business unionism, which focused on the common class interests of all employees and downplayed any divergent racial or ethnic identities.[17]

Some labor historians like Herbert Gutman and David Montgomery in the school of New Labor History argue that it was skilled labor—primarily the AFL and the Railroad Brotherhoods—not the industrial labor in the Congress of Industrial Organizations (CIO), that was discriminatory.[18] However, whether it was skilled or unskilled labor made little difference to employers. Employers discovered that racialization "emerged as a vehicle by which employers could simultaneously exploit white workers and black workers."[19] As the labor historian David Roediger argues, "Status and privileges conferred by race could be used to make up for alienating an exploitive class relationship."[20] While the white working class received low wages, it could count on having better public facilities, like schools and swimming pools, than all those segregated African-Americans. "White workers chose white supremacy on the job and in the union," writes Crain, "even as they recognized its deleterious effects on class solidarity." As a result, "black workers always fought on two fronts, battling both white employers and white workers."[21]

Scholars who study whiteness maintain that white working class solidarity had become embedded by the time the Civil Rights Act was passed in 1964. Title VII, which included the provisions for preventing discrimination in the workplace, did little to break through the color barrier at every union hall.[22] Today, more than 40 years since the passage of civil rights, battles over unionization and racialization still rage in the South with few victories sustained for either white or black labor.

Given the significance and prevalence of racialization, theories that offer explanations abound. Historians of immigration have long argued that ethnic and racial conflict supplanted class conflict. It is theories of whiteness that carried this concept a step further, purporting that racism is an inherent part of American culture. Meanwhile, industrial relations literature has several important explanations that account for this phenomenon.

What makes theories in industrial relations different from most historical treatments is that they concentrate on whether capital or labor is responsible for capitalizing on racial differences. First, proponents of the split labor market theory suggest that although employers favor free competition among workers, they yielded to organized labor's pressure to hire mainly white men.[23] A split labor market emerges when two or more groups of workers, whose price of labor for the same work differs, compete. One group works for less because its resources are fewer and its goals differ from those of the higher paid group. The differences between the groups stem from both large historical forces and cultural conditioning, not necessarily employer bias or prejudice.[24] It is white male labor, as opposed to employers, who are more overtly antagonistic to African-Americans and women.

Split labor market theory is reminiscent of the dual systems idea where patriarchy and capitalism are recognized as two components in a partnership that exploits women. The dual systems argument maintains that male workers had a material interest in exploitation. A woman's low wages kept them dependent on, and subordinate to, their men at work and at home. Similarly, split labor market theory concentrates on how the conflict between capital and labor puts the more privileged workers in a better position than those who are less privileged. "The less privileged," Crain explains, "unwittingly serve capital as a tool to undermine the wages of the more privileged and ultimately become the chief victim in the struggle between employers and labor."[25] The two classes of workers express their conflicts as racial antagonism or gender hostility, hiding the idea that it might just be about class.

By contrast, labor market segmentation theory maintains that working class fragmentation primarily benefits employers, who deliberately promote racial and gender divisions within the working class in order to blunt opposition, to suppress workers' wages, and to weaken their bargaining power. The capital-owning class incites prejudice that perpetuates discrimination in all walks of life.[26] Underscoring the motivation of employers, this version of dual systems theory makes a distinction between patriarchy and capitalism. According to feminist Heidi Hartmann, this latter theory is flexible enough to accommodate variations in the mechanisms of control across cultures and across time. Men use marriage as a means of controlling women's labor power.[27] Further, Iris Marion Young suggests that the marginalization of women and their function as a secondary labor force is a fundamental characteristic of capitalism.[28] Capitalism was founded on a gender hierarchy that defined men as primary and women as secondary. "This arrangement serves capital-owners' interests," she argues, since "women function as a reserve army of labor, available to absorb the slack in the economy in either direction as circumstances change."[29]

Whether it is split labor market or labor market segmentation theories, keeping most women out of the work force benefited employers in two ways. It reduced unemployment, which was particularly crucial during periods of mass unemployment, and diminished the possibility that social unrest would affect production. Turning women into homemakers meant that they could create sanctuaries for their men and boys in which to recuperate from the "degradation of factory labor."[30] Subsequently, when women began entering the work force in large numbers in the 1940s, their positions were ghettoized in certain industries and sectors. Employers offered much lower wages to women than men for comparable work.[31]

Finally, employers profited from the fact that organized labor excluded most women. Initially, labor leaders kept them out of the work force to diminish unemployment. If women competed for jobs, they could depress wages and "undermine the structure of the nuclear family."[32] Although women are no longer excluded, organized labor still makes the white male worker its standard-bearer.[33]

## A faulty foundation: New Deal labor legislation

In addition to the informal divide-and-conquer strategy employers use, the formal collective bargaining framework, designed during the New Deal with the passage of the NLRA or the Wagner Act of 1935, has done little to build worker solidarity and take differences into account. In particular, one basic collective bargaining provision—the notion of exclusive representation—makes it structurally difficult for unions to be accepting of employee differences.[34]

When Senator Robert Wagner, its chief architect, first constructed the NLRA, he included the majority rule principle or the idea of exclusive representation out of political and economic necessity. Without this provision, business would form company unions or unions controlled by employers that ostensibly represented the workers as a means of defeating bona fide unions with workers representing workers. The majority rule provision mandates that one representational structure—a single union—exclusively represents its workers at the collective bargaining table.[35] To certify this one exclusive union, 30 percent of all employees eligible for unionization must sign cards in support. Once this has been completed, and the National Labor Relations Board (NLRB) has verified the cards' validity, this agency oversees a petition for a secret ballot election. If the employees do not elect a majority, the NLRB prohibits collective bargaining.[36] However, if a union wins a majority, the NLRB certifies it as the "exclusive bargaining agent."[37]

Before bargaining begins, however, both employers and employees can challenge the election by calling into question "the appropriateness of the unit" or the union doing the collective bargaining. One of the central questions that immediately emerged was the issue of race. Did employers practice race-baiting or had employees united against the injustices of their bigoted employers?

Examining how race affects a union's election constituted a double-edged sword. On the one hand, a union can charge an employer with committing unfair labor practices under Section 8(a)(1) of the NLRA. This means that the employer "interfere[s] with, restrain[s], or coerce[s] employees in the exercise of the rights guaranteed in the conduct of elections." Just a threat or promise of benefit that had any racial overtones, the NLRB has ruled under this section, means that either an employer *or* a union committed an unfair labor practice.[38] In the *Sewell* decision, a Supreme Court decision rendered in 1962, the NLRB heard that employers tried pitting one employee against another by appealing to their fears of racial integration.[39]

On the other hand, the NLRB has ruled that an employer or a union can bring up race as an issue under Section 9. This provision holds that the NLRB can set aside an election and order a new one.[40] To determine what is appropriate during an election, the NLRB created what it called a "laboratory conditions test," which asks if any conduct on the part of the employer *or* the union has ruined the conditions necessary for a free and fair election.[41] The threshold for this is much wider than under Section 8. In fact, the same day that the Supreme Court handed down *Sewell*, it rendered another decision rejecting the union's challenge against an employer who had distributed letters describing the union's position on racial integration and its support from the National Association for the Advancement of Colored People (NAACP), as well as the possibility that it would sanction local unions that practiced segregation. The Court ruled that the letters were "temperate in tone" and therefore permissible.[42]

Tracing how race has affected organized labor, several labor law professors conclude that the NLRB's rulings have favored employers.[43] Crain and others not only examine the *Sewell* decision, but also *Emporium Capwell*. Handing it down in 1975, Thurgood Marshall, the only black justice, ruled in the latter case that neither the NLRA nor the Civil Rights Act mandated that an employer should bargain with a dissident group of African-Americans who thought that their interests had not been taken into account by either their union or their employer.[44] This department store, Marshall held, need not bargain separately with African-American employees who thought that the union had neglected their interests.[45]

Not only did Marshall's ruling tighten the exclusive representation rule, but it constituted a setback to identity caucuses of all kinds that had begun springing up in the more liberal unions in the 1970s.[46] Identity caucuses had been formed because of rank and file discontent among people of color, women, and gays within unions. Some of the most prominent identity caucuses are the Coalition of Black Trade Unionists (CBTU), the A. Phillip Randolph Institute, the Labor Council on Latin American Advancement (LCLAA), and the Coalition of Labor Union Women (CLUW), which were all founded in the early 1970s. In the 1980s and 1990s, employees formed more identity caucuses like the Asian

Pacific American Labor Alliance (APALA) and Pride at Work (PAW) for gays and lesbians. The intent of the identity caucus was not to bargain separately, but to create a voice for these groups.[47]

Examining the inability for employers or unions to associate with larger causes like desegregation in combination with the exclusive bargaining rule makes some labor lawyers who champion diversity wonder "if the exclusivity and majority rule doctrines have outlived their usefulness."[48] The U.S. is one of the few countries to adopt exclusivity as its organizing industrial relations principle. European countries rely less on majority rule. A union can represent a minority in a workplace.[49]

To be sure, unions carrying less than a majority will encounter difficulties with American employers. Dealing with a multiplicity of groups could well prove to be inefficient and more expensive.[50] Labor law professor Mathew Finkin notes that the problem of multiple bargaining agents already exists under current law, where the NLRB certifies multiple units within a workplace and the employer must bargain with each of them.[51]

But there are benefits that come from not following majority rule. Most notably, in the "absence of majority rule," Crain and Matheny explain, "unions would not need to expend precious resources in a life-or-death struggle to win elections."[52] Community- and identity-based organizing could produce a more nuanced understanding of the form and strategies of economic exploitation.[53]

John Sweeney, the president of the AFL-CIO, was elected on a platform in 1995 that propounded just that.[54] Sweeney, Richard Trumka, and Linda Chavez-Thompson led the labor federation on what they called the "New Voice" slate.[55] After their election, the AFL-CIO made great strides in taking a pro-immigrant position, and hiring bilingual organizers with the same identities as those they were organizing.[56] Union leadership reversed their position on the 1986 Immigration Act, now supporting the 8 million undocumented workers. In June 2001, AFL-CIO launched its Immigration Workers Rights Forum with the theme "Yes we can" or "*Si se puede.*"[57]

### New demographics and a new ideology

This call for labor law reform stems from the fact that organized labor cannot afford to privilege white, working-class men any more.[58] Unionization has dropped to less than 9 percent of the private work force from a high of 35 percent in 1954.[59]

Not only is organized labor hamstrung by the notion of exclusive representation, but the NLRA allows workers to bargain collectively for higher wages and nothing more. The labor relations machinery offers little means of fostering solidarity along racial, gender, or any other social justice grounds. Indeed, if there is no spirit of cooperation between organized labor and a particular employer, this machinery has a difficult time sustaining unionization among any population, let alone women and people of color.

What this machinery does is mandate that employers bargain in good faith over wages and working conditions with collective representatives chosen by their employees.[60]

How can bargaining in good faith be enforced? One of the NLRB's most significant administrative shortcomings is that it is more effective for employers to fire workers who make an effort to organize their workplace than it is to accept unionization. Employers would pay no penalties or punitive damages for wrongfully terminating a worker. The employer simply reinstates the worker with back pay. This strategy was effective from the very beginning of the NLRB's inception and it remains effective today.

It was not until the 1980s, however, when the tide turned against organized labor after President Ronald Reagan defeated the Professional Air Traffic Controllers Organization (PATCO) that employers discovered that firing an employee who sought union representation was a particularly effective weapon in their battle against unionization. This strategy complemented the union-busting campaign that many employers had launched. Then, the NLRB gave employers another tool by ruling that an employer could hire permanent replacements if workers went on strike.[61] Employers now have two effective means of dissuading workers from organizing or punishing them for becoming militant.

Another blow fell against organized labor when the NLRB upheld the new strategy of hiring contingent workers.[62] Employers had begun relying on this type of work force as part of their union-busting campaign. These workers are temporary, part-time, or are full-time but managed by another firm who contracts them out.[63]

While the contingency worker provision was passed in the 1947 Taft-Hartley Act, it did little harm to organized labor during its peak years in the 1950s and 1960s. At that time, many employers cooperated with labor. Low unemployment rates and high productivity rates made it attractive for employers to accept unionization as a way of undermining cutthroat competition and low wage labor. It was only in the late 1970s and 1980s when this spirit of cooperation had collapsed that employers started fighting unionization and increasing the number of contingent workers became a strategy to weaken organized labor.[64]

The narrow concept of unions as economic actors—that is, as business organizations rather than social justice advocacy groups, has contributed significantly to the decline of unionism. The NLRA has ensured that labor is isolated from social justice movements and that its agenda remains narrow: "Legitimate collective action is narrowly self-interested rather than altruistic, directed at maximizing pecuniary rewards rather than influencing the 'basic scope of the enterprise' and confined to the immediate employer-employee relationships rather than involving out-side workers and communities."[65]

As the New Voice Platform indicates, the AFL-CIO and other unions realize that one means of raising unionization rates is by organizing those who were historically disenfranchised—African-Americans and women—who now have the highest rates of organization.[66] Labor leaders like Sweeney are pledging these funds knowing that "exciting new research indicates that this is good news for unions."[67] Unionization rates for women have increased since 1980 to almost 19 percent of women in labor versus 31 percent of men. What is most startling is that nonwhite populations have the highest unionization rates, with approximately 32 percent being organized in comparison to 24 percent of white workers. Furthermore, the white population is projected to decline to 64 percent of the labor force in 2025, down from 74 percent in 1998 and 82 percent in 1980.[68] The new face of labor will be composed of women, African-Americans, Asians, and Latino/a workers wearing pink and white shirts in addition to white men in technical and high-tech industries.

While labor leaders realize that they must attract women and people of color to survive, organizing workers under global capitalism is no small feat. One of the notable features of globalism is that labor became a passive object of technical change. As technology changed work, people had to cope and accommodate.[69]

The fact that information—not a physical good or product—became the primary commodity that employers sought to protect has an additional negative impact on labor. In an important case, Pepsi-Cola successfully prevented William Redmond Jr., its former CEO, from joining Snapple. The company won an injunction that prevented his move, arguing that he would use some of Pepsi-Cola Co.'s trade secrets to market Snapple. While few employees are in Redmond's position, the court established a precedent of placing the company's prerogative of protecting its own knowledge over an employee's right to determine his employment.[70]

Information peddling involves individuals, not collectives.[71] As explained in this chapter's opening, an economy based on information means that the "creatives" or business managers, consultants, and marketing and financial experts as well as science and technology researchers and computer specialists have leverage in the workplace because of their information and ideas. The so-called California ideology governs the workplace. Yet this ideology, with its goal of turning all labor—professional, technical, managerial, or manual—into individual contractors, is antithetical to organized labor.[72]

### The new provocateurs

For organized labor to adapt to the new demographics and the changes to the economy, a whole new perspective must replace the old majority rule one. The AFL-CIO and other unions should continue raising not so much racial consciousness as consciousness about difference, which includes the issues of race, gender, sexuality, and disability.[73]

To revitalize the labor movement in the U.S., Crain proposes that race-conscious reforms be implemented as a means of organizing.[74] The history of the identity caucuses, she argues, shows that they do not impede solidarity, but rather help stimulate it. She challenges industrial relations expert Michael Piore's and others' argument that identity politics divide the work force.[75]

Identity caucuses should not just help people of color and women; the idea of taking into account individuality should be extended to all employees. It is not racial consciousness per se, but a consciousness about individual needs that organized labor must stimulate. A new perspective about the problems associated with majority cultures is needed.

The global work force no longer need be constrained by collective needs or collective desires. Information technology, as the last chapter shows, has transformed this. According to a progressive labor union specialist, the focus for "the new unions must be on individual workers and individual company performance." Specifically, he adds, "Unions can help to negotiate and to finance contract provisions that provide skill training for workers and unions can begin to provide an array of personal services to members." This specialist elaborates, "Unions can help employees attain greater flexibility in many ways. They can agree to eliminate job descriptions and allow employers to assign workers to a variety of jobs."[76]

### Individual employment laws

Given these problems associated with majority-rule culture, should employees simply spurn unionization? After all, advocates of individual employment laws insist that the problem with some union arguments is that they privilege class above all other identities.[77] They argue that individual employment rights are all that is required; and with only 9 percent of the private work force unionized, an overwhelming majority of employees depend on unions to help them enforce individual employment laws. But how do employees fare under these laws?

Before 1970, few restrictions were imposed on employers. Labor law was governed by employment-at-will. That is, employees could be hired and fired at will by employers. Today, over 85 percent of all employees are still governed by employment-at-will. The statutes described below set up some restrictions, but the doctrine still stands.

The only individual employment law that was passed before 1970 was the Fair Labor Standards Act (FLSA) of 1938, which created a minimum wage and set maximum hours. Then, in the late 1960s, just before organized labor had begun its steady decline, an explosion in employment laws occurred. The Occupational Safety and Health Act (OSHA) established a standard for worker safety. The Employee Retirement Income Security Act of 1974 (ERISA) protected employee pensions. The Worker Adjustment and Retraining Notification Act of 1988 (WARN) required employers with 100 or more employees to provide 60 days advance written notice to employees who will suffer an employment loss by virtue of plant closing or a mass layoff. In 1993, the Family Medical Leave Act (FMLA) was passed, providing that employees can return to work after taking 12 weeks of unpaid leave to care for a child or parent.[78]

Another important category of individual employment rights are the antidiscrimination statutes that overtly protect groups of individuals such as the Age Discrimination Employment Act of 1967 (ADEA), Section 504 of the Vocational Rehabilitation Act of 1973, and the ADA.[79] These antidiscrimination acts had been built on the model created by Title VII of the Civil Rights Act of 1964 that bans an employer from using race and gender in hiring and promotion.[80] On the whole, employment discrimination claims are the most successful in terms of volume since this type of claim is 100 percent greater than all other types of civil litigation.[81]

Overall, the question about individual employment laws revolves less around what is included in the statute and more around the means of enforcement.[82] Under labor law, unions represent workers, whereas under individual employment laws, workers must seek their own representation—even if it is just before the Employment Equal Opportunity Commission (EEOC). To examine how well individual employment laws work it is best not to take the weakest ones such as the FLSA and OSHA, but rather the most successful one—Title VII of the Civil Rights Act.

Title VII has had such a great impact that some law professors credit it with changing the workplace culture. As Murray Edelman and Stephen Patterson describe, there is now an expectation that employers be free of bias and exercise fair treatment of all their employees, not just women and people of color.[83] Or as Frank Dobbin puts it, the Equal Employment Office (EEO) "symbolically transformed" members of a disadvantaged group—people of color—from a group that was supposedly uninterested in mobility to one that was upwardly bound.[84]

Yet how much of the EEO is symbolic? Some scholars show that employers subtly sabotage the employment laws by relying on defense attorneys who provide them with the means to engage in what is called "creative compliance" or "preventative advice."[85] Advising companies to "document, document, document," these attorneys have formed a consensus about the general rules of the law, a litigation strategy, and a litigation prevention strategy to diminish employers' liability.[86] Most striking is how these attorneys have created a whole body of literature that offers employers "nonclient-specific advice."[87]

Nonclient-specific advice often masks discriminatory conditions. Evaluators who write in neutral language can obscure workplace bias.[88]

Also, human resource specialists often advise employers to modernize their personnel procedures by creating grievance procedures. These procedures, however, often disguise bias.[89] For the company, the incentive behind instituting grievance procedures is to limit their liability from civil rights claims and other workplace grievances. One way that a grievance structure has done this is by turning workplace disputes into personality conflicts. Employees are asked to vent their frustrations and heal relationships without employers punishing their perpetrators or compensating complainants for losses.[90]

Employers have developed this preventative advice strategy in part because the Supreme Court has rewarded them for doing so. In *Ellerth*, Justice Anthony Kennedy dropped a "litigation bombshell" by making employers liable for sexual harassment. Then, he offered employers a way out. To avoid liability, employers could demonstrate that they acted to prevent and to rectify their employees' behavior. Title VII, Justice Kennedy explained, is "designed to encourage the creation of anti-harassment policies and effective grievance mechanisms." Personnel managers and attorneys, he wrote, could create these policies.[91] Employers, in other words, need an affirmative (read preventative) defense.

An affirmative defense, however, is an affirmation of symbolic compliance and a turn away from prohibiting a truly discriminatory environment. The standard of legal compliance is based on the existence of personnel policies, not the environment itself. An employer does not discriminate, in other words, by having a personnel policy in place. Whether the workplace is hostile or discriminatory remains irrelevant.[92]

Arbitration is another recent development that has affected and promises to continue to affect employees in a negative way.[93] Arbitration agreements have been called the modern-day yellow-dog contract. The nineteenth century yellow-dog contract, law professor Katherine Stone explains, prohibited employees from joining a union. The late-twentieth century version is that employees must "waive their statutory rights in order to obtain employment."[94] Employers mandate that their employees sign an arbitration agreement as a condition of employment. This agreement removes all their employment grievances from the courtroom.[95] Employees cannot seek redress in court and must arbitrate almost all of their disputes.[96]

However, arbitration overwhelmingly benefits employers. First, it cuts down on court costs. Employers no longer need to pay for expensive legal counsel. Earlier some employees who threatened a lawsuit might gain compliance or a settlement because an employer did not want to incur these costs. Second, the rulings are largely in favor of employers and there is no possibility for punitive damages. Answering a chorus of law professors and amicus curiae briefs claiming that arbitration agreements are unfair to employees, the Supreme Court ruled in 2001 that "mere inequality in bargaining power" between an employer and an employee is not enough to make an arbitration agreement unenforceable.[97]

Few individual employment laws have been as beneficial for workers as unionization. Individual protection has failed to provide substantially better work conditions for most employees.[98] Most employees, however, do not realize how few rights they have in the workplace. They do not know that employment-at-work is alive and well. And they discover too late how little recourse they have—after being terminated without cause.[99]

This is understandable on two levels. On one level, most Americans take pride in the wide array of rights available to them as a general proposition. On another level, some politicians claim credit for appealing to this sense of rights when they are in actual fact doing the opposite. Some members of Congress and presidents disguise their motives by passing laws with benevolent and benign titles. The Family Working Flexibility Bill is a prime example.[100] This bill strips employees of overtime pay, giving an employer the authority to award compensation time instead of the time-and-a-half pay rate provided by the minimum wages and maximum hours law. The flexibility is given to the employer, not the family, yet it is touted as a labor law that will benefit employees.

## A reasonable accommodations model: good for goose and gander

Neither labor laws nor individual employment laws provide employees with enough protection in the workplace. The most effective means of ensuring that they have better work conditions is a marriage of these two types of laws. Few employment statutes, however, allow organized labor to help individual employees. One notable exception is the ADEA, which borrowed a remedial provision from the FLSA that allows a class to seek redress.[101] Nothing prevents a union from representing this class. Labor leaders could also report violations in occupational health and safety standards. Despite these provisions, organized labor has played a small role in helping employees enforce their rights under individual employment laws.

Separating labor laws that affect organized labor and individual employees was not a foregone conclusion. One of the first drafts of what became the FLSA put organized labor in the unique position of policing employers.[102] Had this bill passed, labor unions would have been called upon to report all those firms and factories that violated minimum wage and maximum hours. This legislative draft, however, was not enacted. When individual employment laws sprang up in the 1970s, no such role for organized labor was proposed again as it had been in the late 1930s. These laws were partially designed to compensate for the absence of collective bargaining agreements.[103]

If organized labor utilized the ADA, it could alter this historic trajectory. The reasonable accommodations model provides a means of circumventing the individual rights versus collectives divide. Quite simply, labor leaders could help individual employees negotiate reasonable accommodations. A union could help an individual employee in the interactive process as he or she discusses with an employer what the essential and nonessential tasks of a position are and what reasonable accommodations are. A union's size and strength would offset the structural disadvantage that a single employee has against a large company or even a small office. After all, it is the employer and not the individual employee who understands the overall employment context.

Title I of the ADA could be broadly construed since it is not employees but employers who cannot divulge why or what type of reasonable accommodations are offered. The statute does not prevent an employee from spreading the word about a particular accommodation. As described in the last chapter, the employee with a disability could become the saboteur, providing his or her colleagues with information about how their employers control the workplace. This would transform employees with disabilities into becoming agents of resistance as Michel Foucault imagines. This type of resistance could cause more chaos than ever before since the new economy relies on information.

Furthermore, organized labor could have a hand in helping achieve this liberating resistance. Having an individual employee negotiate with an employer in the interactive process provides no guarantee that this employee knows what reasonable accommodations could be obtained. While the federal courts have imposed a duty on employers to explain what accommodations are possible, this duty would be more effectively enforced if there were a safeguard. Like an employer, a union would gain experience and therefore be able to provide an employee with a disability with an idea of what type of reasonable accommodations are available. Armed with this information, a disabled employee has a much greater chance of obtaining an accommodation that gives him or her the ability to step into the workplace or maintain his or her position after an illness or an injury.

Employers can also obtain preventative information from attorneys who give them advice about how to avoid litigation, particularly about civil rights. This practice is considered part of their normal business routine. By contrast, the most savvy and sophisticated employee secures legal counsel only when a conflict arises. If a company learns that an employee has retained an attorney, moreover, this could erode his or her bargaining power by making employers and their teams of lawyers more wary. Relying on unions and labor lawyers rather than individual lawyers would give employees with disabilities a greater chance of success in gaining reasonable accommodations.

As discussed earlier, the problem with unionization is its majority-rule culture. Not only do labor laws insist that unions represent all members equally, but a culture that fosters majority rule dominates most unions.

Unions could change this culture, however. As Michael Harper and Ira Lupu have suggested, organized labor could rely on a constitutional configuration rather than a majority-rule framework to determine which policies to pursue.[104]

Organized labor has the capacity to represent persons with disabilities. The question is not whether labor leaders can, but whether they want to. Taking on the task of representing persons with disabilities would mean that organized labor would have to modify the seniority system. This system does not take into account reasonable accommodations. A personnel system featuring seniority was enacted to promote a sense of fairness in the workplace. It also originated during the postwar period when employers had to compete for labor. Factories and firms with seniority systems, retirement benefits, and vacation plans had less employee turnover.[105]

Historically, American unions have neither had, nor sought, much control over setting work conditions. Labor historians argue that organized labor turned its back on legitimate worker demands for respect and autonomy at the workplace in "exchange for bargaining higher wages and bigger benefit packages."[106] Labor-management expert Randy Hodson elaborates that unions have undermined "their own long-term legitimacy with workers by trading off the pursuit of solutions to workers' daily complaints for collective bargaining over wages and benefits."[107]

Labor law, moreover, has codified organized labor's position. As law professor Stephen Befort states, "The NLRA, itself, has never mandated any substantive terms of the employment relationship."[108] The one way of securing some control was creating seniority rules that the employer, who set work conditions, could not alter. Jobs were set. It was not the person but the job that was stipulated, which a particular person then filled. Jobs were doled out on a "first come-first served" basis, setting up a seniority ladder system.

Seniority rules, however, constitute a crude means of controlling managerial prerogative power. These rules are more of a reflection of organized labor's weakness than its strength. American unions are exceptional not just for their notion of business unionism and exclusionary practices, but also because they respect business's "right to manage."[109] Few other industrialized nations have unions that play such a small part in controlling the labor process as America has.

Seniority systems as well as other hiring and firing practices included in collective bargaining agreements were first introduced as businesses sought help from organized labor to maintain group discipline. Managerial experts thought organized labor could help firms create and maintain this discipline, which would make the business organization more efficient. In Chester Barnard's classic book, *The Functions of the Executive*, he wrote that group discipline can become so effective that "even individuals who have exhausted their promotional prospects can thereby be induced to comply."[110] In fact, Barnard and the internal market economist Oliver Williamson each underscore how helpful organized labor has been in instilling the type of group discipline necessary for the workplace.[111] Given organized labor's emphasis on seniority and setting wages to job descriptions, rather than the individuals who fill them, unions—particularly industrial unions during the postwar economic boom—have helped promote and maintain this discipline.[112]

Organized labor and American business established this special arrangement after World War II. Experiencing an unprecedented boom in the economy and strong unions, firms accepted organized labor. During organized labor's heyday, many factories and firms accepted unions as one means of retaining labor. The bargain many companies struck was that organized labor would be accepted as long as it kept control over the workplace.

Since organized labor began its rapid decline in the 1980s, workers have been asking for more control in the labor process, not less. In a country that has little faith in unionization, this is one of the roles that most employees want from organized labor. According to labor-management experts Robert Freeman and James Medoff, there is a large participation gap between employers and employees, which shows that the latter want more of a voice in the workplace.[113] Workers may not endorse unionization, but they do want a greater role in determining the labor process.

With its provision for the interactive process, the ADA would give organized labor an unprecedented role in helping set work conditions. If labor leaders bargained for individual employees on a case-by-case basis rather than only when a collective bargaining agreement (which covers the entire work force) expired, this would give organized labor a great deal of power to help determine work conditions on a continual basis.

In the concluding chapter, this book suggests how the ADA could be transformed from a disability rights law into a statute that interjects the concept of needs into the workplace. Employers would have to address the individuality of each employee. Given the functional definition of a disability, which is expansive, organized labor can maintain that most of its employees now or in the future have disabilities that will need to be accommodated. Our bodies are in a permanent state of flux. Few people escape life without some health mishap, illness, or injury. Rather than perceiving a healthy person as a standard for all others, it is best to recognize each individual and the different needs that he or she has. It is not about being disabled, but about doing things differently.

CHAPTER 7

# Critical Care

The Americans with Disabilities Act (ADA) is the most significant statute enacted by the president and Congress since the Great Society. As this book shows, the Act's reasonable accommodations provisions are groundbreaking. They are not affirmative action provisions that compensate a group of individuals for past injustices; they are not antidiscrimination provisions that prevent employers from exercising any bias against a people based on their group identity; nor are they a new form of collective bargaining. The reasonable accommodations provisions give affirmative or substantive rights to no identifiable group, but rather to individuals who have physical and mental needs that must be satisfied for these individuals to work.

Put simply, these provisions create a model for interjecting a notion of workplace need that is based on our individuality rather than our group identity. Anyone can need anything at any time. Yet hearing one individual's voice could bring help to the collective. The accommodations offered to one individual can be passed on to a collective of individuals, albeit on a case-by-case basis. The ADA's employment provisions issue a Three Musketeers-like cry of "all for one and one for all."

Reasonable accommodations are not merely tangible goods like a chair or a ramp. They are also work conditions like offering flexitime or job sharing, the feasibility of which can only be understood if an employee has a full understanding of a company's routine operations. Organized labor could play a significant role in this process. Using the reasonable accommodations model, labor leaders could get more involved in setting work conditions. In the high-tech industry, as shown in chapter 5, unions might gain information that would help them negotiate at the bargaining table. First, if employees with disabilities gain an overview of a plant's or an office's operations, they would have access to information that could help them bargain for optimal work conditions. Second, armed with this knowledge and information, employees with disabilities can help their colleagues reclaim their subjectivity.

Employers have incentives and programs that induce employees to identify with them though their interests might well be best served by identifying with their colleagues. Many employees participate in programs like "employee of the month," not realizing how these programs erode their subjectivity and conflict with their own self-interest.

Most employers prefer that information about the operation of a workplace remain ambiguous to employees. Employers benefit from employees not having a comprehensive understanding of how a factory or an office is run. Indeed, this was one of the fundamental principles in Adam Smith's pin factory.[1] It also explains why Congress and a pro-business Republican President, George H. W. Bush, passed the Worker Adjustment and Retraining Notification Act of 1988 (WARN) to compel employers to inform their work force about plant shutdowns.[2]

This concluding chapter provides a concrete outline of how organized labor can work for persons with disabilities, broadly construed. First, it explores how prejudice creates the biggest stumbling block in expanding the role that the ADA could play in the work force. Second, it shows how this interpretation of the ADA exemplifies a critical conception of an ethic of care by showing why disabled and able-bodied employees should embrace the reasonable accommodations model in the workplace.

## Overcoming otherness

The tallest hurdle for organized labor to jump is the same one that all groups must clear when they encounter persons with disabilities—that of bias and prejudice. Persons with disabilities are now seeking employment rights after great strides have been made toward mainstreaming them into society.[3] Not only has deinstitutionalization been a policy that both the state and federal governments have successfully implemented for several decades, but the ADA's greatest court victory has been the Supreme Court's defense of it.[4]

However, disability is still mistakenly viewed as something someone else has. Persons with disabilities are viewed as the other, or worse yet, freaks.[5] Presenting a historical perspective, Rachel Adams shows how the perception of disability has evolved. Featured in carnival sideshows in the late nineteenth century, persons with disabilities were freaks of nature or human curiosities.[6] By the turn of the century, Fiona Whittington-Walsh explains, "The Protestant ethic combined with Victorian morality helped turn audiences away from the Freak Shows."[7] In part because of the large number of veterans who became injured during World War I, and the even larger number during World War II, disability became medicalized. Offering a medical diagnosis and then treating him or her, the physicians helped turn the freak into a clinical version of the other.

Today, despite mainstreaming and all the strides the disability rights movement has made, persons with disabilities are still seen as the other. Some avant-garde artists, Adams argues, now characterize them as unique oddities. Although the venue has changed, with persons with disabilities moving from the seedy carnival booth to the upscale art exhibit hall, they are still regarded as freaks. Instead of being freaks of human nature, some avant-garde artists have transformed persons with disabilities into a human counterpoint or point of contrast in their running commentary about mainstream society and normality.

Furthermore, the historian Catherine Kudlick argues that the media's emphasis on "normality, youth, and bodily perfection" subtly entrenches bias and prejudice against disabled persons.[8] It is part of common parlance, she observes, to turn a physical and mental condition like blindness into an adjective that describes both unhealthy and undesirable amounts of obedience, rage, or ambition. The one phrase that journalists pulled out of a sensational political tell-all book about George W. Bush, for example, was former Treasury Secretary Paul O'Neill's description of the president behaving "like a blind man in a room full of deaf people."[9]

Being a champion of the rights of previously disenfranchised people, moreover, does not make one any less susceptible to practicing this type of discrimination. Well-known feminists have used disability in the same pejorative way. Iris Marion Young, for instance, described "women in a sexist society" as "physically handicapped."[10]

Adams's and Kuklick's work represent just a few of the many studies that delve into the very nature of prejudice against persons with disabilities. Peeling back the many layers of prejudice is as vital to disability studies as it was to African-American studies. Yet discrimination against persons with disabilities could prove more difficult to eradicate than racial prejudice. Many people who identify themselves as liberal and tolerant have well thought out explanations for their prejudice. For instance, Justice Byron R. White, who ruled in favor of many civil rights cases, explained that discrimination based on disability can be distinguished from that based on race and gender since persons with disabilities are "different."[11]

That disability is about uniqueness, about how disabled persons break standards, and about how they can help unions negotiate better work conditions for all workers can be recognized only if able-bodied people suspend their discomfort, biases, and prejudice against them. One of the strategies for "educating" people so that they can be free of their prejudices involves giving those without disabilities first-hand experience to learn about those with disabilities.

A great place to start is the workplace. Myths about hiring persons with disabilities could be dispelled by close proximity. Employers and able-bodied employees have anxiety about hiring employees with disabilities. When persons with disabilities actually enter the work force they become less of an abstraction and consequently less of a concern to their nondisabled colleagues who gain a better understanding of their daily activities. The improbable "what if a blind person applies for a position as an air-traffic controller" is exposed for what it is: an expression of angst rather than a real employment dilemma. (It is highly improbable that someone with a severe vision problem would seek employment as an air-traffic controller. And if this happened, he or she would not be hired on the grounds of a lack of qualifications. A person with a severe visual impairment is clearly not qualified for a position that requires excellent vision.)

Another strategy involves having labor leaders show the rank and file that the ADA's employment provisions are so broad that they could include providing privacy for women pumping breast milk on the job. Interestingly enough, most of the Supreme Court's ADA employment provisions cases involved persons not with traditional disabilities like paraplegia or blindness, but with carpal tunnel syndrome, breast cancer, and hypertension.[12] Organized labor should therefore alert its members and potential members that disabled persons cannot be classified as the "other," but are just like them. As described in chapters 1 and 6, new working mothers, older employees, and people with a genetic predisposition for disease also fit this bill.

## A caring union: all for one and one for all

Within the workplace, labor leaders could educate their employees so that they understand that helping individual workers with disabilities does not necessarily put them in a zero-sum position with other employees. Reasonable accommodations set precedents. Labor leaders could show them how these accommodations represent needs—not special needs, but essential needs that every employee, provided he or she works long enough, is likely to request some day.

Working on a case-by-case basis, moreover, means that standardized treatment of employees is no longer necessary. While an exclusive bargaining unit could be established, labor leaders would be bargaining perpetually. The union would be responsive to employee needs as they were formulated. Organized labor could rely on the ADA to break its historic turn away from workers by pledging formally and informally not to interfere in management's right to manage the shop floor or the daily operations in an office.

Richard Freeman's and Joel Rogers's landmark study, "What Workers Want," indicates that employees would greatly prefer that organized labor get involved in shop floor operations.[13] The workers themselves would like to help their employers design the shop floor or the office space; and just as employers no longer need to standardize their work conditions, so too labor leaders can offer collective bargaining agreements that are not entirely standardized.

Yet how does one envision the practical operations of a nonstandardized workplace that takes into account individual needs? Do specific provisions about collective bargaining interfere with the ADA's employment provisions? In 2002, the Supreme Court ruled in *U.S. vs. Barnett* that seniority rights take precedence over accommodations.[14] While this decision limits the rights of persons with disabilities, it does not stop organized labor from including a provision on its own about accommodations in a collective bargaining agreement. The flexibility necessary to include accommodations could be part of the collective bargaining agreement that is ratified by the rank and file.

What the *Barnett* decision indicates is that the Supreme Court has opened a door for organized labor to play a vital role in setting work conditions. It also gives the disability rights community an incentive to work with organized labor. Indeed, labor unions are a natural place for disabled people to turn. Organized labor has had more success in resolving workplace conflicts with grievance structures than employers. An accommodation is certainly not a grievance, however. Labor leaders should create an accommodations structure that would not determine, but would rather advise employees about what are the essential and nonessential duties of positions to help them formulate requests for specific accommodations. This type of approach would give employees greater strength in the interactive process with employers. Organized labor would gain too since able-bodied employees could benefit from the information gathered. This information would give labor leaders a better understanding of the day-to-day operations of a firm or a factory, which in turn could help them negotiate for better work conditions.

A whole body of industrial relations literature shows that union-led grievance structures best promote issues that involve workplace justice.[15] This literature purports that workplace justice is a crucial aspect of creating an efficient company or corporation, and that organized labor, not management, has the best rate of success in implementing a grievance structure.[16] What such a structure does is regularize conflicts at the workplace as a means of avoiding formal strikes as well as informal acts of resistance.[17]

Most grievance structures are based on the principle of due process or the idea that every individual has the right to fair and equal treatment. A perception of fairness is an essential part of the calculation.[18] Employees are more likely to accept a negative outcome if they believe this outcome is decided fairly by the people operating the grievance structure.[19]

So why would persons with disabilities turn to employers without relying on organized labor's support? Why should they believe that employers will recognize their interests more than labor leaders? Part of the reason stems from how employers try to divide-and-conquer their work force as outlined in the last chapter. Not only is this strategy effective in workplaces that are racially divided or gendered, but it works for those employers who balk at providing accommodations to persons with disabilities.

The emotion that causes an able-bodied employee to resent an employee receiving an accommodation comes from the feeling of "why not me?" The accommodation reminds able-bodied employees of how poor their work conditions really are. Employers can capitalize on this resentment by turning it into a zero-sum game between the able-bodied and disabled employees.

To fuel the fire, employers often play the cost card—maintaining that their firm or company cannot afford an accommodation. Persons with disabilities could contest this. In their quest for understanding the essential and nonessential functions of a position, employees with disabilities would discover the costs of a firm's operation, including reasonable accommodations. One study shows that two-thirds of all accommodations cost nothing, that the average accommodation costs $120, and that 70 percent of all accommodations cost less than $500, with only 3 percent costing more than $1,000.[20] Employers would then have more difficulty using the threat of costs and lay-offs to force the union to rethink the issue.

A grievance structure for accommodations could create a system for labor leaders to present the employee's resentment to management. While not everyone can park as close to the store as those with disabilities, it would represent a watershed in thinking if employers gave out parking on the basis of need. They could give preferences to those who ride-share, have long commutes, or have small children to pick up, in addition to the most productive worker, let alone someone with a mobility problem.

The reasonable accommodations model impresses upon employers that their employees' needs must be taken into account. This idea is radical in that it violates one of the fundamental principles within the classical concept of capitalism. It spurns the notion that employers own their workers' time. The reasonable accommodations model contests the idea that the workers' right to exit should be their only means of protesting the lack of support in a workplace.

Interjecting the notion of needs into the workplace with an alternative conception of an ethic of care allows women and people of color to transcend the rights discourse with its restrictions about equal treatment and special protection. The ADA is the first law that creates a framework with potential for a care ethic.

Given its emphasis on truth and morality, however, an ethic of care initially lacked a critical edge. As feminist legal theorist Kathryn Abrams writes, the first wave of the literature about an ethic of care was "marred ... by [the authors'] depiction of care as a moral or cognitive attribute reflecting women's essence."[21] The second wave of care-ethic literature replaces essentialism with social construction. By abandoning gender altogether, a care ethic could lay the groundwork for a third wave. Applying this feminist morality to the workplace could also turn into a rejection of Max Weber's notion of standardization and rationalization as well as being an indictment of liberalism and capitalism.

## Sociability rather than standardization

The care ethic behind this book relies on Gilles Deleuze's and Felix Guattari's interpretation of Benedict de Spinoza. These French critical theorists extend the notion that people are deeply embedded in relationships to include Spinoza's conception of sociability. The book then interjects the notion of sociability into the ethic of care. For the workplace this means that no employee would stand alone. United they stand—not by virtue of what they hold in common, but by what makes each of them distinctive.

Put differently, a sociable workplace resembles a puzzle, with each person fitting in because of his or her unique curves and edges. Work conditions are created for each individual on a case-by-case basis. For instance, flexitime could help someone with diabetes who took medication that prevented him or her from arriving at work early in the morning. It would also give someone who could not drive the chance to have a daytime-only schedule that would correspond with the suburban bus schedule he depended on. Or new mothers and fathers might prefer job sharing while their children are under school age.

But how could work conditions be turned into puzzle pieces without jeopardizing the economic health of the companies that provide them in the first place? How could these conditions be set in accordance with each employee's needs in a way that does not erode a company's profits? The life/work literature in management journals reflects some of this call for utilizing an employee's distinctiveness given the employee's and the employer's mutual benefits.[22] Employees who believe that their employers respect and appreciate them put more energy and effort into their performance.[23]

More important, it is the very structure of high-tech industrialism that helps determine how workplace conditions could change to reflect an employee's individuality. Employers have begun setting individual rather than standard work conditions because of the high-tech industrial revolution. Mass industrialization changed the rules for industrialization. Before that, industrialization altered the principles underlying mercantilism. Similarly, high-tech industrialization, as shown in chapter 5, has changed the very assumption about standardization that underlies mass industrialization. What was described as the California ideology, which determines every individual's contribution to the workplace, now prevails in many an industry, not just the computer industry.[24]

What has happened is that robotics and computers encourage employers overseeing high-tech workplaces to promote individuality. Offices and factories no longer need standardized equipment or machinery built for the average person to maintain high worker productivity. In fact, the well-known management expert Peter Drucker places what he describes as the new "knowledge worker" in context with the old manufacturing worker, emphasizing that the former needs his or her autonomy, which is in turn an expression of individuality, if employers want to increase worker productivity.[25] Drucker uses the term knowledge worker expansively, describing not just those in the high-tech industry, but almost all workers, since technology has become important in almost every factory or office. Unless the U.S. and other first world nations understand that this transformation is as fundamental as standardization was to scientific management, Drucker warns, the First World's competitive edge, separating it from the Third World, will be eroded.

To Drucker, the high-tech informational economy has dramatically altered how employers should view employees. Employees can no longer be regarded as a cost. Instead, they should be recognized as an asset that must be nurtured and cultivated. "Making knowledge workers more productive requires changes in basic attitude, whereas making the manual worker more productive only required telling the worker how to do the job. . . . Changes in attitude . . . [are required] not only on the part of the individual knowledge worker, but on the part of the whole organization," he suggests.[26]

According to Drucker, this change in attitude is best understood by recognizing what components go into making knowledge workers productive. First, he explains, employees and employers must carefully define what a company's task is. For example, U.S. Caterpillar discovered early on that it was not selling heavy machinery, like tractors, but selling machinery that would run businesses.[27] It was the service it provided in combination with finding the right machinery for a specific company that made U.S. Caterpillar successful. Drucker then notes that knowledge workers must manage themselves rather than have supervisors that manage them. Another key component is that these workers must perpetually learn *and* continuously teach other knowledge workers.[28] Finally, Drucker insists that the quality of goods or services provided is as important as the quantity or amount that the knowledge worker produces.

Ultimately, Drucker is arguing that innovation must be built into most jobs. It is not enough for companies to tell and to direct their work force about how to perform. Knowledge workers *are* the means of production. Therefore, they must be self-motivated. Self-motivation, however, must not be confused with self-discipline.

The employers described in chapter 5 who use technology for surveillance and control are not fulfilling the notion of interdependence that self-motivation propels. Taking into account the individual's performance pushes the person to his or her limit to fulfill the corporation's interest. Teamwork under concertive control represents another example where the employer, not the employee, profits from the individual's initiative and ingenuity.

While management experts purports that teamwork reinvigorates employee morale, increases efficiency, and boosts productivity, many employees realize that it was the company, not they, that profited from their collective know-how and ingenuity.[29] While some employees, manipulated into believing that their self-interests are fulfilled by serving the company, may surrender their subjectivity to the company, many do not. Self-discipline means that employers have deceived employees into increasing productivity that they profit from, whereas self-motivation is accompanied by self-awareness that would not permit such deception.

It is self-motivation resulting from a knowledge worker's individuality, not self-discipline substituting a corporate mentality for an individual one, that Drucker sees as the key. To him, viewing workers as an asset rather than a cost means employers must take into account not just the economic but the individual contribution of each employee, including his or her physical well-being.

Meanwhile, other studies underscore how worker productivity, for instance, has increased when employers address physical well-being.[30] As long ago as 1930, the Kellogg Company discovered that a 6-hour working day increased worker productivity by 3 percent.[31] While today some employers operate under the premise that better work conditions improve worker productivity, most employers reach the same bottom line by pushing their employees and recovering cost by lowering wages. Sweatshops certainly still exist in the U.S., but for those employers who reject this type of management, many have given workers better work conditions knowing that these conditions help them operate within the parameters of just-in-time production.

That profits and better work conditions need not be in conflict is nowhere better demonstrated than with teamwork or what is called module production. Most retail companies rely on just-in-time production to reduce the high cost of maintaining a large inventory. This represents retail's response to a public that makes faster fashion-conscious or fad-oriented purchasing decisions than ever before. To maximize their profits in such a volatile market, in other words, these companies insist on having no real inventory. Factories producing the goods for retail had to adapt to this request, which they could not do with the outdated progressive bundling system created by scientific management in the 1910s and used up until the 1990s. This system breaks down tasks into distinct and separate operations conducted by employees who are paid on the basis of individual piece rates. Having work performed in pieces created a large inventory that was waiting to be assembled. Just-in-time production, by contrast, works better with module production where a team of workers assemble an entire product. In fact, module production has been such a help in reducing inventory costs in addition to manufacturing space, supervisory and service functions, and quality inspections that some companies engage in this type of production even if they anticipate that the productivity of the work force would fall.[32]

Whether they are addressing knowledge workers or factory workers in quality circles or practicing some type of teamwork, what these management studies show is that standardization is a thing of the past.[33] Taking into account the individuality of the whole work force, not just workers with disabilities, has become an important means of increasing worker productivity and/or cutting costs in the office or on the factory floor.

Many manufacturing firms that have given employees better work conditions by following quality circles and different forms of team participation do so because they depend on continuous learning and teaching. Most studies reveal that teamwork increases worker productivity.[34] One study showed that team participation increased productivity by 14 percent. This study complements Drucker's argument by showing that the heterogeneous teams were more productive than the homogenous ones. That is, teams with highly productive workers in combination with less productive ones still increased a factory's overall rate of productivity. The faster workers taught the slower workers.[35] Continuous teaching and learning represent the key to increasing productivity.

This finding contradicts the classic free-rider problem, in which the weaker employees profit from the work of the stronger ones, bringing down average overall productivity or keeping it the same. Yet why did the highly productive workers in this study decide to be on teams, risking that they would receive less payment for their work? One management study shows that highly productive individuals prefer to gain higher social status in teams or stronger bargaining power than to maximize their pay. The more productive workers enjoy helping their less productive colleagues.[36] Nonpecuniary rewards are very important to most employees.

### If not honey, what about vinegar?

Another reason why employers would find it in their interest to provide work conditions that cater to their individual employees' needs is that their employees have an expensive means of getting back at them for being too harsh or unsympathetic. Employee sabotage is not only more ubiquitous than ever, but it represents a more costly problem than it did under mass industrialization. Up until the mid-1980s, throwing a wrench into that factory machine might temporarily stop a line from moving. This deed, however, would not go unpunished, even if the individual culprit was not found. More importantly, a supervisor could pinpoint the problem immediately and fix it without too much cost and difficulty.

Employees, ex-employees, or friends of employees can plant a logic bomb, or a program designed to cause chaos, in a computer system so that it wipes out records.[37] According to the Federal Bureau of Investigation (FBI), "Every 30 seconds a hack takes place on the Internet and every three minutes an intranet is under siege."[38] During a month-long strike, communications workers committed 450 acts of sabotage, including cutting off 30,000 local customers. A disgruntled employee of a Fort Worth insurance company (the manager of company security no less) erased 168,000 pay records from its database.[39] While the police, the FBI, and company investigators find some of these saboteurs, most escape punishment.[40]

Who are these disgruntled employees? According to the FBI, more than half of all security breaches are inside jobs. Disgruntled employees, former workers, and unscrupulous associates with access to your network are more likely to wreak havoc than the random criminal.[41] "During times of an economic slowdown, it is common to see an increase in security incidents caused by frustrated and hostile former employees," said Michael Rasmussen, an analyst at Giga Information Group in Boston.[42]

A more important question is how many people commit acts of workplace vengeance. Are these lone rogue employees? Daniel Dana, president and director of program development for the Mediation Training Institute maintains that "it is estimated that over 65 percent of performance problems result from strained relationships between employees, not from deficits in individual employees skill or motivation." One management study showed that 85 percent of all employees admit to having committed some act of sabotage. A full 90 percent admit that it is an everyday occurrence.[43] "Unmanaged employee conflict is perhaps the largest reducible cost in organizations today and probably the least recognized" adds Dana. While all 50 states and the federal government have passed laws prohibiting sabotage, it is nonetheless a serious, intractable problem.[44] It also often goes unreported. A company would prefer to handle it quietly, as shown in chapter 5, rather than let its stockholders or customers know how much it suffers from employee sabotage.[45]

If management opts not to cultivate individual employee work conditions, sabotage represents means of compelling employers to do so. Moreover, workers with disabilities, with their access to workplace operations, can help the saboteurs. In the absence of what a collective of employees deem to be good work conditions, employees could foster sociability and further a constructive form of resistance by utilizing the ADA's employment provisions. Instead of just committing acts of petty resistance and sabotage, they could use the ADA's provisions about asking for more information about the essential and nonessential tasks of a job to gain insight about an office's or a factory's operations. This information could help employees unite around gaining better work conditions for each employee on a case-by-case needs basis.

Once mobilized, employers could be cooperative in making accommodations or they could fight them. In either case, employees with knowledge of daily operations are in a good position for negotiating better work conditions.

The individualizing capacity of high-tech equipment has turned labor-management relations into a strategic game about information. How much does a new computer program increase productivity? Who benefits? Thus far the evidence indicates that employers profit most from this change in technology. Yet a mutually inclusive situation fostering Spinoza's notion of sociability would cause the greatest, most long-lasting changes.

## A caring economy

A care ethic based on individuality highlights the infinite possibilities of the mind and the body in the new, nonstandardized modern workplace. First by uniting around the body—rather than the female or male body—a critical care ethic can render a critique of American liberalism. Identity politics often works within a classical liberal framework. This means that some previously excluded group of people begins participating in the political process. When such a new group enters the political arena, it often has little influence. They are a minority not just numerically, but also in terms of directing the political climate.[46] Thus, the theory of whiteness was developed to explain how little influence African-Americans have had in the political process.

Civil rights protections for women and people of color underscore this point. As women and people of color enter the workplace, they have little power to change it. A critical workplace care ethic, by contrast, could ensure that a worker with physical or mental needs could not only get into the workplace, but the accommodations he or she receives would change the atmosphere. "The ADA goes beyond and asks employers to restructure the jobs themselves" explain Stewart Schwab and Steven Willborn. "We suggest that, over time, this sort of inquiry will spill over into Title VII cases as well and, from there, into general conceptions of discrimination across the entire range of discrimination law."[47]

Similarly, in another study, feminist Salli Westwood shows how women feminized a workplace by adding a social element that reflected life's different stages.[48] Exploring the impact of feminization in one factory, Westwood reveals that social functions like wedding and baby showers, retirement parties, and potluck dinners helped the women in this factory forge a strong bond. This bond helped them bargain more effectively with their employers for better work conditions.

While Westwood's research discusses feminization on an informal level, the ADA's employment provisions could offer persons with disabilities a formal means of changing the workplace atmosphere. Taking care of Jane and John would have the effect of making the workplace a more humane environment.

A critical care ethic also offers no less than a new vision of political economy. The feminist morality makes little distinction between the public and the private spheres, which is counter to the American conceptions of capitalism and liberalism. Both ideologies are governed by an ethic of rights, which depends on a clear distinction between the private and public domains. Whereas liberalism draws the line between the personal and the public spheres, capitalism does not. Capitalism certainly draws the line at public interference in private property, but it makes no distinction between private life and work. One's personal life and one's public work life are both part of the private sphere. A critical ethic of care erodes this idea, making the private workplace an extension of the private home.

By providing health benefits, employers reinforce this idea that the personal life and one's employment history are in the private domain. All other industrialized nations have made health care a public benefit, not a private one. Having private health benefits hides some of the costs associated with governmental involvement. Nonetheless, there are specific costs associated with a predominantly employer-paid health care system. If an employer refuses to insure an employee or an employee's family, the government picks up the tab—either indirectly with public hospitals treating those people who lack insurance in emergency rooms—or directly through Medicare and Medicaid.

Capitalism has long benefited from the private/public dichotomy in contradictory ways. In *The Great Transformation*, Karl Polanyi maintains that one of the fundamental contradictions within capitalism is this idea that there is (or should be) a strict dichotomy between the public and the private domains.[49] The history of capitalism has a dubious birth. "The tradition of the classical economists," he notes, "attempted to base the law of market on the alleged propensities of man in the state of nature."[50] The march of capitalism, in other words, represents the development of a theory, not history. Capitalism is therefore universal and transhistorical. To Polanyi, the ideological function of the idea of the market propounded by classical economists is as important as its scientific function.

Polanyi argues, by contrast, that capitalism belongs within the realm of history. The "economy does not exist apart from or as a subset of activity within society, but rather is deeply embedded in social institutions and social relations at all levels."[51] The market is only one such institution or set of relations. "The economic system was submerged in general social relations;" writes Polanyi, "markers were merely an accessory feature of an institutional setting controlled and regulated more than ever by social authority."[52]

After making this argument, Polanyi insists that the government should prevent capitalism from undermining the very society that supports it.[53] All the major social movements of the nineteenth and early twentieth centuries, like labor union organizing, the rise of nationalism, and indeed the emergence and growth of political democracy, he argues, can be attributed to societal groups trying to defend themselves from the less humane side of this economic system.[54]

The employment provisions within the ADA should be interpreted as society's recognition that people with physical and mental needs belong in the work force and that it should not be considered entirely within the private domain. Employers, moreover, should shoulder the burden of providing reasonable accommodations. By rendering a functional definition of disability, the Supreme Court opened Pandora's box to all physical and mental needs. While it may not be in the short-term interests of capital, it is in capital's long-term interest as well as in the interest of the government and society at large to accommodate persons with physical and mental needs in the workplace.

People currently live longer than they used to and are therefore more likely to develop disabilities. At the same time, persons who experience disabilities at an early age live longer than ever before. Also, medical technologies and genetic testing increasingly determine who has a predisposition to certain conditions and diseases and might develop a disability. All of this underscores the larger theoretical issue of the myth of independence and the quest for perfection. People are neither independent at home nor in the workplace. The sooner the quest for the perfect mind and body is abandoned, the sooner private enterprise, the government, and society can recognize needs.

## Critical care

This book concludes that Enlightenment principles of Cartesian dualism, standardization, and rationalization have run their course in the workplace. Information technology now affords us the luxury of looking at the individual *and* the collective. Accommodating one person at a workplace shows how we can accommodate all. Methods of accommodation, in other words, should be viewed as large puzzles that a body of people in a work force can solve collectively.

This puzzle has the potential to work since employers and employees have the capacity to anticipate their needs and the needs of others. This is particularly true for all employees, whether they have disabilities or not. Once employees understand that the Spinozian critical care ethic fosters individuality and promotes the notion of interdependence at the workplace, they might be more accommodating of each other.

This stems from the idea that accommodations are not based on altruism or benevolence. Rather, they should be made on the basis of self-preservation. The question is not *if* you need help (read accommodations), but *when* will you need it. As Spinoza explains, people must "strive together, as far as they can, to preserve their being; and that all, together, should seek for themselves the common advantage of all." If we are "joined to one another, they compose an individual twice as powerful as each one."[55]

The accommodations model, with its underlying critical care ethic, is premised upon powerful ideas. And ideas matter. While the Supreme Court and the lower federal courts may ensure that the definition of a disability is not broadly construed, the power of the ideas behind the accommodations model might not be so easily discounted, rebuffed, or rejected.

# ENDNOTES

## Chapter 1: A Subversive Act

1. Irving K. Zola, "Disability statistics, what we count and what it tells us," *Journal of Disability Policy Studies* 4 (1993).
2. Rosemarie Garland-Thomson, "Integrating disability, transforming feminist theory," *National Women's Studies Association Journal* 14 (2002), 2. She argues that "disability studies can benefit from feminist theory and feminist theory can benefit from disability studies."
3. Quoted from Garland-Thomson, "Integrating disability, transforming feminist theory," 5. See Mariam Corker, "Disability discourse in a postmodern world" in *The Disability Reader: Social Science Perspectives*, Tom Shakespeare, ed. (London: Cassell, 1998); and Eve Kofofsky Sedgwick, *Epistemology in the Closet* (Berkeley: University of California, 1990). Also see Rosemarie Garland-Thomson, "Redrawing the boundaries of feminist disability studies," *Feminist Studies* 20 (1994), 582–99. Simi Linton, *Claiming Disability* (New York: New York University, 1998), 118.
4. Max Weber, *The Theory of Social and Economic Organization* (New York: Free, 1947).
5. Scientific management or Taylorism, founded by Frederick Winslow Taylor, was the first management technique to identify discrete manufacturing activities and reunify them into an integrated production system. After World War II, Fordism replaced Taylorism, continuing the trend of centralizing control by transferring workers' knowledge to managers, incorporating workers' "know how" into production machinery, and creating "taller managerial hierarchies." Fordism continues fragmenting tasks, specializing work activities, and most characteristically it reincorporates different tasks into an assembly line. Neo-Fordism, which emerges with the beginnings of global production in the mid-1980s, further extends Taylorism's emphasis on centralized control, but by computerizing information flows. See Harland Prechel, "The labor process and the transformation of corporate control in the global economy" in *Labor and Capital in the Age of Globalization: The Labor Process and the Changing Nature of Work in the Global Economy* (Lanham: Rowan & Littlefield, 2002); and James Rinehart, "Transcending Taylorism and Fordism? Three decades of work restructuring" in *The Critical Study of Work: Labor, Technology, and Global Production*, Rick Baldoz, Charles Koeber, and Philip Kraft, eds. (Philadelphia: Temple University, 2001), 185. Also see John Micklethwait and Adrian Wooldridge, *The Witch Doctors* (London: Heinemann, 1996), 32. They argue it is the "first management theory to use computers as a starting [point] rather than a neat addition." It eliminates layers of lower and middle management, and reduces the decision-making authority of lower and middle managers. Both Fordism and neo-Fordism applied their principles not just to assembly lines but also to white-collar workers, including professionals.
6. Ruth Colker, "The ADA: A windfall for defendants," *Harvard Civil Rights–Civil Liberties Law Review* 99 (1999), 34.

151

7. Ruth O'Brien, *Crippled Justice: The History of Modern Disability Policy in the Workplace* (Chicago: University of Chicago, 2001).

8. *Sutton v. United Air Lines*, 527 U.S. 471 (1999); *Albertsons v. Kirkinburg*, 527 U.S. 555 (1999); and *Murphy v. United Parcel Service*, 527 U.S. 516 (1999).

9. *Toyota v. Williams*, 534 U.S. 184 (2002); *U.S. Airways v. Barnett*, 535 U.S. 391 (2002); and *Chevron v. Echazabal*, 536 U.S. 391 (2002).

10. See Martha Albertson Fineman, *The Neutered Mother, the Sexual Family and Other Twentieth Century Tragedies* (New York: Routledge, 1995), 24.

11. Ibid., 25.

12. Americans with Disabilities Act Stat. 1990a. U.S. Code Vol. 42 Sec. 101 Defin. 42 USC 12111 (10) (A). The reference to the mind should not be confused with spirituality. It refers to physical changes in the mind such as those caused by mental illness.

13. See Marion Crain and Ken Matheny, "Labor's divided ranks: Privilege and the united front ideology," *Cornell Law Review* 84 (1999), 1542–1626.

14. I use the term "animality" for two reasons. First, it captures the connection between the body and Michel Foucault's notion of bio-power and resistance. "Bio-power" is a term that describes the subjugation of people through the control of the body and the control of the species. Yet it also means that people can seek liberation with Foucault's idea of resistance. To liberate someone, Foucault agrees political struggle is essential. However, one does not struggle against power to achieve justice, a term bogged down by a universal notion of truth, but rather to take power or to exercise counterpower. Power may have formed disciplined individuals, who are rational, responsible, productive subjects, yet Foucault suggests that their action should not be confused with their nature as human beings. Being an obedient subject does not reflect one's human nature. By contrast, resistance relies on strategic knowledge and represents Foucault's ideas of revolutionary action. Animality best describes how universalizing our notion of disability means that persons with disabilities can become agents of resistance. See Michel Foucault, *The History of Sexuality, An Introduction, Vol. 1*, Robert Hurley, trans. (New York: Vintage, 1980). Second, Gilligan's work differentiated between an ethic of justice or rights and an ethic of care, and put emotionality on par with rationality, but it neglects our animality. See Carol Gilligan, *In a Different Voice: Psychological Theory and Women's Development* (Cambridge: Harvard University, 1982). Humans are not merely sentient automatons. Rather than purely mechanical creatures designed to optimize intellectual creativity and emotion, *Homo sapiens* is an *animal* species. Our bodies affect our existence and thus how we think and feel. Animality influences both rationality and emotionality. Most theorists and social scientists ignore the role human animality plays because they identify people's mental and physical conditions with restrictions. If someone has *x*, then she or he cannot do *y*. Theories of human thought and action usually focus on abstract potential, while overlooking limitations. By contrast, the term animality is used not to convey an individual's limitations but rather her or his capabilities.

15. Slavoj Zizek in *The Sublime Object of Ideology* (New York: Verso, 1989) views structures of fantasy that define and constitute the production of social scapegoats. See Michelle Jarman, Sharon Lamp, David Mitchell, Denise Nepeux, Nefertiti Nowell, and Sharon Snyder, "Theorising disability as political subjectivity: Work by the UIC Disability Collective on political subjectivities," *Disability & Society* 17 (2002), 557.

16. Joan Tollifson, "Imperfection is a beautiful thing" in *Staring Back: The Disability Experience from the Inside Out*, Kenny Fries, ed. (New York: Plume, 1997), 106.

17. Jack M. Balkin, "Ideology as constraint," *Stanford Law Review* 43 (1991), 1156.

18. David M. Trubek, "Complexity and contradiction in the legal order: Balbus and the challenge of critical society thought about law," *Law & Society* 11 (1977), 1156–57.

19. Sally Engle Merry, "Everyday understandings of the law in working-class America," *American Ethnologist* 13 (1986), 253–70.

20. Clifford Geertz, *The Interpretation of Cultures: Selected Essays* (New York: Basic, 1973).

21. Pierre Bourdieu, *Outline of a Theory and Practice*, Richard Nice, trans. (Cambridge: Cambridge University, 1977), 16.

22. Merry, "Everyday understandings of the law in working-class America," 253–54.

23. Merry, "Resistance and the cultural power of law," *Law & Society Review* 29 (1995), 14.

24. Ibid., 16. Also see Michael W. McCann, *Rights at Work: Pay Equity Reform and the Politics of Legal Mobilization* (Chicago: University of Chicago, 1994), 5–12.
25. Merry, "Resistance and the cultural power of law," 23.
26. Ibid., 24.
27. James Scott, *Domination and the Art of Resistance: Hidden Transcripts* (New Haven: Yale University, 1991).
28. Paul Pierson, "Increasing returns, path dependence, and the study of politics," *American Political Science Review* 94 (2000), 251–67.
29. See O'Brien, *Crippled Justice*, chapter 2.
30. This book applies the law as ideology literature to a statute since it treats the national political institutions, both the officials in the legislative and executive branches, as actors who have ideas that stem from their association with epistemic communities. See O'Brien, *Crippled Justice*, 18–22. For more on how American political development and historical institutionalism regards national institutions as actors, imbued with all the characteristics of judges, for instance, see Karen Orren and Stephen Skowronek, "Beyond the Iconography of Order: Notes for a 'New Institutionalism'" in *The Dynamics of American Politics: Approaches and Interpretations*, Lawrence C. Dodd and Calvin Jillson, eds. (Boulder: Westview, 1994); and Karen Orren and Stephen Skowronek, *The Search for American Political Development* (New York: Cambridge University, 2004), chapters 3–4.
31. O'Brien, *Crippled Justice*, 119.
32. See Peter David Blanck and Michael Millender, "Before disability civil rights: Civil War pensions and the politics of disability in America," *Alabama Law Review* 52 (2000), 1; Peter Blanck and Chen Song, "Civil War pension attorneys and disability politics," *University of Michigan Journal of Law Reform* 35 (2001–2002), 137; and Theda Skocpol, *Protecting Soldiers and Mothers* (Cambridge: Harvard University, 1992).
33. This provision for preventative relief is the same one that was allowed under Section 504, which in turn had been modeled after Title VI of the Civil Rights Act. See Richard K. Scotch, *From Goodwill to Civil Rights* (Philadelphia: Temple University, 1984), 52.
34. *Alexander v. Choate*, 469 U.S. 287 (1985). See O'Brien, *Crippled Justice*, 150–51.
35. See Scotch, *From Goodwill to Civil Rights*; and Kent Hull, *The Rights of Physically Handicapped People* (New York: Avon, 1979).
36. James I. Charlton, *Nothing About Us Without Us: Disability Oppression and Empowerment* (Berkeley: University of California, 1998).
37. Colker, "The ADA: A windfall for defendants."
38. *Sutton* 1999; *Murphy* 1999; *Albertsons* 1999; and Leslie Francis and Anita Silvers, "Introduction: Achieving the right to live in the world: Americans with Disabilities Act and the civil rights tradition" in *Americans with Disabilities Act*, Leslie Francis and Anita Silvers, eds. (New York: Routledge, 2000), xxiii–xxiv.
39. *Sutton* 1999, 60.
40. *Bragdon v. Abbott*, 524 US 624 (1998).
41. Julie Manning Magid, "Pregnant with possibility: Reexamining the Pregnancy Discrimination Act," *American Business Law Journal* 38, 819 (2001), 821.
42. Leslie A. Perlow, "Boundary control: The social ordering of work and family in a high-tech corporation," *Administrative Science Quarterly* 43 (1998), 330–31.
43. Mary A. Gowan and Raymond A. Zimmerman, "The impact of the FMLA: Results of an employer survey," *Journal of Compensation and Benefits* 11 (1996), 33–38.
44. See *Barrash v. Bowen*, 846 F. 2d 927 (4th Cir. 1988), where a court upheld an employer's refusal to grant an employee a six-month maternity leave.
45. Sue Shellenbarger, "Legal Climate Favorable for Pregnant Workers," *Arizona Republic*, January 15, 1998, D1.
46. See *Fejes v. Gilpin Ventures, Inc.*, 960 F. Supp 1487 (D. Colo. 1997).
47. Stewart J. Schwab and Steven L. Willborn, "Reasonable accommodation of workplace disabilities," *William and Mary Law Review* 44 (2003), 1246. Some law professors argue that new protections are needed. See Lara M. Gardner, "A step toward true equality in the workplace: Requiring employer accommodation for breastfeeding women," *Wisconsin Women's Law Journal* 17 (2002), 259.

48. Paulette T. Beatty and Lisa Burroughs, "Preparing for an aging work force: The role of higher education," *Educational Gerontology* 25 (1999), 595–97.
49. Francis J. Winn, "Structural impediments to the efficient use of older workers in the U.S.," *Experimental Aging Research* 25 (1999), 452.
50. The increase in older workers coincides with the shift in the U.S. from a manufacturing economy to a service one. By 1990, only 18 percent of civilian jobs were in manufacturing, whereas 33 percent were in the service industries. This shift to a service economy is of particular relevance to older workers as older workers are over represented in many of the service industries and in part-time work. See Nancy L. Marshall, "Health and illness issues facing an aging work force in the new millennium," *Sociological Spectrum* 21 (2001), 432.
51. Winn, "Structural impediments to the efficient use of older workers in the US," 454.
52. Ibid.
53. Ibid., 452.
54. Michael A. Veresej, "Left in the lurch: Aging work force exacerbates an already tight labor market," *Industry Week*, March 5, 2001, 14.
55. Jim Parkel, "The cost of doing nothing about the maturing," *Executive Speeches* 17 (Oct./ Nov. 2002), 15–19.
56. Beatty and Burroughs, "Preparing for an aging work force," 595–597.
57. Quoted from Margaret Morganroth Gullette, *Aged by Culture* (Chicago: University of Chicago, 2004), 25. See Jeff Madrick, "Enron, the media, and the new economy," *The Nation*, April 1, 2002, 17–20. See Gullette, *Aged by Culture*, for an insightful critique of age ideology and culture.
58. Beatty and Burroughs, "Preparing for an aging work force," 602–03.
59. Amanda Griffiths, "Work design and management—the older worker," *Experimental Aging Research* 25 (1999), 417.
60. President George W. Bush, Remarks by the president on stem cell research, August 9, 2001. Transcript available at <http://www.whitehouse.gov/news/releases/2001/08/20010809-2.html>. Bush allowed National Institutes of Health (NIH) funding on human embryo research and stem cells. He decreed that all stem cell lines extracted from embryos prior to August 9, 2001, would become eligible for funding after the NIH had developed guidelines. No new stem cell research could be funded. Bush hoped to remove the incentive for additional stem cell lines that would destroy more embryos.
61. Alissa Johnson, "State genetic discrimination in health insurance laws," National Conference of State Legislatures. Available at <http://www.astho.org/templates/display_pub.php?u=JnB1Yl9pZD00MzY=>.
62. Deborah Hellman, "What makes genetic discrimination exceptional?" *American Journal of Law and Medicine* 29 (2003), 88.
63. Ibid., 105.
64. Monica Konrad, "From secrets of life to the life of secrets: Tracing genetic knowledge as genealogical ethics in biomedical Britain," *Journal of the Royal Anthropological Institute* 9 (2003), 343.
65. Erick Parens and Adrienne Asch, "The disability rights critique: Prenatal genetic testing: Reflections and recommendations," *Hastings Center Report* 29 (1999), 2. Also see Erick Parens and Adrienne Asch, *Prenatal Testing and Disability Rights* (Washington, D.C.: Georgetown University, 2002).
66. Nina Foster Hallowell, C., Eeles, R., Ardern-Jones, A., Murday, V., Watson, M., "Balancing autonomy and responsibility: The ethics of generating and disclosing genetic information," *Journal of Medical Ethics* 29 (2003), 74.
67. Lisa Soleymani Lehmann, "A population-based study of Ashkenazi Jewish women's attitudes toward genetic discrimination and BRCA1/2 testing," *Genetics in Medicine* 4 (September/October 2002), 346–53.
68. Harriet McBride Johnson, "Unspeakable conversations," *New York Times Magazine*, February 16, 2003.
69. Kelly Dahlgress Childress, "Genetics, disability, and ethics: Could applied technologies lead to a new eugenics?" *The Journal of Women and Religion* 19/20 (2003), 165.
70. Ibid., 165–66.
71. In 1947, Dr. Sheldon Reed created the term "genetic counseling" as a means of masking genetic hygiene—tainted by eugenics. Counselors are coached to practice "nondirective-

ness" when informing parents about genetic screening. See Hellman, "What makes genetic discrimination exceptional?" 107–110. Also see Annette Patterson and Martha Satz, "Genetic counseling and the disabled: Feminism examines the stance of those who stand at the gate," *Hypatia* 17 (2002), 118–42; and Keith Sharp and Sarah Earle, "Feminism, abortion and disability: Irreconcilable differences?" *Disability & Society* 17 (2002), 137–45 in which they claim that the two movements are fundamentally at odds.

72. Childress, "Genetics, disability, and ethics," 169.
73. Hellman, "What makes genetic discrimination exceptional?" 110.
74. Parens and Asch, "The disability rights critique."
75. Josephine Wong and Felice Lieh-Mak, "Genetic discrimination and mental illness: A case report," *Journal of Medical Ethics* 27 (2001), 393–97.
76. Childress, "Genetics, disability, and ethics," 158.
77. Ibid.
78. See Jacob Hacker, *The Divided Welfare State: The Battle Over Public and Private Social Benefits in the U.S.* (New York: Cambridge University, 2002), chapter 5.
79. Also, the Pregnancy Discrimination Act addresses this dilemma about cost. Who should bear the cost of women bearing children? This legislation mandated that employers shoulder this responsibility. The legislation stipulated that during their childbearing years, women cannot be treated differently from men because they might or they do have children, using medical benefits to bear the children and recuperate from childbirth. While the federal courts have not upheld this legislation, this was its intent. See Magid, "Pregnant with possibility: Reexamining the Pregnancy Discrimination Act."
80. Hellman, "What makes genetic discrimination exceptional?" 82.
81. Ibid., 94.
82. See Lani Guinier and Gerald Torres, *The Miner's Canary: Enlisting Race, Resisting Power, Transforming Democracy* (Cambridge: Harvard University, 2002), 11.
83. Tricia Rose, Symposium Proceedings: "Building a multiracial social justice movement: Session three," *New York University Review of Law and Social Change* 27 (2001/2002), 63. Rose added the italics.
84. See Shawn Richard Perreaulit, "Family law—'side-stepping' the marriage laws: The contradiction created by the Texas Appeals Court in *Littleton v. Prange*," *Suffolk Journal of Trial and Appellate Advocacy* 7 (2002), 149.
85. See Jennifer Marie Albright, "Comment: Gender assessment: A legal approach to transsexuality," *Southern Methodist University Law Review* 55 (2002), 594.
86. See Perreaulit, "Family law—'side-stepping' the marriage laws," 149.
87. The case of *Anonymous v. Mellon*, 91 Misc. 2d 375, 383, 398 (N.Y. Sup. Ct. 1977) involved a postoperative female seeking to have her name and sex changed to show her as a male. The Bureau of Vital Records issued a new birth certificate but left no indication of her sex. The court found that it could deny modifications to sex on birth certificates in regards to transsexuals. Also in *Matter of Anonymous*, 64 Misc. 2d 309, 309 (N.Y. Sup. Ct. 1970), a postoperative female transsexual requested that the name and sex on her birth certificate be changed and the New York Superior Court denied this request.
88. See *Ulane v. Eastern Airlines*, 742 F. 2d 1081, 1081 (1984). A postoperative female transsexual fired after undergoing treatment sought protection under Title VII and under appeal, the federal court maintained that given her maleness, she had no standing to sue. On the other hand, in *Richards v. U.S. Tennis Assoc.*, 93 Misc. 2d 713 (N.Y. Sup. Ct. 1977), the federal court held that it was discriminatory for Richards to have to take a sex chromatin test and that she was protected class under the "sex" class of antidiscrimination statutes.
89. Massachusetts courts must first decide whether the person is a male or female and then they must determine the legality of the couple's marriage. Only Hawaii and Vermont permit same sex marriages. Meanwhile, Congress and the president passed the Defense of Marriage Act (DOMA) to protect the "institution of marriage." The legislation was introduced on May 7, 1996.The bill number is H.R. 3396 and it was introduced in the 104th Congress, 2nd Session (1996). See <http://www.lectlaw.com/files/leg23.htm> for a good summary. (Last visited March 11, 2003.)
90. Two states accept transsexual lesbian same sex marriages. On Sept 16, 2000, Jessica Wicks and Robin Manhart Wicks were married in San Antonio, Texas. On October 15, 2000,

Bonnie Earle and Donna Schwartz were legally allowed to marry. See Perreaulit, "Family law—'side-stepping' the marriage laws."

91. See *Littleton v. Prange*, 9 S.W. 3d 223, 224 (Tex. App. 1999) where a couple's marriage was declared void when the spouse sought damages for malpractice.

92. See Jerold Taitz, "Judicial determination of the sexual identity of post-operative transsexuals: A new form of sex discrimination," *American Journal of Law and Medicine* 13 (1987), 53; and Julie A. Greenberg, "When is a man a man, and when is a woman a woman?" *Florida Law Review* 52 (2000), 74, explaining sex designations on official records as inconsistent with marrying according to sex roles.

93. See Laura Hermer, "Paradigms revised: Intersex children, bioethics & the law," *Annals of Health Law* 11 (2002), 195. Intersexuals were made famous by the mythological fable of Hermaphroditus, Aphrodite's and Hermes' child, who had the complete external genitalia of both a man and a woman.

94. Several cases were filed where the child sued because of the loss of sexual function, an "unreasonable invasion of their bodily integrity" and their psychosexual and psychosocial identities. See Hazel Glenn Beh and Milton Diamond, "An emerging ethical and medical dilemma: Should physicians perform sex assignment surgery on infants with ambiguous genitalia?" *Michigan Journal of Gender & Law* 7 (2000), 1. Also see Intersex Society of North America <http://isna.org/faq/frequency.html>. (Last visited March 7, 2003.) Also see Milton Diamond and H. Keith Sigmundson, "Sex reassignment at birth: Long-term review and clinical implications," *Archives of Pediatric Adolescent Medicine* 151 (1997), 298; and Hermer, "Paradigms revised," 197.

95. See Greenberg, "When is a man a man, and when is a woman a woman?" 133.

96. See Peter Halewood, "Law's bodies: Disembodiment and the structure of liberal property rights," *Iowa Law Review* 81 (1996), 1333–42 for an excellent overview about personhood and property rights under law, which reveals how significantly science has changed our conception of the body.

97. Americans with Disabilities Act Stat. 1990a. U.S. Code Vol. 42. Defin. 42 USC 12111 5(A).

98. *Sutton* 1999; *Albertsons* 1999; and *Murphy* 1999.

99. *Taylor v. Phoenixville School Dist.*, 184 F.3d 296 (3rd Cir.(Pa.)1999).

100. Senate Report on the ADA 1989, 35; House Report on the ADA 1990, 66; and *Barnett v. U.S. Airways*.

101. *Franklin v. Consolidated Edison Co. of New York, Inc.*, 1999 WL 796170 (S.D.N.Y.).

102. Jeremy Rifkin, *The End of Work: The Decline of the Global Labor Force and the Dawn of the Post-Market Era* (New York: G. P. Putnam's Sons, 1996), 10; Americans with Disabilities Act Stat. U.S. Code Vol. 42. Sec. 101 Defin. 42 USC 12111 (10) (A).

103. Equal Employment Opportunity Committee's (EEOC) Regulations Defining Disability 29 CFR Pt. 1630, App. Section 1630.9, 2001.

104. *Franklin v. Consolidated Edison Co.*

105. *Geneva M. Smith v. Midland Brake, Inc.*, 180 F.3d 1154; 1999 U.S. App. Lexis 13185, U.S. Court of Appeals for the 10th circuit.

106. *Taylor v. Phoenixville School Dist.*

107. American capitalists were particularly hostile to the labor movement, using Pinkerton private detectives, called private guns for hire, who expressed little trepidation about using violence to prevent unionization. See Jeremy Brecher, *Strike* (Boston: South End, 1972), 55–58; and Paul Krause, *The Battle for Homestead, 1880–1892: Politics, Culture, and Steel* (Pittsburgh: University of Pittsburgh, 1992).

108. According to *Black's Legal Dictionary*, employment-at-will provides that "absent express agreement to the contrary, either employer or employee may terminate their relationship at any time, for any reason." Aside from private agreements like a collective bargaining agreement, there are a number of federal laws that prevent employers from firing employees without cause. The Civil Service Reform Act has a provision for whistleblowers that *Black's* states is "designed to protect employees from retaliation for a disclosure of employer's misconduct." State and federal antidiscrimination statutes also prohibit wrongful discharge.

109. The American courts developed employment-at-will from English master–servant law, which had been established by the British to deal with yearly hirings of agricultural and domestic workers. Unlike the American version of the doctrine, the original interpretation of the

doctrine created an equitable relationship between the employer and the employee. "[I]njustice would result," explained William Blackstone, the famous eighteenth-century jurist, "if . . . masters could have the benefit of servants' labor during planting and harvest seasons but discharge them to avoid supporting them during the unproductive winter." Quoted from Andrew Hill, *Wrongful Discharge and the Derogation of the At-Will Doctrine, Labor Relations and Public Policy Series, No. 3.* (Philadelphia: University of Pennsylvania, 1987), 2. According to legal historians, the American conception of employment-at-will also imposed duties on employers until the industrial revolution when the Woods rule was adopted by the judiciary. This rule was taken from Horace Wood's treatise on master–servant relations law, which was written in 1877. See Deborah Ballam, "The traditional view on the origins of the employment-at-will doctrine: Myth or reality?" *American Business Law Journal* 33 (1995), 1. Quoted from *Criscione v. Sears Roebuck Co.*, 1978 384 N.E. 2d 91 Illinois App. Ct.

110. Jay Feinman, "The development of the employment-at-will rule," *American Journal of Legal History* 20 (1976), 132–34.
111. See Michael J. Phillips, "Toward a middle way in the polarized debate over employment-at-will," *American Business Law Journal* 30 (1992), 447.
112. Ibid.
113. Ibid., 450.
114. Investigating wage and hour violations would always be difficult for the Wage and Hour Division, in large part because the victims of these violations could offer little help. Employers violating the FLSA had few worries about being reported by their employees who rightfully feared for their jobs. What would concern employers, by contrast, were routine investigations or spot checks. Congress, however, has never allocated the extensive resources needed for this type of investigation. In fact, the number of investigators has fallen steadily since the FLSA passed. In 1939, there were 0.05 investigators per thousand employees, whereas in 1988 the figure had dropped to 0.01 investigators per thousand. The Wage and Hour Division has long been perceived as so ineffectual that some scholars suggest that employers who abide by the FLSA do so voluntarily. See Ruth O'Brien, " 'A sweat shop of the whole nation': The Fair Labor Standards Act and the failure of regulatory unionism," *Studies in American Political Development* 15 (Spring 2001), 33–52.
115. Ruth O'Brien, " 'A sweat shop of the whole nation': The Fair Labor Standards Act and the failure of regulatory unionism," *Studies in American Political Development* 15 (Spring 2001), 33–52.
116. Julie Waters, "Does the battle over mandatory arbitration jeopardize the EEOC's war in fighting workplace discrimination?" *St. Louis Law Journal* 44 (2000), 1156. Civil rights claims are 100 percent greater than all other types of civil litigation.
117. Sexual harassment represents an exception. Feminist law professor Kathryn Abrams defines this type of discrimination as "the devalutive sexualization or derogation of women in the workplace." Protecting a woman from sexual harassment involves removing hostility, not fostering tolerance and difference in the workplace. Being freed from this negative environment, however, is different than the positive workplace climate that the ADA could help foster. See Kathryn Abrams, "Title VII and the complex female subject," *Michigan Law Review* 92 (1994), 2479.
118. Ruth Milkman, Review of Eileen Appelbaum and Rosemary Batt, *The New American Workplace: Transforming Work Systems in the U.S.* in *Administrative Studies Quarterly* 39 (1993), 679–80; Michael Goldfield, *The Color of Politics: Race, Class, and the Mainsprings of American Politics* (New York: New, 1997); and Elizabeth M. Iglesisas, "Structures of subordination: Women of color at the intersection of Title VII and the NLRA. Not!" *Harvard Civil Rights–Civil Liberties Law Review* 28 (1981) 395.
119. Molly S. McUsic and Michael Selmi, "Postmodern unions: Identity politics in the workplace," *Iowa Law Review* 82 (1997), 1344.
120. The problem with unionization is the majority rule culture it creates. Not only do labor laws insist that unions represent all members equally, but a culture that fosters majority rule dominates most unions. Unions could change this culture, however. As Michael C. Harper and Ira C. Lupu in "Fair representation as equal protection," *Harvard Law Review* 98 (1985) 1215, have suggested, organized labor could rely on a constitutional configuration rather than a majority-rule framework to determine which policies to pursue. This leads to the

question not of whether unions have the capacity, but of why they would be compelled to represent persons with disabilities seeking accommodations. Also see McUsic and Selmi, "Postmodern unions"; and Michael Piore, *Beyond Individualism* (Cambridge: Harvard University, 1995).

121. McUsic and Selmi, "Postmodern unions: identity politics in the workplace," 1348. They cite Marion Crain, "Women, labor unions and hostile work environment sexual harassment: The untold story," 4 *Texas Journal of Women and the Law* 9 (1995), 66–77.

122. Iris Marion Young, "Americans with disabilities: Exploring the implications of the law for individuals and institutions," in *Americans with Disabilities: Exploring Implications of the Law for Individuals and Institutions*, Leslie A. Francis and Anita Silvers, eds. (London: Routledge, 2000), 171.

123. David Knights and Theo Vurdubakis, "Foucault, power, resistance and all that" in *Resistance and Power in Organizations*, John M. Jermier, David Knights, and Walter R. Nord, eds. (London: Routledge, 1994), 169.

124. Brent L. Pickett, "Foucault and the politics of resistance," *Polity* 28 (1996) 453.

125. Ibid., 458.

126. Jessica J. Kulynych, "Performing politics: Foucault, Habermas, and postmodern participation," *Polity* 30 (1997), 315–46.

127. Dierter Freundlieb, "Foucault's theory of discourse and human agency" in *Reassessing Foucault: Power, Medicine, and the Body*, Colin Jones and Roy Porter, eds. (London: Routledge, 1994), 147.

128. Knights and Vurdubakis, "Foucault, power, resistance and all that," 177–79.

129. Pickett, "Foucault and the politics of resistance," 459.

130. Ibid., 463–64.

131. Rosemarie Garland-Thomson, *Extraordinary Bodies: Figuring Physical Disability in American Culture and Literature* (New York: Columbia University, 1997), 25.

132. John W. McCarthy was the attorney representing Ragdon Brandon in *Bragdon v. Abbott*. David G. Savage, "Supreme Court HIV case tests disability law," *Los Angeles Times*, March 31, 1998, A1.

133. Lennard J. Davis, *Enforcing Normalcy: Disability, Deafness, and the Body* (New York: Verso, 1995).

134. Garland-Thomson, *Extraordinary Bodies*, 6.

135. Ibid., 42–43.

136. Eric A. Taub, "The blind leading the sighted," *New York Times*, October 28, 1999, G1.

137. "People with disabilities are very resourceful, and they figure out ways to do things," maintains Paul Longmore, a historian and a disability cultural studies expert at San Francisco State University. See Peter Monaghan, "Pioneering field of disability studies challenges established approaches and attitudes," *Chronicle of Higher Education* (January 23 1998) for an interview with Longmore.

138. See Heidi Hartmann, *The Unhappy Marriage of Marxism and Feminism* (London: Pluto, 1981).

139. See Ben Fine, *Women's Employment and the Capitalist Family* (New York: Routledge, 1992), 22–44 for a good overview of the literature about patriarchy and capitalism.

140. Virginia Held, *Feminist Morality: Transforming Culture, Society, and Politics* (Chicago: University of Chicago, 1993), 183.

141. Ibid., 183–84.

142. Martha Albertson Fineman, "Cracking the foundational myths: Independence, autonomy, and self-sufficiency," *Journal of Gender, Social Policy & the Law* 8 (1999), 101–16.

143. See Held, *Feminist Morality*, 181–83.

144. Phone interview, Patricia Wright, Disability Rights and Education Defense Fund (DREDF), 1999.

## Chapter 2: The Life of the Body

1. Michel Foucault, *The Birth of the Clinic: An Archaeology of Medical Perception*, A.M. Sheridan Smith, trans. (London: Tavistock, 1973); and Michel Foucault, *The History of Sexuality, Volume 1: An Introduction*, Robert Hurley, trans. (New York: Vintage, 1980).
2. Maurice Merleau-Ponty, *The Phenomenology of Perception*, Colin Smith, trans. (London: Routledge and Kegan Paul, 1962); Francis Barker, *Tremulous Body: Essays on Subjection* (Ann Arbor: University of Michigan, 1995); Jean Baudrillard, *Selected Writings*, Mark Poster, ed. (Cambridge: Polity, 1988); Pasi Falk, *Consuming Body*, (London: Sage, 1994); Emily Martin, *Flexible Bodies: Tracking Immunity in American Culture from the Days of Polio to the Age of AIDS* (Boston: Beacon, 1994); Margrit Shidrick, *Leaky Bodies and Boundaries: Feminism, Postmodernism and (Bio)Ethics* (London: Routledge, 1997).
3. See Christopher Norris, *Spinoza and the Origins of Modern Critical Theory* (London: Basil Blackwell, 1991).
4. Man explains that becoming animal therefore means that the mind and matter stem from one underlying process or *substantia* "that is materially grounded in extension but is also absolute and infinite." Eva Kit Wah Man, "Contemporary feminist body theories and Mencius's ideas of body and mind," *Journal of Chinese Philosophy* 27 (2000), 159.
5. Ibid.
6. Gilles Deleuze, *Negotiations: 1972–1990*, Martin Joughin, trans. (New York: Columbia University, 1995), 20.
7. Quoting Moira Gatens, *Imaginary Bodies: Ethics, Power and Corporeality* (London: Routledge, 1996), 169. The radical feminist Australian school of thought is composed of theorists such as Elizabeth Grosz, Genevieve Lloyd, Moira Gatens, and Claire Colebrook. In addition to Gatens' book, see Elizabeth Grosz, *Volatile Bodies: Toward a Corporal Feminism* (Sydney: Allen & Unwin, 1994), 196, for an important radical feminist interpretation of Spinoza, Delueze, and Guttari. For an overview of this interpretation see Claire Colebrook, "From radical representations to corporeal becomings: The feminist philosophy of Lloyd, Grosz, and Gatens," *Hypatia* 15 (2000), 76–93.
8. Grosz, *Volatile Bodies*, 5. Also see Gatens, *Imaginary Bodies*, 21–35; and Judith Butler, *Bodies that Matter: On the Discursive Limits of "Sex"* (New York: Routledge, 1993), 40–53; and Man, "Contemporary feminist body theories and Mencius's ideas of body and mind," 157.
9. Grosz, *Volatile Bodies*, 5.
10. Richard Shusterman, "Somaesthetics and care of the self: The case of Foucault," *Monist* 83 (2000), 530–53.
11. Man, "Contemporary feminist body theories and Mencius's ideas of body and mind," 157.
12. Shusterman, "Somaesthetics and care of the self."
13. Grosz, *Volatile Bodies*, 6.
14. Quoted from Bente Meyer, "Extraordinary stories: Disability, queerness, and feminism," *Nordic Journal of Women's Studies* 10 (2002), 170.
15. William Merrin, "To play with phantoms: Jean Baudrillard and the evil demon of the simulacrum," *Economy & Society* 30 (2001), 92.
16. Pasi Falk, "Corporeality and its fates in history," *Acta Sociologica* 2 (1985), 117. This list later became the medieval moral code of the eight sins.
17. Ibid.
18. Grosz, *Volatile Bodies*, 6.
19. Ibid.
20. Falk, "Corporeality and its fates in history," 120–21.
21. Grosz, *Volatile Bodies*, 6. Also see René Descartes, *The Philosophical Works of Descartes*, 2 vols. E.S. Haldane, G.T.R. Ross, eds. (Cambridge: Cambridge University, 1931), 34 for original.
22. The critical question for feminists as Man puts it is "How can something that inhabits space affect or be affected by something non-spatial? How can consciousness ensure the body's movements, its receptivity to conceptual demands and requirements? How can the body inform the mind of its needs and wishes? How is bilateral communication possible?" Man, "Contemporary feminist body theories and Mencius's ideas of body and mind," 158.

160 • Bodies in Revolt

23. Catherine Roach, "Loving your mother: On the woman–nature relation," *Hypatia* 6 (1991), 46–59.
24. See Susan Bordo, "The Cartesian masculinization of thought," *SIGNS: Journal of Women in Culture and Society* 11 (1986), 439–56. Also see Victor J. Seidler, *Recreating Sexual Politics: Men, Feminism and Politics* (London: Routledge, 1991); and Lawrence D. Berg, "Masculinity, place and a binary discourse of 'theory' and 'empirical investigation' in the human geography of Aotearoa/New Zealand," *Gender Place & Culture: A Journal of Feminist Geography* 1 (1994): 245–62.
25. Richard T. Twine, "Ma(r)king essence—ecofeminism and embodiment," *Ethics and the Environment* 6 (2001), 38.
26. Grant Duncan, "Mind–body dualism and the biopsychosocial model of pain: What did Descartes really say?" *Journal of Medicine and Philosophy* 25 (2000), 485–513.
27. According to Raymond Barlow, "Medicine at the Millennium," *Tikkun* (March/April 2002), 17, the body in the Middle Ages was imbued with astrological meaning. It is something individual—a bordered territory, possessed by its owner.
28. Gilles Deleuze, *Expressionism in Philosophy: Spinoza*, Martin Joughin, trans. (New York: Zone, 1990), 227–28. "With the anti-Cartesian reaction, on the other hand, it is a matter of re-establishing the claims of a Nature endowed with forces or power. But a matter also of retaining the chief discovery of Cartesian mechanism: every power is actual, in act; the powers of Nature are no longer virtualities referred to occult entities, to souls or minds through which they are realized, Leibniz formulates the program perfectly: to counter Descartes by restoring to Nature the force of action and passion, but this without falling back into a pagan vision of the world, an idolatry of Nature. Spinoza's program is very similar (with this difference, that he does not rely on Christianity to save us from idolatry)."
29. Quoted in Merrin, "To play with phantoms: Jean Baudrillard and the evil demon of the simulacrum," 92–93.
30. Quoted in Barlow, "Medicine at the Millenium," 17.
31. Ibid.
32. Charles Darwin, *On the Origin of Species* (Cambridge: Harvard University, 1964).
33. Alphonse Bertillon was the chief of criminal identification for Paris. He created anthropometry or "Bertillonage," which used a series of body measurements, a physical description, and photographs to help the police identify criminals. Meanwhile, Cesare Lombroso, an Italian psychiatrist, published *Criminal Man* (*L'uomo delinquente*) in 1876, which relied on Darwin. See Allan Sekula, "The body and the archive," *October 39* (1986), 3–64.
34. Falk, "Corporeality and its fates in history," 123.
35. Ibid.
36. Quoted in Roy Porter, "Matrix of Modernity," *History Today* 52 (April 13, 2001), 25. Also see Edward Gibbon, *Decline and Fall of the Roman Empire*, ed., abridged, with a critical foreword by Hans-Friedrich Mueller; introduction by Daniel J. Boorstin; illustrations by Giovanni Battista Piranesi (New York: Modern Library, 2003).
37. Porter, "Matrix of modernity," 31.
38. Ibid., 31. By contrast, John Milton in *Paradise Lost* explored "man's" relationship with God. Adam's great offense occurred because he violated God's command. This was a transcendental revelation. John Milton, *Paradise Lost*, in *Twelve Books* (McLaughlin, 1804 ed., orig., 1663). Also in Pope's "Essay on Man," he rejected human pride as hubristic." See Pope's "Essay on Man," A. D. Nuttall, ed. (Boston: Allen & Unwin, 1984).
39. Porter, "Matrix of modernity," 30.
40. Alexandra Winter, "Writing and skin," *Hectate* 27 (2001), 176.
41. Ibid. Winter refers to Gayatri Chakrovorty Spivak's definition in "Three women's texts and a critique of imperialism" in *Race, Writing and Difference*, Henry Louis Gates, Jr., ed. (Chicago: University of Chicago, 1985), 263. She also refers to Thomas J. Csordas, "Embodiment and cultural phenomenology" in *Perspectives on Embodiment: The Intersections of Nature and Culture*, Gail Weis and Honi Fern Haber, eds. (New York: Routledge, 1999), 144.
42. Colebrook, "From radical representations to corporeal becomings, 77.

43. Martha C. Nussbaum, "Experiments in living," *The New Republic* 222 (1), March 1, 2000, 31–37.
44. See Mary Russo, *The Female Grotesque-Risk, Excess & Modernity* (London: Routledge, 1994), 62–63. Quoted from Twine, "Ma(r)king essence—ecofeminism and embodiment," 45.
45. Twine, "Ma(r)king essence—ecofeminism and embodiment," 46.
46. Quoted in Ibid.
47. Melvin D. Williams, "Biophobia, social boundaries, and racism: Prologue to a macroanthropology," *Journal of Social & Evolutionary Systems* 19 (1996), 171–85.
48. Patricia Foster, ed., *Minding the Body: Women Writers on Body and Soul* (New York: Doubleday, 1994).
49. Twine, "Ma(r)king essence—ecofeminism and embodiment," 42–43.
50. Anthony Synnott, *The Body Social: Symbolism, Self, and Society* (New York: Routledge, 1993); and Twine, "Ma(r)king essence—ecofeminism and embodiment," 43.
51. Edward Hall, "Workspaces: refiguring the disability/employment debate" in *Mind and Body Spaces: Geographies of Illness, Impairment and Disability*, Ruth Butler and Hester Parr, eds. (New York: Routledge, 1999), 144.
52. Lennard Davis, *Enforcing Normalcy: Disability, Deafness, and the Body* (New York: Verso, 1995), 24.
53. Ibid.
54. Helen Meekosha, "Body battles: Bodies, gender and disability," in *The Disability Reader: Social Science Perspectives*, Tom Shakespeare, ed. (London: Continuum, 1998).
55. The prevailing medical perspective before the 1940s had doctors examining what caused, and how they could prevent or cure, a disability. See Glenn Gritzer and Arnold Arluke, *The Making of Rehabilitation: The Political Economy of Medical Specialization: 1890–1980* (Berkeley: University of California, 1985); and James I. Charlton, *Nothing About Us Without Us: Disability Oppression and Empowerment* (Berkeley: University of California, 1998). For a model that attempts to strike a balance between the medical and the social models see M.R. Bury, "Social constructionism and the development of medical sociology," *Sociology of Health and Illness* 8 (1986), 137–69; Liz Crow, "Including all of our lives: Renewing the social model of disability" in *Exploring the Divide: Illness and Disability*, Colin Barnes and Geof Mercer, eds. (Leeds: The Disability, 1996); M. Kelly and D. Field, "Medical sociology, chronic illness and the body," *Sociology of Health and Illness* 18 (1996), 241–57.
56. See K. Walter Hickel, "Medicine, bureaucracy, and social welfare: The politics of disability compensation for American veterans of World War I" in *The New Disability History: American Perspectives*, Paul K. Longmore and Lauri Umansky, eds. (New York: New York University, 2001).
57. See Paul Abberley, "The spectre at the feast: Disabled people and social theory" in *The Disability Reader: Social Science Perspectives*, Tom Shakespeare, ed. (London: Casswell, 1998), 79; Simon Brisenden, "Independent living and the medical model of disability" in *The Disability Reader: Social Science Perspectives*, Tom Shakespeare, ed. (London: Cassell, 1998), 24; and Paul K. Longmore, "Medical decisionmaking and people with disabilities: A clash of cultures," *Journal of Law, Medicine & Ethics* 23 (1995), 82–87; and Douglas Bilker, "The myth of clinical judgment," *Journal of Social Issues* 44 (1988), 127–40.
58. Brisenden, "Independent living and the medical model of disability," 23.
59. Ibid., 24.
60. Edward D. Berkowitz, "The cost-benefit tradition in vocational rehabilitation" in *Measuring the Efficiency in Public Programs*, Monroe Berkowitz, ed. (Philadelphia: Temple University, 1988), 12.
61. Abberley, "The spectre at the feast: Disabled people and social theory," 79.
62. Ernest Becker, *The Denial of Death* (New York: Free, 1973), 51.
63. David W. Orr, "The coming biophilia revolution," *Earth Island Journal* 9 (1994), 3–40.
64. Williams, "Biophobia, social boundaries, and racism."
65. Orr, "The coming biophilia revolution," 38–40.
66. Ibid., 38.
67. Anthropologists report that one of the most significant social constructions is the identification of one's human group as distinct, superior, and connected to supernatural

powers as was no other form of life, plant or animal. See Williams, "Biophobia, social boundaries, and racism;" Twine, "Ma(r)king essence—ecofeminism and embodiment;" and Irene Diamond, *Fertile Ground—Women, Earth, and the Limits of Control* (Boston: Beacon, 1994).

68. Williams, "Biophobia, social boundaries, and racism," 173.

69. Shannon Sullivan, "Pragmatist feminism as ecological ontology: Reflections on living across and through skins," *Hypatia* 17 (2002), 202.

70. Sullivan bolsters her definition with Maurice Merleau-Ponty's conception of the "neutral, generic core to bodily existence shared by all human beings such that we are interchangeable with one another." Sullivan, "Pragmatist feminism as ecological ontology," 204.

71. Sullivan, "Pragmatist feminism as ecological ontology," 210–11.

72. Quoted in Ibid., 211. Also see Elizabeth Grosz, *Architecture from the Outside: Essays on Virtual and Real Space* (Cambridge: MIT, 2001), 168. Also see Donna J. Haraway, *Simians, Cyborgs, and Women: The Reinvention of Nature* (New York: Routledge, 1991).

73. This said, some studies in radical feminism fall into a postmodernist trap, which hails the death of man, reason, history, and subject. See Abigail Bray and Claire Colebrook, "The haunted flesh: Corporeal feminism and the politics of (dis)embodiment," *SIGNS: Journal of Women in Culture and Society* 24 (1998), 39.

74. See Colebrook, "From radical representations to corporeal becomings," 76.

75. Mariam Fraser, "Visceral futures: Bodies of feminist criticism," *Social Epistemology* 15 (2001), 97.

76. Bray and Colebrook, "The haunted flesh," 43–46. Grosz concurs by rejecting any "inside out" approach where the body would be a projection of the mind. Also see Jane Gallop, *Thinking Through the Body* (New York: Columbia University, 1992).

77. Twine, "Ma(r)king essence—ecofeminism and embodiment," 37. Twine suggests one also see Rosemary Radford Ruether's idea of body-people. See Rosemary R. Ruether, *New Woman, New Earth: Sexist Ideologies and Human Liberation* (Boston: Beacon, 1975).

78. Twine, "Ma(r)king essence—ecofeminism and embodiment," 36, 49.

79. Bray and Colebrook, "The haunted flesh," 42.

80. Miriam Fraser, "Visceral futures: bodies of feminist criticism," *Social Epistemology* 15 (2001), 95.

81. Elizabeth Grosz, "A thousand tiny sexes: feminism and rhizomatics" in *Gilles Deleuze and the Theatre of Philosophy*, Constanin V. Boundas and Dorothea Olkowski, eds. (New York: Routledge, 1994), 197–98.

82. Fraser, "Visceral futures," 106.

83. Camilla Griggers, *Becoming–Woman* (Minneapolis: University of Minnesota, 1997).

84. Deleuze, according to the radical feminist theorist Mariam Fraser, suggests that the biological body resists "either an essentialist or biological deterministic position." Fraser, "Visceral futures," 92–93.

85. Rosi Braidotti, *Patterns of Dissonance: A Study of Women in Contemporary Philosophy*, Elizabeth Guild, trans. (Cambridge: Polity, 1991), 89.

86. Quoted from Alexandra Winter, "Writing and skin," 175. Quoting Michel Foucault, "Nietzsche, genealogy, history" in *Language, Counter-Memory, Practice: Selected Essays and Interviews*, Donald F. Bouchard, ed., Donald F. Bouchard and Sherry Simon, trans. (Ithaca: Cornell University, 1997), 148.

87. Winter, "Writing and skin," 176. Citing Michel Foucault, *Discipline and Punish: The Birth of the Prison*, A. M. Sheridan, trans. (New York: Vintage, 1977), 29.

88. Gilles Deleuze and Felix Guattari, *A Thousand Plateaus: Capitalism and Schizophrenia*, Brian Massumi, trans. (London: Althone, 1988), 37.

89. Fraser, "Visceral futures," 94.

90. Deleuze and Guattari, *A Thousand Plateaus*, 159.

91. Man, "Contemporary feminist body theories and Mencius's ideas of body and mind," 159.

92. Ibid.

93. Ibid.

94. Ibid.

95. Deleuze, *Expressionism in Philosophy*, 229.

96. Gatens, "Power, ethics and sexual imaginaries." Similarly, ecofeminist Catherine Dale contends that a person's capacity is determined by the body, "but also by everything which makes up the context in which that body is acted upon and acts." Catherine Mary Dale, "A queer supplement: Reading Spinoza after Grosz," *Hypatia* 14 (1999), 7.
97. Gilles Deleuze, *Spinoza's Practical Philosophy*, Robert Hurley, trans. (San Francisco: City Lights, 1988).
98. Deleuze, *Expressionism in Philosophy*, 220.
99. Ibid., 217.
100. Ibid., 220–21.
101. Colebrook, "From radical representations to corporeal becomings," 88.
102. Ibid., 86.
103. Quoted in Gatens, *Imaginary Bodies*, 31.
104. Colebrook, "From radical representations to corporeal becomings," 89.
105. Quoted in Elizabeth Grosz, "Deleuze's Bergson: Duration, the virtual and a politics of the future" in *Deleuze and Feminist Theory*, Ian Buchman and Claire Colebrook, eds. (Edinburgh: Edinburgh University, 2000).
106. Dale, "A queer supplement," 7–8.
107. Deleuze, *Expressionism in Philosophy*, 218.
108. Gilles Deleuze and Claire Parnet, *Dialogues*, Hugh Tomlison and Barbara Habberjam, trans. (London: Althone, 1987), 60.
109. Colebrook, *Deleuze*, 4. While he recognizes that women have been compromised, Deleuze goes on to qualify this macropolitics of the female subject in an unfortunate and even hackneyed way, cautioning that it is dangerous to confine oneself to such a subject.
110. Jerry Aline Flieger, "Becoming-woman: Deleuze, Schreber and molecular identification" in *Deleuze and Feminist Theory*, Ian Buchanan and Claire Colebrook, eds. (Edinburgh: Edinburgh University, 2000), 40.
111. Colebrook, *Deleuze*, 7–8.
112. Ibid., 8.
113. Ibid., 126.
114. Ibid.
115. Deleuze, *Expressionism in Philosophy*, 218.
116. Ibid., 221.
117. Ibid, 127. To Deleuze, "An affection of our body is only a corporeal image, and the idea of the affection as it is in our mind an inadequate idea, an imagining." "While our body exists, it endures, and is defined by duration;" he elaborates, "its present state is thus inseparable from a previous state with which it is linked in a continuous duration. Thus *to every idea that indicates an actual state of our body, there is a necessarily inked another sort of idea that involves the relation of this state to the earlier state.*" Spinoza explains that this should not be thought of as an abstract intellectual operation by which the mind compares two states. "Our feelings are in themselves ideas which involve the concrete relation of present and past in a continuous duration: they involve the changes of an existing mode that endures." Quoted from Deleuze, *Expressionism in Philosophy*, 219–20.
118. Deleuze and Guattari, *A Thousand Plateaus*, 243–44.
119. Colebrook, *Deleuze*, 133–36.
120. Gatens and Lloyd, *Imaginings: Spinoza, Past and Present*, 111.
121. Ibid., 100.
122. Ibid.
123. Ibid., 101.
124. Ibid.
125. Ibid., 102.
126. Deleuze, *Expressionism in Philosophy*, 221.
127. Colebrook, *Deleuze*, 135–36.
128. See the fifth thesis of Max Horkheimer and Theordor W. Adorno, *Dialectic of the Enlightenment: Philosophical Fragments*, Gunzelin Schmid Noerr, ed., Edmund Jephcott, trans. (Stanford: Stanford University, 2002).
129. See Jack Sidnell, "An ethnographic consideration of rule following," *Journal of the Royal Anthropological Institute* 9 (2003), 429–45.

130. See Deleuze, *Expressionism in Philosophy*; and Deleuze, *Difference and Repetition*, Paul Pratton, trans. (New York: Columbia University, 1994).

131. Grosz, *Volatile Bodies*, 21–23.

132. Ibid, 23. Grosz argues that should also demonstrate some sort of internal or constitutive articulation between the biological and the psychological. Finally, she suggests we should not adhere to one side of the binary.

133. Rosemarie Garland-Thomson, *Extraordinary Bodies: Fighting Physical Disability in American Culture and Literature* (New York: Columbia, 1997), 7.

134. It would be a mistake to read Deleuze's and Guattari's references about the mind and body literally. They certainly argue that "the body's power of suffering has as its equivalent in the mind the power of imagining and of experiencing passive feelings." But the idea of suffering is not about the body. Words themselves are inadequate for Deleuze and Guattari to express this notion. They do not ascribe adequate ideas to healthy minds and bodies, leaving the inadequate ones to unhealthy minds and bodies. Deleuze does juxtapose joy to suffering, yet it is the adequate ideas that persons with disabilities produce given the perpetual connection between their minds and bodies. See Deleuze, *Expressionism in Philosophy*, 222.

135. Alasdair MacIntyre, *Dependent Rational Animals: Why Human Beings Need the Virtues* (Chicago: Open Court, 1999), 4.

136. Ibid., 8.

137. Liz Crow, "Including all of our lives: renewing the social model of disability" in *Exploring the Divide: Illness and Disability*, Colin Barnes and Geof Mercer, eds. (Leeds: The Disability Press, 1996); and Williams, "Is anybody there? critical realism, chronic illness and the disability debate."

138. Williams, "Theorizing disability," 139.

139. Irving Kenneth Zola, "An appreciation," *Sociology of Health and Illness* 18 (1996), 107–25.

140. See Ruth Pinder, "Bringing back the body without the blame? The experience of ill and disabled people at work," *Sociology of Health and Illness* 19 (1995), 605–31; Jeffrey Benoist and P. Cartherbras, "The body: From one immateriality to another," *Social Science and Medicine* 36 (1993), 857–65; and G.H. Williams, "The genesis of chronic illness: Narrative reconstruction," *Sociology of Health and Illness* 6 (1984), 175–200.

141. First, impairments are multiple and various. Second, "Making notions of impairment equivalent to forms of human variation would reduce the need to decide who is 'in' and who is 'out' of the group of people counted as persons with disabilities, which has become one of the major methods of denying people protection under the employment provisions of the Americans with Disabilities Act." Third, people with various conditions have a range of needs that influence their ability to take advantage of legal entitlements to education or employment or public services. See Adrienne Asche, "Critical race theory, feminism, and disability: Reflections on social justice and personal identity," *Ohio State Law Journal* 62 (2001), 391, 400. Disability could be defined as an extension of the variability in physical and mental attributes beyond the present—but not the potential—ability of social institutions to routinely respond." For Richard Scotch, who with Pamela Brandwein has a postmodern edge in creating the human variation model, disability is "an extension of the natural physical, social, and cultural variability of the human species." See Richard K. Scotch and Pamela Brandwein, "The gender analogy in the disability discrimination literature," *Ohio State Law Journal* 62 (2001) 465.

142. Mariam Corker, "Disability discourse in a postmodern world" in *The Disability Reader: Social Science Perspectives*, Tom Shakespeare, ed. (Cassell: London, 1998).

143. Brisenden, "Independent living and the medical model of disability," 23. The first struggle the disability rights movement undertook was with the rehabilitation experts. In the mid-Seventies, the movement successfully confronted the cult of experts in public education when the Education for All Handicapped Children Act was passed. This legislation gave students an individualized educational program that the parents, sometimes the students themselves, and teachers devised together. Educational experts no longer dictated what students needed. Also see Edward D. Berkowitz, *Disabled Policy: America's Programs for the Handicapped* (New York: Cambridge University, 1987); Ruth O'Brien, *Crippled Justice: The History of Modern Disability Policy in the Workplace* (Chicago: University of Chicago, 2001);

and Paul F. James, "The Education for All Handicapped Children Act of 1975: What's left after *Rowley*?" *Willamette Law Review* 19 (1983), 721.

144. Abberley, "The spectre at the feast," 79.
145. Brisenden, "Independent living and the medical model of disability," 24.
146. Jenny Morris, "Impairment and disability: An ethics of care that promotes human rights," *Hypatia* 16 (2001), 1–16. Morris goes so far as to argue that disability is a term that should not be substituted for impairment. Rather, it should be tantamount to the word racism or sexism. Also, the human rights approach equates disability rights with human rights. See Charlton, *Nothing About Us Without Us*. First, Charlton suggests that disabled people have experienced a human rights tragedy of epic proportions. Second, the poverty isolation in the independence of these 500 million people is a human rights catastrophe and a fundamental critique of the existing world system. Third, the scant attention to the theorized conditions of everyday life for persons with disabilities is incomplete or fundamentally flawed because of the medicalization and the depoliticalization of disability. Fourth, disability-based consciousness is emerging throughout the world and has begun to contest the oppression of these people. Fifth, the political-economic and sociocultural dimensions of disability determine who is affected and the form resistance takes. Sixth, all the individuals and organizations that have taken up the cause of disability rights in the last twenty years have embraced the concept of empowerment and human rights, independence and integration, self-help, and self-determination. Seventh, these themes suggest a fundamental re-ordering of global priorities and resources by the people that need them.
147. Brandwein and Scotch, "The gender analogy in the disability discrimination literature," 465, 468.
148. Ibid., 468.
149. Roy Bhaskar, *Reclaiming Reality: A Critical Introduction to Contemporary Philosophy* (New York: Verso, 1989), 92.
150. Oliver Sacks, *The Man Who Mistook His Wife for a Hat and Other Clinical Tales* (New York: Summit, 1985).
151. Shelley Tremain, "On the government of disability," *Social Theory and Disability* 27 (2001), 617–636. Tremain argues that this "timeless entity (impairment) is a historically specific effect of knowledge/power." She takes a nominalist position.
152. Ibid.

## Chapter 3: An Alternative Ethic of Care

1. Francis Carleton and Jennifer Nutt Carleton, "An ethic of care and the hazardous workplace," *Wisconsin Women's Law Journal* 10 (1995), 289.
2. Catherine MacKinnon, "Feminism, Marxism, method, and the state: Toward feminist jurisprudence," *SIGNS: Journal of Women in Culture and Society* 8 (1983), 635–58; Robin West, *Caring for Justice* (New York: New York University, 1997); and Judith Baer, *Our Lives Before the Law: Constructing a Feminist Jurisprudence* (Princeton: Princeton University, 1999). For other work on an ethic of care from a legal perspective see Leslie Bender, "From gender differences to feminist solidarity: Using Carol Gilligan and an ethic of care in the law," *Vermont Law Review* 15 (1990), 1; and Martha Albertson Fineman, *The Neutered Mother, the Sexual Family and Other Twentieth Century Tragedies* (New York: Routledge, 1995).
3. Catherine A. MacKinnon, *Feminism Unmodified: Discourses on Life and Law* (Cambridge: Harvard University, 1987), 44, 166-67, 179. Also see Ellen DuBois, Mary C. Dunlap, Carol Gilligan, Catherine MacKinnon and Carrie Menkel-Meadow, "Feminist discourse, moral values, and the law—a conversation," *Buffalo Law Review* 34 (1985), 70.
4. Inspired by Gilligan, West's earlier work is essentialist. In "Jurisprudence and gender," for example, West identified categorical and essentialist differences in terms of culture, biology, and materialism. Robin West "Jurisprudence and gender," *University of Chicago Law Review* 55 (1988), 1. See Linda McClain, "The liberal future of relational feminism: Robin West's *Caring for Justice*," *Law and Social Inquiry* 24 (1999), 478, for a thorough critique.
5. Quoted from McClain, "The liberal future of relational feminism: Robin West's caring for justice," 479. Critics like Linda McClain argue that her key concepts are liberal—she relies on the choosing, caring self.

6. Baer, *Our Lives Before the Law* 199.

7. Carol Gilligan, *In a Different Voice: Psychological Theory and Women's Development* (Cambridge: Harvard University, 1982). Also see Nel Noddings, *Caring: A Feminine Approach to Ethics* (Berkeley: University of California, 1984), whose work was criticized for being essentialist.

8. Joy Kroeger-Mappes, "The ethic of care vis-á-vis the ethic of rights: A problem for contemporary moral theory," *Hypatia* 9 (1994), 108. Also Diemut Elisbet Bubeck, *Care, Gender, and Justice* (Oxford: Oxford University, 1995) is concerned with overcoming the supposedly "misleading disjuncture of justice and care."

9. Joan C. Tronto, *Moral Boundaries and Political Change: A Political Argument for an Ethic of Care* (New York: Routledge, 1993), 6.

10. Ibid., 7–9.

11. Ibid., 102–03. She cites four phases of caring: Caring about; taking care of; caregiving; and care-receiving.

12. See Diana Fuss, *Essentially Speaking: Feminism, Nature, and Difference* (New York: Routledge, 1989). Gilligan herself challenges the essentialist reading of her book. See Tronto, *Moral Boundaries and Political Change*, 82–85. Also see Martha C. Nussbaum, "Human functioning and social justice: In defense of Aristotlean essentialism," *Political Theory* 20 (1992), 202–46 for a good overview of this debate.

13. Sara Ruddick, *Maternal Thinking: Toward a Politics of Peace* (Boston: Beacon, 1989).

14. Claire Colebrook, "From radical representations to corporeal becomings: The feminist philosophy of Lloyd, Grosz, and Gatens," *Hypatia* 15 (2000), 77. Social constructionism was first introduced in linguistic and anthropological theories. See Manuel De Landa, "Deleuze, diagrams, and the open-ended becoming" in *Becomings: Explorations in Time, Memory, and Future*, Elizabeth Grosz, ed. (Ithaca: Cornell University, 1999), 30.

15. Sheila Greeve Davaney, "The limits of the appeal to women's experience" in *Shaping New Vision: Gender and Values in American Culture*, Clarissa W. Atkinson, Constance H. Buchanan, and Margaret R. Miles, eds. (The Harvard Women's Studies in Religion Series, no. 5., Ann Arbor: UMI Research, 1987), 42.

16. Ibid., 46.

17. Nancy Hirschmann, "Toward a feminist theory of freedom," *Political Theory* 24 (1996), 52.

18. Colebrook, "From radical representations to corporeal becomings."

19. Kathryn Abrams, "The second coming of care," *Chicago-Kent Law Review* 76 (2001), 1606.

20. De Landa, "Deleuze, diagrams, and the open-ended becoming" 32.

21. Hirschmann, "Toward a feminist theory of freedom," 58.

22. Martha Fineman, "Cracking the foundational myths: Independence, autonomy, and self-sufficiency," *Journal of Gender, Social Policy & the Law* 8 (1999), 101–16.

23. Hirschmann, "Toward a feminist theory of freedom," 63.

24. Daryl Koehn, *Rethinking Feminist Ethics: Care, Trust and Empathy* (New York: Routledge, 1998), 6.

25. Seyla Benhabib, "The generalized and the concrete other" in *Feminist Contentions: A Philosophical Exchange* Linda Nicholson, ed. (New York: Routledge, 1995), 80–81.

26. Cristiana L.H. Traina, *Feminist Ethics and Natural Law: The End of the Anathemas* (Washington, D.C.: Georgetown University, 1999), 2–3.

27. Davaney, "The limits of the appeal to women's experience," 47.

28. Joan C. Tronto, Review of *Moral Voices, Moral Selves* by Susan Hekman; *Caring: Gender-Sensitive Ethics* by Petra Bowden; and *Care, Gender, and Justice* by Diemut Elisbet Bubecke, *Hypatia* 14 (1999), 117.

29. Tronto, *Moral Boundaries*, 3.

30. Ibid., 6.

31. Ibid., 19–20.

32. Koehn, *Rethinking Feminist Ethics*.

33. Ibid., 15.

34. Ibid., 16–17.

35. Hirschmann, "Toward a feminist theory of freedom;" and Zillah Eisenstein, *The Female Body and The Law* (Berkeley: University of California, 1988).

36. Isaiah Berlin, *Liberty: Incorporating Four Essays on Liberty* (New York: Oxford University, 2002).

37. Hirschmann, "Toward a feminist theory of freedom," 49.

38. Ibid., 55–56.

39. Eisenstein, *The Female Body and The Law*.

40. Ibid., 79–80. For an important exchange about difference see Susan Moller Okin, "Gender inequality and cultural differences," *Political Theory* 22 (1994), 5–24. Also see Rita Felski, "The doxa of difference," *SIGNS: Journal of Women in Culture and Society* 23 (1997), 1–21 for an excellent survey of the debate about the notion of difference and its political significance.

41. The three classic Supreme Court decisions that relied on protectionism were *Muller v. Oregon*, 198 U.S. 45 (1905), which protected women from working long hours; *Bradwell v. Illinois* 83 U.S. 130 (1872), which barred women from practicing law; and *Hoyt v. Florida*, 208 U.S. 412 (1908), which exempted women from jury duty on the basis of their family responsibilities.

42. Eisenstein, *The Female Body and The Law*, 207.

43. Jerry Aline Flieger, "Becoming-woman: Deleuze, Schreber and molecular identification," 38–63 in *Deleuze and Feminist Theory*, Ian Buchanan and Claire Colebrook, eds. (Edinburgh: Edinburgh University, 2000), 40.

44. Colebrook, *Deleuze*, 3. While he recognizes that women have been compromised, Deleuze goes on to qualify this macropolitics of the female subject in an unfortunate and even hackneyed way, cautioning that it is dangerous to confine oneself to such a subject.

45. Gilles Deleuze and Felix Guattari, *A Thousand Plateaus: Capitalism and Schizophrenia*, Brian Massumi, trans. (Minneapolis: University of Minnesota, 1987), 254.

46. Christopher Norris, *Spinoza & and the Origins of Modern Critical Theory* (London: Basil Blackwell, 1991), 143.

47. Ibid., 153.

48. Quoted in Ibid., 167.

49. Moira Gatens and Genevieve Lloyd, *Imaginings: Spinoza, Past and Present* (London: Routledge, 1999), 132.

50. Fourth Part, Proposition 35 in *Spinoza's Ethics*, edited with revised trans., G. H. R. Parkinson (London: J.M. Dent & Sons, 1989), 163.

51. Ibid.

52. Gatens and Lloyd, *Imaginings: Spinoza, Past and Present*, 133.

53. Critics of the communitarian view see it as value-laden, conservative, and as having an unrealistic and romantic perception of history. Also see Elizabeth Frazer and Nicola Lacey, *The Politics of Community: A Feminist Critique of the Liberal-Communitarian Debate* (Buffalo: University of Toronto, 1993).

54. See Warren Montag, *Bodies, Masses, Power: Spinoza and his Contemporaries* (London: Verso, 1999), 91.

55. Douglas Den Uyl, *Power, State, and Freedom: An Interpretation of Spinoza's Political Philosophy* (Assen, The Netherlands: Van Gorcum, 1983), 19.

56. Gatens and Lloyd, *Imaginings: Spinoza, Past and Present*, 107.

57. Montag, *Bodies, Masses, Power*, 91.

58. Ibid., 92.

59. Third Part, Proposition 9 in *Spinoza's Ethics*, 62.

60. Gatens and Lloyd, *Imaginings: Spinoza, Past and Present*, 104.

61. See Fourth Part, Propositions 37–40 in *Spinoza's Ethics*, 165–70.

62. See Second Part, Proposition 18 in *Spinoza's Ethics*, 66–67.

63. See Gatens and Lloyd, *Imaginings: Spinoza, Past and Present*, 105.

64. Ibid.

65. Ibid., 13.

66. Ibid., 105.

67. Ibid., 106.

68. Ibid.

69. Ibid., 109. Spinoza suggests that the governing body cannot rob people of their power of judging, or make them "regard" with honor things that excite ridicule or disgust. Nor can it systematically flout its own laws or engage in corruption without ceasing to be a

commonwealth. Spinoza's view is that to engage in such activities is to fail to be, or cease to be, a government. Individuals living under such a power are not bound by the social contract if that contract no longer has utility for them. Peace, as Spinoza maintains, consists not in mere absence of war, but in a union or agreement of minds.

70. Ibid., 112.
71. Pickett, "Foucault and the politics of resistance," 461.
72. Knights and Vurdubakis, "Foucault, power, resistance and all that," 175.
73. Ibid., 186.
74. John M. Jermier, David Knights, and Walter Nord, "Introduction" in *Resistance and Power in Organizations*, John M. Jermier, David Knights, and Walter Nord, eds. (London: Routledge, 1994), 16.
75. Knights and Vurdubakis, "Foucault, power, resistance and all that," 169.
76. Dierter Freundlieb, "Foucault's theory of discourse and human agency" in *Reassessing Foucault: Power, Medicine, and the Body*, Colin Jones and Roy Porter, eds. (London: Routledge, 1994), 147.
77. Pickett, "Foucault and the politics of resistance," 463–64.
78. Jessica J. Kulynych, "Performing politics: Foucault, Habermas, and postmodern participation," *Polity* 30 (1997), 315–46.
79. Knights and Vurdubakis, "Foucault, power, resistance and all that," 177–79.
80. Pickett, "Foucault and the politics of resistance," 459.
81. Ibid., 453.
82. Ibid., 458.
83. Kulnynch, "Performing politics," 330.
84. Vic Finkelstein, "Emancipating disability studies" in *The Disability Reader: Social Science Perspectives*, Tom Shakespeare, ed. (London: Casswell, 1998), 29.
85. Ibid., 30.

## Chapter 4: The Body at Work

1. Grant Duncan, "Mind–body dualism and the biopsychosocial model of pain: What did Descartes really say?" *Journal of Medicine and Philosophy* 25 (2000), 487.
2. E. P. Thomson, "Time, work-discipline, and industrial capitalism," *Past & Present* 38 (1967), 60.
3. Ibid., 61, 89.
4. Geoffrey Godbey, "No time to waste: An exploration of time use, attitudes toward time, and the generation of municipal solid waste," *Social Research* 65 (1998), 101–41; and Daniel Bell, "The end of scarcity," *Saturday Review of the Society* (May, 1975), 13.
5. Winter, "Writing and skin," 176.
6. Philip Hancock, "Baudrillard and the metaphysics of motivation: A reappraisal of corporate culturalism in the light of the work and ideas of Jean Baudrillard," *Journal of Management Studies* 36 (1999), 158.
7. Ibid., 157–158. The critics of capitalism also followed the Enlightenment. For Karl Marx, the worker suffers from alienation under a capitalist economic system when he or she is cut off from deciding how to execute his work. Marx's version of alienation is therefore an expression of the corruption of this ideal ontological state. It is a literally "distancing from" both the natural and social universe. The subjective self feels "disempowered" with little or no control over either the activity or conditions of his/her own lab or material products from it. The only solution to alienation is to overthrow the capitalist mode of production and "return of the human species to its central place within both the natural and social universe."
8. Len Doyal and Ian Gough, *A Theory of Human Need* (New York: Guilford, 1991), 10.
9. Karl Polanyi, *The Great Transformation* (Boston: Beacon, 1971), 101.
10. Henry J. Bittermann, "Adam Smith's empiricism and the law of nature, I," *Journal of Political Economy* 48 (1940), 511–14.
11. Omid Nodoushani, "A postmodern theory of general economy: The contribution of Georges Batille," *Studies in Cultures, Organizations, and Societies* 5 (1999), 333–34. Also see Polanyi, *The Great Transformation*, 110.

12. Bittermann, "Adam Smith's empiricism and the law of nature, I," 488. Also see Emma Rothschild, *Economic Sentiments: Adam Smith, Condorcet, and the Enlightenment* (Cambridge: Harvard University, 2001), 123.
13. Bitterman argues that Smith's difficulty was not to account for selfishness but rather how to explain "sentiments about matters not directly affecting individual interests, actions of others involving third parties, emotions aroused by the feelings of others, or even the sentiments occasioned by literature and remote history." Smith followed David Hume with his definition of sympathy, which created this link. Sympathy is not a moral or ethical principle. Instead, it is a psychological process that involves someone's sense of what events happen to others. Bitterman, "Adam Smith's empiricism and the law of nature, I," 510. Also see Jeffrey T. Young, *Economics as a Moral Science: the Political Economy of Adam Smith* (Cheltenham: Edward Elgar, 1997), 32–34.
14. Doyal and Gough, *A Theory of Human Need*, 9.
15. Amartya Sen, *Inequality Reexamined* (New York: Russell Sage Foundation; Cambridge: Harvard University, 1992), 6. Utilitarian economics ignores achievements other than those reflected in one of these mental metrics.
16. See Clifford W. Cobb, *Measuring Tools and the Quality of Life* (San Francisco: Redefining Progress, 2000), 7, for a good definition.
17. Doyal and Gough, *A Theory of Human Need*, 11.
18. Under utilitarianism, wealth and consumer power has a moral priority. This theory cannot distinguish between different types of pleasure and pain. Everything other than total utility is overlooked and ignored. Amartya Sen, "Rights and capabilities" in *Morality and Objectivity: A Tribute to J. L. Mackie* (London: Routledge and Kegan Paul, 1985).
19. David Wiggins, "Claims of need" in *Morality and Objectivity: A Tribute to J. L. Mackie*, Ted Honderich, ed. (London: Routledge and Kegan Paul, 1985), 159–60.
20. Ibid., 165.
21. Brian Massumi, *A User's Guide to Capitalism and Schizophrenia: Deviations from Deluze and Guattari* (Cambridge: MIT, 1999), 130.
22. See Robert L. Heilbroner, *The Nature and Logic of Capitalism* (New York: Norton, 1985), 68. See Frederick Engels, *On Authority*. Engels wrote: "Wanting to abolish authority in large-scale industry is tantamount to wanting to abolish industry itself." Quoted from Stephen Marglin, "What do bosses do? The origins and functions of hierarchy in capitalist production," *Review of Radical Political Economy* 6 (1974), 33.
23. Massumi, *A User's Guide to Capitalism and Schizophrenia*, 130.
24. See Heilbroner, *The Nature and Logic of Capitalism*, 66–67.
25. Quoted in Marglin, "What do bosses do?" 54.
26. Heilbroner also explains that "under a wage labor system workers are entirely free to enter or leave the work relationship as they wish" and that this is what gives the mainstream economists the moral justification for this system. The "contractual right of refusal"—a right that protects both employee and employer from the coercive use of property—he states is the "essential political foundation of capitalism" or "its justification of a moral order." See Heilbroner, *The Nature and Logic of Capitalism*, 66–67.
27. Heidi Hartmann, "Capitalism, patriarchy, and job segregation by sex" in *Women, Class, and the Feminist Imagination*, Karen V. Hanson and Ilene J. Philipson, eds. (Philadelphia: Temple University, 1990), 138.
28. Making hierarchical control patriarchical gave men considerable personal and material benefits. See Sylvia Walby, *Theorizing Patriarchy* (Oxford: Basil Blackwell, 1990). In *Sexual Politics*, Kate Millett, a leading radical feminist, brought the concept of patriarchy to the forefront by using Weber's idea of Herrschaft or the relationship of domination and subordination to understand it. See Kate Millett, *Sexual Politics* (London: Sphere, 1971). By contrast, Shulamith Firestone maintains that it is an "imbalance of power in favor of men." See Shulamith Firestone, *The Dialectic of Sex* (London: Women's, 1979). Zillah Eisenstein in *Capitalist Patriarchy and the Case for Socialist Feminism* (New York: Monthly Review, 1979) views it as sexual hierarchy in which the woman is mother, domestic laborer, and consumer. For an excellent overview of the debate see Mary Murray, *The Law of the Father?: Patriarchy in the Transition from Feudalism to Capitalism* (London: Routledge, 1995), 7–8.

29. Hartmann, "Capitalism, patriarchy, and job segregation by sex," 137.
30. Ibid., 139.
31. Marglin, "What do bosses do?," 35.
32. Ibid., 36.
33. Ibid., 39.
34. Ibid., 34.
35. Ibid.
36. See Stephen R. Barley and Gideon Kunda, "Design and devotion: Surges of rational and normative ideologies of control in managerial discourse," *Administrative Science Quarterly* 37 (1992), 364–66.
37. Barley and Kunda, "Design and devotion," 364; Loren Baritz, *The Servants of Power: A History of the Use of Social Science in American Industry* (Middletown, Conn.: Wesleyan University, 1960); and Daniel A. Wren, *The Evolution of Management Thought* (New York: John Wiley, 1994, 4th edition).
38. By 1879, 39 YMCAs existed. See Barley and Kunda, "Design and devotion," 366.
39. It was the prominent Congregationalist minister, Washington Gladden, who created the philosophy underlying it. To him, laborers needed to follow "simple control." See Barley and Kunda, "Design and devotion," 365.
40. Quoted in Barley and Kuda, "Design and devotion," 369. Joseph A. Litterer, "Systematic management: Design for organizational recoupling in American manufacturing firms," *Business History Review* 37 (1963), 360–91.
41. Samuel Haber, *Efficiency and Uplift: Scientific Management in the Progressive Era, 1880–1920* (Chicago: University of Chicago, 1964); Richard Edwards, *Contested Terrain: The Transformation of the Workplace in the Twentieth Century* (New York: Basic, 1979), and David A. Hounsell, *From the American System to Mass Production, 1880–1934: The Development of Manufacturing in the United States* (Baltimore: Johns Hopkins University, 1984).
42. See Melvyn Dubofsky, *We Shall Be All: A History of the Industrial Workers of the World* (Urbana: University of Illinois, 1988, 2nd edition).
43. Webster and Robins, "I'll be watching you," 254–55; and Edward L. Bernays, *Public Relations* (Norman: University of Oklahoma, 1952), 159.
44. Frederick Winslow Taylor, *The Principles of Scientific Management* (New York: Harper & Row, 1911), 140.
45. Ibid.
46. In 1914, Ford increased the pay from $2.34 to $5.00 for a nine-hour day. This was one year after he introduced the assembly line. "On the job," *Business Week* Issue 3630A (Summer, 1999), 28.
47. Scientists like Louis Pasteur and artists such as Edward Manet became interested not in the world as it was, but what it *could* be. See Terrie C. Reeves, W. Jack Duncan, and Peter M. Ginter, "Motion study in management and the arts," *Journal of Management Inquiry* 10 (2001), 139.
48. Reeves, Duncan, and Ginter, "Motion study in management and the arts," 137–38.
49. Taylor also had a mission to serve the community the "American way." Kyle Bruce and Chris Nyland, "Scientific management, institutionalism, and business stabilization, 1903–1923," *Journal of Economic Issues* 35 (2001), 956.
50. Hancock, "Baudrillard and the metaphysics of motivation," 159.
51. Bernays, *Public Relations*, 159.
52. Beverly H. Burris, "Braverman, Taylorism, and technocracy" in *Rethinking the Labor Process*, Mark Wardell, Thomas L. Steiger, and Peter Meiksins, eds. (Buffalo: SUNY, 1999), 42–43.
53. Frank Webster and Kevin Robins, "I'll be watching you: Comment on Sewell and Wilkinson," *Sociology* 27 (1993), 245.
54. Bruce and Nyland, "Scientific management, institutionalism, and business stabilization," 956.
55. Webster and Robins, "I'll be watching you," 244–45.
56. Frank B. Gilbreth expanded on Taylor's conception of scientific management to create the motion study of the body at work. See his book *Motion Study, A Method for Increasing the Efficiency of the Workman* (New York: Van Nostrand, 1911).

57. Hancock, "Baudrillard and the metaphysics of motivation," 157.
58. Quoted from Michael Freeman, "Scientific management: 100 years old; poised for the next century," *SAM Advanced Management Journal* 61 (1996), 35–43.
59. Fess B. Green and Victor B. Wayhan, "Reengineering: Clarifying the confusion," *SAM Advanced Management Journal* 61 (1996), 37.
60. Rudolph H. Ehrenberg and Ronald J. Stupak, "Total quality management: its relationship to administrative theory and organizational behavior in the public sector," *Public Administration Quarterly* 18 (1994), 76.
61. John Wheatcroft, "Organizational change, the story so far," *Industrial Management & Data Systems* 100 (2000), 5–6.
62. Ibid.
63. William G. Scott, *Chester I. Barnhard 7 The Guardians of the Managerial State* (Lawrence: University Press of Kansas, 1992), 25.
64. See Barley and Kunda, "Design and devotion," 369–70 for an excellent overview of the different stages in scientific management.
65. Taylor himself established close ties with progressives. Not only did he write an influential legal opinion for the "people's lawyer" Louis Brandeis's rate-making case against the Interstate Commerce Commission, but he borrowed Walter Lippman's emphasis on administration and rationalization. To Lippmann, society has attained a "complexity now so great to be humanly unmanageable." The central government has been compelled to assume responsibility for the control and coordination of this diffuse social structure. As in the Taylorist factory, this depends on systematic intelligence and information control: the gathering of social knowledge, Lippmann argues, must become the normal accompaniment of action. For social control to be effective, information must be controlled. See Walter Lippmann, *Public Opinion* (New York: Harcourt, Brace, 1922), 394; and Webster and Robins, "I'll be watching you," 254–55.
66. Martin Albrow, *Max Weber's Construction of Social Theory* (New York: St. Martin's, 1990), 184.
67. Ibid., 179.
68. Quoted from "Charisma and its transformation" in *Economy & Society*, Guenther Roth and Claus Wittich, eds., Ephraim Fischoff, trans. (New York: Bedminister, 1968), 1111, 1117.
69. Joan C. Tronto, Book Review of *Max Weber*, by Anthony Kronman: "Law and Modernity: The Significance of Max Weber's Sociology of Law," *Texas Law Review* 63 (1984), 565; Stephen Kalberg, "Max Weber's types of rationality: Cornerstones for the analysis of rationalization processes in history," *American Journal of Sociology* 85 (1980), 114; and Levine, "Rationality and freedom: Weber and beyond" *Sociological Inquiry* 51 (1981), 5.
70. Julien Freund, *The Sociology of Max Weber* (New York: Pantheon, 1968), 18.
71. Albrow, *Max Weber's Construction of Social Theory*, 183.
72. Ibid., 180.
73. Ibid., 180–81.
74. Turner, *From History to Modernity*, 118.
75. Harland Prechel, "The labor process and the transformation of corporate control in the global economy" in *Labor and Capital in the Age of Globalization: The Labor Process and the Changing Nature of Work in the Global Economy*, Berch Berberoglu, ed. (Lanham: Rowan & Littlefield, 2002), 51.
76. Michael Rosen and Jack Baroudi, "Computer-based technology and the emergence of new forms of managerial control" in *Skill and Consent: Contemporary Studies in the Labor Process*, Andrew Sturdy, David Knights, and Hugh Willmott, eds. (London: Routledge, 1992), 216.
77. A renewed faith in welfare capitalism after World War I had laid the groundwork for Gilbreth's human relations approach to scientific management. The U.S. Bureau of Statistics began collecting information on vacations, sick leaves, and health care—employee benefits—in 1919. Gilbreth combined this information with data about productivity to show employers why they should provide better work conditions. Instead of improving the worker themselves, changing work conditions would lead to more efficiency and

productivity. Barley and Kunda, "Design and devotion," 371; and Baritz, *The Servants of Power*.

78. Lillian E. Gilbreth, *The Psychology of Management: The Function of the Mind in Determining, Teaching and Installing Methods of Least Waste* (New York: Sturgis & Walton, 1914).

79. Also see Baritz, *The Servants of Power*; and Abraham Maslow, *Motivation and Personality* (New York: Harper, 1954).

80. See Hancock, "Baudrillard and the metaphysics of motivation," 160. Also see Barley and Kunda, "Design and devotion," 373. Oliver Sheldon in 1923 and Mary Parker Follette in 1918 had written of social-psychological aspects. Their model of the human subject was both alienated from and yet receptive to strategies of motivation. This information was not gathered to aid one person, however. Rather, the experts collected it to help the expert formulate general rules of workplace behavior. Another psychologist, Elton Mayo, had a great influence on the human relations approach to scientific management—he relied on psychodynamics. Believing that labor conflict could be perceived as a form of group psychopathy, Mayo thought worker solidarity represented the single most important factor in regulating individual output since it created a healthy atmosphere. Maslow's ideas strayed little from the traditional conception of empiricism. They were based on positivistic assumptions about human behavior. Experts, he insisted, could study human behavior by using scientific investigation and then offer clear and objective analysis about it. Maslow objectified the subjective domain, reducing people and their needs to not much more than variables calculated by pseudo-mathematical equations.

81. Barley and Kunda, "Design and devotion," 363.

82. See Hancock, "Baudrillard and the metaphysics of motivation," 159–60.

83. Scott, *Chester I. Barnard*, 89. Chester Barnard's intellectual debt was to Einstein. Relativity and bureaucracy dominated the thought of Barnard's generation and he had a managerial epistemology. Control of human behavior in the workplace was the most pressing management need at the time, therefore the use of social sciences for purposes of social engineering had a high priority. Hancock, "Baudrillard and the metaphysics of motivation," 157; Barley and Kunda, "Design and devotion," 372; and Sanford Jacoby, "Masters to managers: An introduction" in *Masters to Managers: Historical and Comparative Perspectives on American Employers*, Sanford Jacoby, ed. (New York: Columbia University, 1991). The Ford Foundation and the Carnegie Corporation issued reports that argue that managerial education lacked a coherent core and that managerial training should be as rigorous as other disciplines. Most notably, the University of Chicago founded the Committee on Human Relations in 1943 to emphasize a multidisciplinary approach. There was corporate experimentation on strategies for enhancing loyalty, motivation, and satisfaction with innovative compensation systems like participatory decision-making, job enrichment, and attitude surveys. Human relations also shaped the labor-management centers at Cornell, Yale, and the University of Illinois. Part of the penchant for the testing movement had grown out of the War Department's support for ability assessment during World War II. This department created procedures for selecting and placing employees in the tight labor market. While the tests had been constructed to promote employee welfare, their utility stemmed from their chance to enhance workplace performance. The tests gathered objective knowledge about employees' well-being to serve the entire firm or factory.

84. Scott, *Chester I. Barnard*, 25.

85. Edwards, *Contested Terrain*, 4.

86. Hancock, "Baudrillard and the metaphysics of motivation," 159.

87. Scott, *Chester I. Barnard*, 178. Although this new psychological perspective about scientific management reified the individual worker no less than the rational perspective, it raised the issue of human agency by exploring why employees accepted their supervisor's authority. This aspect of human relations scientific management was drawn not from psychology but rather from law and political science. It involved the consent theory of Ehrlich who was influenced by psychodynamics and gestalt theory. Adopting Eugene Ehrlich's *Fundamental Principles of the Sociology of Law* (New Brunswick, N.J.: Transaction, 2002), Barnard argued that workers tacitly gave their employers consent. To Ehrlich, the center of gravity in law rested in neither the legislatures nor the judiciary, but in society itself. This did not mean that the people themselves had consented to law. Instead, Ehrlich found that law was rooted

in associations or other subsidiary social units that people joined. Since these were informal as opposed to formal sources, he argued that authority was based on customs and norms that could be described as bubbling up from below. Someone attained authority because of the tacit consent of the people, not because of a decision rendered from the higher level of the state. If Ehrlich's conception of law was true for the state, Barnard reasoned, then it could be extended to the workplace. Employers attained the authority to manage the workplace when employees accepted employment, giving their tacit approval of this authority. Employers maintained tight hierarchical control despite the layer upon layer of bureaucracy because the employees thought they had the legitimate right to rule. Ehrlich and Michels were influenced by Weber, who argued that coercion is not a viable basis for compliance, and his theory of domination treated bureaucratization as an effective solution to the problem of labor contacting and control in advanced societies. See Aren L. Kalleberg and Torger Reve, "Contracts and commitment: Economic and sociological perspectives on employment relations," *Human Relations* 45 (1992), 1110; and Scott, *Chester I. Barnard*, 99.

88. Scott, *Chester I. Barnard*, 98; and Douglas M. McGregor, *The Human Side of Enterprise* (New York: McGraw Hill, 1960). In the mid-1950s, scientific management took another direction, being influenced by contingency theory or bounded rationality in organizational theory. This meant that rational calculation and cognitive decision making replaced Maslow's theories of motivation. See Barley and Kunda, "Design and devotion," 377; and Fred Luthans, "Contingency theory of management: A path out of the jungle," *Business Horizons* 16 (1973), 67–72. As the organizational theorists James March and Herbert Simon explained, people make decisions based upon what information they have in front of them. No best way of performing a task could be prescribed by scientific management experts, though they could identify that some ways were better than others. Instead of emphasizing categorical differences, bounded rationality emphasized that difference should be calculated in amounts or degrees. See James G. March and Herbert A. Simon, *Organizations* (New York: Wiley, 1958).

89. In addition to Williamson and Barnard, see Archibald Cox, who observed that the collective bargaining agreement "should be understood as an instrument of government as well as an instrument of exchange." Archibald Cox, "The legal nature of collective bargaining agreements," *Michigan Law Review* 57 (1958), 22.

90. See Morris Llewellyn Cooke, *Organized Labor and Production* (New York: Arno, 1971). He parted ways with Gilbreth and other industrial psychologists.

91. Barley and Kunda, "Design and devotion," 374–75.

92. Howell John Harris, *The Right to Manage: Industrial Relations Policies of American Business in the 1940s* (Madison: University of Wisconsin, 1982).

93. Oliver E. Williamson, *Markets and Hierarchies, Analysis and Anti-trust Implication: A Study in the Economics of Internal Organization* (New York: Free, 1975), 74–75.

94. Cox, "The legal nature of collective bargaining agreements," 22.

95. Ibid.

96. See Williamson, Wachter, and Harris, "Understanding the employment relation," 4. Also see John Dunlop, Clark Kerr, Richard Lester, and Lloyd Reynolds, *How Labor Markets Work: Reflections on Theory and Practice*, Bruce E. Kaufman, ed. (Lexington, Mass.: Lexington, 1988). This became known as the internal labor market literature introduced by Peter B. Doeringer and Michael Piore, *Internal Labor Markets and Manpower Analysis* (Lexington, Mass.: Heath, 1971), which relies on institutional literature for the purpose of identifying the structural elements associated with internal labor markets.

97. Marc Granovetter, "Economic action and social structure: The problem of embeddedness," *American Journal of Sociology* 91 (1985), 481–510; and Oliver E. Williamson, *The Economic Institutions of Capitalism: Firms, Markets, Relational Contracting* (New York: Free, 1985), 66–67.

98. Williamson, *Markets and Hierarchies*, 71.

99. Ibid., 81.

100. Williamson, *Markets and Hierarchies*, 74; Williamson, Wachter, Harris, "Understanding the employment relation," 273.

101. Kalleberg and Reve, "Contracts and commitment: economic and sociological perspectives on employment relations."

102. Williamson, *Markets and Hierarchies*, 73.
103. Ibid., 73–74.
104. Ibid.
105. Williamson, Wachter, and Harris, "Understanding the employment relation: The analysis of idiosyncratic exchange," 268.
106. Williamson, *The Economic Institutions of Capitalism*, 218.
107. Michael Burawoy, *Manufacturing Consent: Changes in the Labor Process under Monopoly Capitalism* (Chicago: University of Chicago, 1979).
108. Richard Edwards, *Contested Terrain: The Transformation of the Workplace in the Twentieth Century* (New York: Basic, 1979).
109. David M. Gordon, *Fat and Mean: The Corporate Squeeze of Working Americans and the Myth of Managerial "Downsizing"* (New York: Martin Kessler, 1996), 41.
110. Ibid., 35.
111. Ibid., 40, 66.
112. Harry Braverman, *Labor and Monopoly Capital* (New York: Monthly Review, 1974).
113. Ibid. Bell used the same data as Braverman had, but he came to different, more optimistic conclusions.
114. Braverman, *Labor and Monopoly Capital*, 52–53.
115. Gordon, *Fat and Mean*.
116. Mark Wardell, "Introduction" in *Rethinking the Labor Process*, Mark Wardell, Thomas L. Steiger, and Peter Meiksins, eds. (Buffalo: SUNY, 1999), 1–3.
117. Peter B. Webb and Harold L. Bryant, "The challenge of *kaizen* technology for American business competition," *Journal of Organizational Change* 6 (1993), 10–11.
118. Cited from "The Financial Page: The Cultural Excuse," *The New Yorker* (January 27, 2003), 31.

## Chapter 5: Unmasking Control

1. Max Weber, *The Theory of Social and Economic Organization* (New York: Free, 1947).
2. Friedrich A. Hayek, *Full Employment at Any Price?* (London: Institute of Economic Affairs, 1975).
3. Anthony King, "Legitimating post-Fordism: A critique of Anthony Giddens' later work," *Telos* 115 (1999), 61–78.
4. Ibid.
5. Jean Baudrillard, *The Mirror of Production* (St. Louis: Telos, 1975).
6. See Philip Hancock, "Baudrillard and the metaphysics of motivation: A reappraisal of corporate culturalism in the light of the work and ideas of Jean Baudrillard," *Journal of Management Studies* 36 (1999), 166.
7. Brian Massumi, *A User's Guide to Capitalism and Schizophrenia: Deviations from Deleuze and Guattari* (Cambridge: MIT, 1999), 129–31.
8. Ibid., 131.
9. Nick Land, "Machine desire" in *Textual Practice* 7 (1993), 479. One company is trying to patent the human genome. See Massumi, *A User's Guide to Capitalism and Schizophrenia*, 133.
10. Massumi, *A User's Guide to Capitalism and Schizophrenia*, 138–39.
11. Ibid., 137.
12. Ibid., 127.
13. See Peter F. Drucker, *The Practice of Management* (New York: Perennial, 1986, c. 1954); and Charles Handy, *Gods of Management: The Changing Work of Organizations* (New York: Oxford University, 1995).
14. See Manuel Castells, *The Rise of the Network Society* (Cambridge, Mass.: Blackwell, 1996).
15. Terence Turner, "Bodies and anti-bodies: Flesh and fetish in contemporary social theory" in *Embodiment and Experience*, Thomas Csordas, ed. (Cambridge: Cambridge University, 1994), 27.
16. Hancock, "Baudrillard and the metaphysics of motivation," 156.
17. Ibid.

18. See Hancock, "Baudrillard and the metaphysics of motivation," 156–57; and Frederick Winslow Taylor, *The Principles of Scientific Management* (New York: Harper & Bros., 1915), 233.
19. Hancock, "Baudrillard and the metaphysics of motivation," 160–64.
20. Ibid., 160.
21. Beverly H. Burris, "Braverman, Taylorism, and technocracy" in *Rethinking the Labor Process*, Mark Wardell, Thomas L. Steiger, and Peter Meiksins, eds. (Buffalo: SUNY, 1999), 44.
22. Leslie A. Perlow, "Boundary control: The social ordering of work and family time in a high-tech corporation," *Administrative Science Quarterly* 43 (1998), 330; and Mark Wardell, "Introduction" in *Rethinking the Labor Process*, Mark Wardell, Thomas L. Steiger, and Peter Meiksins, eds. (Buffalo: SUNY, 1999), 1.
23. Robert Reich, *The Work of Nations: Preparing Ourselves for 21st-Century Capitalism* (New York: Knopf, 1990).
24. Perlow, "Boundary control," 330–31.
25. Jeremy Rifkin, *The End of Work: The Decline of the Global Labor Force and the Dawn of the Post-Market Era* (New York: G. P. Putnam's Sons, 1996), 6.
26. James Rinehart, "Transcending Taylorism and Fordism? Three decades of work restructuring" in *The Critical Study of Work: Labor, Technology, and Global Production*, Rick Baldoz, Charles Koeber, and Philip Kraft, eds. (Philadelphia: Temple University, 2001), 185.
27. Francis Wilson, "Cultural control within the virtual organization," *Sociological Review* 47 (1999), 675.
28. Quoted from Wilson, "Cultural control within the virtual organization," 682.
29. John Micklethwait and Adrian Wooldridge, *The Witch Doctors* (London: Heinemann, 1996), 32.
30. Rinehart, "Transcending Taylorism and Fordism?," 186–88.
31. Wilson, "Cultural control within the virtual organization," 672.
32. Ibid., 673.
33. Wilson, "Cultural control within the virtual organization," 685, who cites D. L. Jacobs, "The perils of policing employees," *Small Business Reports* 19 (1994), 22–26.
34. Gene Bylinsky, "How companies spy on employees," *Fortune* (November 4, 1991), 131.
35. Philip Kraft, "To control and inspire: U.S. management in the age of computer information systems and global production" in *Rethinking the Labor Process*, Mark Wardell, Thomas L. Steiger, and Peter Meiksins, eds. (Buffalo: SUNY, 1999).
36. Barbara Garson, *The Electronic Sweatshop* (New York: Penguin, 1988).
37. Wilson, "Cultural control within the virtual organization," 680.
38. Kraft, "To control and inspire," 18.
39. See Peter Blackman and Barbara Franklin, "Blocking big brother: Proposed law limits employers' right to snoop," *New York Law Journal* (August 19, 1993), 5.
40. See Peter T. Kilborn, "Workers using computers find a supervisor inside," *New York Times* December 23, 1990, N1.
41. Secretary-Treasurer of Committee on Labor Relations of New York County Lawyers Association quoted in S. Elizabeth Wilborn, "Revisiting the public/private distinction: Employee monitoring in the workplace," *Georgia Law Review* 32 (1998), 825, footnote 217.
42. See Ron Sakolosky, "'Disciplinary power' and the labour process" in *Skill and Consent: Contemporary Studies in the Labour Process*, Andrew Sturdy, David Knights, and Hugh Willmott, eds. (London: Routledge, 1992), 235; Stewart Clegg, "Power relations and the constitution of the resistant subject" in *Resistance and Power in Organizations*, John M. Jermier, David Knights, and Walter Nord, eds. (London: Routledge, 1994), 275.
43. While the interests of capitalists and the proletariat were antithetical, Marx believed that both classes suffered from "false consciousness." Nonetheless, it was the proletariat who would benefit more than the capitalists from a revolution (the latter of whom in neo-Hegelian terms lost some of their humanity by cultivating this consciousness). See David McLellan, *Selected Writings/Karl Marx* (New York: Oxford University, 2000), chapter 19.
44. See Sakolosky, "'Disciplinary power' and the labour process," 235; Clegg, "Power relations and the constitution of the resistant subject," 275.

45. Randy Hodson, "Good jobs and bad management: How new problems evoke old solutions in high-tech settings" in *Sociological and Economic Approaches to Labor Markets*, Paula England and George Farkas, eds. (New York: Plenum, 1988).

46. John M. Jermier, David Knights, and Walter Nord, "Introduction" in *Resistance and Power in Organizations*, John M. Jermier, David Knights, and Walter Nord, eds. (London: Routledge, 1994), 8.

47. See Nickolas Rose, *Governing the Soul: The Shaping of the Private Life* (London: Routledge, 1989).

48. See Michael Burawoy, *Manufacturing Consent: Changes in the Labor Process under Monopoly Capitalism* (Chicago: University of Chicago, 1979), 27–30. Worker consent, Burawoy argues, "is expressed through, and is the result of, the organization of activities."

49. See Paul Thompson and Stephen Ackroyd, "All quiet on the workplace front? A critique of recent trends in British industrial sociology," *Sociology* 29 (1995), 615–35.

50. Sakolosky, "'Disciplinary power' and the labour process," 249.

51. This is not to say that the subject has no agency. As political scientist Neve Gordon writes, Foucault creates "a balance between agency and structure, activity as passivity." See Neve Gordon, "Foucault's subject: An ontological reading," *Polity* 31 (1999), 396. Also see Clegg, "Power relations and the constitution of the resistant subject," 278.

52. Clegg, "Power relations and the constitution of the resistant subject," 278.

53. Ibid.

54. Michel Foucault, *Foucault Live* (New York: Semiotext(e), 1989), 188.

55. Sakolosky, "'Disciplinary power' and the labour process," 236, quoting Michel Foucault, *Discipline and Punish: The Birth of the Prison*, A. M. Sheridan, trans. (New York: Vintage, 1977); Richard Edwards, *Contested Terrain: The Transformation of the Workplace in the Twentieth Century* (New York: Basic, 1979), 237.

56. Clegg, "Power relations and the constitution of the resistant subject," 299–301.

57. Felix Driver, "Bodies in space: Foucault's account of disciplinary power" in *Power, Medicine, and the Body*, Colin Powers and Roy Porter, eds. (London: Routledge, 1994), 113.

58. See Brent L. Pickett, "Foucault and the politics of resistance," *Polity* 28 (1996), 461, for a good overview.

59. David Knights and Theo Vurdubakis, "Foucault, power, resistance and all that" in *Resistance and Power in Organizations*, John M. Jermier, David Knights, and Walter Nord, eds. (London: Routledge, 1994), 172–73.

60. William G. Ouchi, *Theory Z: How American Business Can Meet the Japanese Challenge* (Reading, Mass.: Addison-Wesley, 1981); William G. Ouchi, "Markets, bureaucracies, and clans," *Administrative Science Quarterly* 25 (1980), 129–41; and Terrence E. Deal and Allan A. Kennedy, *Corporate Cultures: The Rites and Rituals of Corporate Life* (Reading, Mass.: Addison-Wesley, 1982). Also see Thomas J. Peters and Robert H. Waterman, *In Search of Excellence: Lessons from America's Best-Run Companies* (New York: Harper & Row, 1982).

61. Stephen R. Barley and Gideon Kunda, "Design and devotion: Surges of rational and normative ideologies of control in managerial discourse," *Administrative Science Quarterly* 37 (1992), 381–82.

62. Deal and Kennedy, *Corporate Cultures*, 15. Other revisionist treatments of Braverman are Andrew L. Friedman, *Industry and Labour: Class Struggle at Work and Monopoly Capitalism* (London: McMillan, 1977); and Burawoy, *Manufacturing Consent*.

63. J. Richard Hackman and Ruth Wageman, "Total quality management: Empirical, conceptual, and practical issues," *Administrative Science Quarterly* 40 (1995), 310–11.

64. Ibid.

65. Ibid.

66. Barley and Kunda, "Design and devotion," 381–82.

67. Ibid., 364.

68. Yet, not all management experts agree that total quality control management or any other participatory human resource program were representative of the American workplace in comparison to Swedish socio-technical systems, Japanese lean production, Italian flexible specialization, and German diversified quality production. While these practices were used in Xerox, Saturn, and Fed Ex, they constituted the exception rather than the rule. See Ruth Milkman, Review of Eileen Appelbaum and Rosemary Batt, *The New American Workplace:*

*Transforming Work Systems in the United States* (Ithaca: ILR Press, 1994) in *Administrative Studies Quarterly* 39 (1994), 679.

69. Rosen and Baroudi, "Computer-based technology and the emergence of new forms of managerial control," 217.

70. Hackman and Wageman, "Total quality management," 309.

71. Wilson, "Cultural control within the virtual organization," 674, quoting Henry J. Johansson et al., *Business Process Reengineering: Breakpoint Strategies for Market Dominance* (Chichester, U.K.: Wiley, 1993).

72. See Masaaki Imai, *Kaisen* (New York: Random House Business Division, 1986).

73. Peter B. Webb and Harold L. Bryant, "The challenge of *kaizen* technology for American business competition," *Journal of Organizational Change* 6 (1993), 10.

74. See Webb and Bryant, "The challenge of *kaizen* technology for American business competition," 10. Also see Lester Thurow, "A weakness in process technology," *Science* 238 (December 18 1987), 1661.

75. Ibid., 9.

76. The management expert Peter Drucker created a blueprint of a postmodern factory in 1999 that incorporated statistical quality control techniques as one of its managerial practices. See Peter F. Drucker, "The emerging theory of manufacturing," *Harvard Business Review* 90 (1990), 94.

77. See Fess B. Green and Victor B. Wayhan, "Reengineering: clarifying the confusion," *SAM Advanced Management Journal* 61 (1996), 37. Another classic is Michael Hammer, "Reengineering work: Don't automate, obliterate," *Harvard Business Review* 90 (July–August 1990), 104–12. Quoting Michael Hammer and James Champy, *Reengineering The Corporation: A Manifesto for Business Revolution* (New York: Harper Business, 1993).

78. Wilson, "Cultural control within the virtual organization," 674.

79. W. Edwards Deming, *Out of the Crisis* (Cambridge: MIT, Center for Advanced Engineering Study, 1992); and W. Edwards Deming, *Some Theory of Sampling* (New York: Dover, 1950). Deming, who was one of the new gurus of TQM, was a statistician. He developed fourteen points about reengineering. Also see *The 14 Points* [video-recording] featuring Deming (Chicago, Films Incorporated, 1992).

80. John Wheatcroft, "Organizational change, the story so far," *Industrial Management & Data Systems* 100 (2000), 6. Wheatcroft is quoting David Kearns, The Chief Executive officer of Xerox.

81. Ibid., 7.

82. Frank Webster and Kevin Robins, "I'll be watching you: Comment on Sewell and Wilkinson," *Sociology* 27 (1993), 243.

83. Ibid., 244. Also see Kevin Robins and Frank Webster, "The revolution of the fixed wheel: Information, technology and social Taylorism" in *Television in Transition*, Phillip Drummond and Richard Paterson, eds. (London: British Film Institute, 1985).

84. Terry Austrin, "Positioning resistance and resisting position: human resource management and the politics of appraisal and grievance hearings" in *Resistance and Power in Organizations*, John M. Jermier, David Knights, and Walter R. Nord, eds. (London: Routledge, 1994).

85. Sakolosky, "'Disciplinary power' and the labour process," 241.

86. Michael Rosen and Jack Baroudi, "Computer-based technology and the emergence of new forms of managerial control" in *Skill and Consent: Contemporary Studies in the Labor Process*, Andrew Sturdy, David Knights, and Hugh Willmott, eds. (London: Routledge, 1992), 224–26.

87. Wilson, "Cultural control within the virtual organization," 675.

88. Webster and Robins, "I'll be watching you," 254–55. Also see Anthony Giddens, *Modernity and Self-Identity: Self and Society in the Late Modern Age* (Stanford: Stanford University, 1991); and Geoff Mulgan, *Communications and Control: Networks and the New Economies of Communication* (New York: Guilford, 1991).

89. Management does not trying shifting every employee. Only those employees who have highly productive work habits are sought after. See Austrin, "Positioning resistance and resisting position," 202.

90. Rosen and Baroudi, "Computer-based technology and the emergence of new forms of managerial control," 224.

91. Robins and Webster, "I'll be watching you," 255.

92. Jean-Paul de Gaudemar, *L'Ordre et la Production: Naissance et Formes de la Discipline d'Usine* (Paris: Dunod, 1982). This idea was popularized, however, by Shoshana Zuboff, *In the Age of the Smart Machine: The Future of Work and Power* (New York: Basic, 1988) chapter 9.

93. Foucault, *Discipline and Punish*, 200–28.

94. Webster and Robins, "I'll be watching you," 243.

95. Zuboff, *In the Age of the Smart Machine*, 322.

96. Robins and Webster, "'The revolution of the fixed wheel;'" and "Cybernetic capitalism: information, technology, everyday life" in *The Political Economy of the Information Industry*, Vincent Mosco and Janet Wasko, eds. (London: MacMillian, 1988) were much more pessimistic than Zuboff, who ironically had an optimistic message.

97. Graham Sewell, "The discipline of teams: The control team-based industrial work through electronic and peer surveillance," *Administrative Science Quarterly* 43 (1998), 403.

98. Ibid.

99. Alan McKinlay and Phil Taylor, "Power surveillance and resistance: Inside the 'factory of the future'" in *The New Workplace and Trade Unionism*, Peter Ackers, Chris Smith, and Paul Smith, eds. (London: Routledge, 1996), 279. See also Rosen and Barudi, "Computer-based technology and the emergence of new forms of managerial control," 224.

100. Harley Shaiken, *Work Transformed: Automation and Labor in the Computer Age* (New York: Holt, Rinehart, and Winston, 1984).

101. See Kraft, "To control and inspire," 17–36. Also see James B. Rule, *Private Lives and Public Surveillance: Social Control in the Computer Age* (New York: Schocken, 1974).

102. See Kraft, "To control and inspire," 18.

103. Thompson and Ackroyd argue, however, that this position can lead to an obsessive focus on the effectiveness of systems of surveillance at the expense of the traditional issues of labor process theory, such as the underlying reasons for increased control and the ways in which it might be resisted. Paul Thompson and Stephen Ackroyd, "All Quiet on the Workplace Front? A critique of recent trends in British industrial sociology," *Sociology* 29 (1995), 615–33.

104. Brett M. Wright and James R. Barker, "Assessing concertive control in the team environment," *Journal of Occupational and Organizational Psychology* 73 (2000), 245; See also Webster and Robins, "I'll be watching you?" 243; Philip Garrahan and Paul Stewart, *The Nissan Enigma* (London: Mansell, 1992); and James R. Barker, "Tightening the iron cage: Concertive control in self-managing teams," *Administrative Science Quarterly* 38 (1993), 408–37.

105. Zuboff, *In the Age of the Smart Machine*, 324.

106. Graham Sewell, "The disciple of teams: The control team-based industrial work through electronic and peer surveillance," *Administrative Science Quarterly* 43 (1998), 411.

107. Graham Sewell and Barry Wilkinson, "Empowerment or emasculation? Shopfloor surveillance in a total quality organization" in *Reassessing Human Resource Management*, Paul Blyton and Peter Turnbull, eds. (London: Sage, 1992), 103–110.

108. Test results were relayed to a central inventory control database and, by referring to the batch number, the source of the error could be traced to a particular individual instantaneously.

109. Graham Sewell and Barry Wilkinson, "Empowerment or emasculation? Shopfloor surveillance in a total quality organization" in *Reassessing Human Resource Management*, Paul Plyton and Peter Turnbull, eds. (London: Sage, 1992), 103–110.

110. Kay employee quoted in Sewell and Wilkinson, "Empowerment or emasculation? Shopfloor surveillance in a total quality organisation," 110.

111. Nissan created another mechanism for team surveillance and concertive control called a neighborhood check system. See Wilson, "Cultural control within the virtual organization," 684–85.

112. Pickett, "Foucault and the politics of resistance," 461.

113. David Knights and Theo Vurdubakis, "Foucault, power, resistance and all that" in *Resistance and Power in Organizations*, John M. Jermier, David Knights, and Walter R. Nord, eds. (London: Routledge, 1994), 175.
114. Jermier, Knights, and Nord, "Introduction," 16.
115. Michel Foucault, *The Will to Know: Volume One of the History of Sexuality*, Robert Hurley, trans. (New York: Vintage/Random House, 1980), 95.
116. Pickett, "Foucault and the politics of resistance," 463–64.
117. Knights and Vurdubakis, "Foucault, power, resistance and all that," 177–79.
118. Foucault, *The Will to Know*, 219.
119. Pickett, "Foucault and the politics of resistance," 459.
120. Ibid., 453, 458.
121. The theorists Frederic Jameson, Jean Baudrillard, and Gilles Deleuze have all highlighted how Foucault's notion of resistance and the idea of the saboteur demonstrates the "strong strain of anti-statism, libertarianism or anarchism" in his writing. See Rick Fantasia, *Cultures of Solidarity: Consciousness, Action, and Contemporary American Worker* (Berkeley: University of California, 1988).
122. Danny LaNuez and John M. Jermier, "Sabotage by managers and technocrats: neglected patterns of resistance at work" in *Resistance and Power in Organizations*, John M. Jermier, David Knights, and Walter R. Nord, eds. (London: Routledge, 1994), 221.
123. Graham Sewell, "The discipline of teams," 400.
124. David L. Collinson, "Strategies of resistance: Power, knowledge and subjectivity in the workplace" in *Resistance and Power in Organizations*, John M. Jermier, David Knights, and Walter R. Nord, eds. (London: Routledge, 1994), 33.
125. Peter Fleming and Graham Sewell, "Looking for the good soldier, Svejk: Alternative modalities of resistance in the contemporary workplace," *Sociology* 36 (2002), 858.
126. Ibid. Some of the authors Fleming and Sewell criticize for being too pessimistic that this book relies on are James R. Barker, "Tightening the iron cage: Concertive control in self-managing teams," *Administrative Science Quarterly* 38 (1993): 408–37; and Gideon Kunda, *Engineering Culture: Control and Commitment in a High-Tech Corporation* (Philadelphia: Temple, 1992).
127. Ibid., 857.
128. Ibid., 861–62, 867–68.
129. James Scott, *Weapons of the Weak: Everyday Forms of Peasant Resistance* (New Haven: Yale University, 1985).
130. Collinson, "Strategies of resistance," 25.
131. Ibid., 50.
132. Peter Ackers and John Black, "Watching the detectives: Shop stewards' expectations of their managers in the age of human resource management" in *Skill and Consent: Contemporary Studies in the Labour Process*, Andrew Sturdy, David Knights, and Hugh Willmott, eds. (London: Routledge, 1992), 186.
133. Whistle-blowing follows a different pattern, however, since the whistle-blowers themselves are usually loyal employees who try to stop specific abuses. Having blown the whistle because these typically hardworking employees had faith that the business or company would seek reform, they become disillusioned when it doesn't. Whistle-blowers realize what some of their colleagues already understood—that the business or company had operated like this all along. To succeed, whistle-blowers need not bother convincing their employers, but rather their fellow employees that reform is imperative. See Joyce Rothschild and Terence D. Miethe, "Whistle blowing as resistance in modern work organizations: the politics of revealing organizational deception and abuse" in *Resistance and Power in Organizations*, John M. Jermier, David Knights, and Walter R. Nord, eds. (London: Routledge, 1994); and Jermier, Knights, and Nord, "Introduction," 20.
134. Another form of resistance takes the form of co-opting inspectors. Surveillance can be evaded if a damaged piece in a factory, for instance, can be attributed not to the employee's error, but a faulty part. Supervisors will help out new workers by explaining this means of accounting for errors. See Webb and Palmer, "Evading surveillance and making time: an ethnographic view of the Japanese factory floor in Britain," 618.

135. Labor process theory studies have been comparatively silent about a theory of resistance. Knights and Vurdubakis, "Foucault, power, resistance and all that." Also see Stanley Aronowitz, "Marx, Braverman, and the logic of capital," *Insurgent Sociologist* 8 (1978), 126–46; and Edwards, *Contested Terrain.*
136. Zuboff, *In the Age of the Smart Machine,* 354.
137. Collinson, "Strategies of resistance," 34.
138. Webb and Palmer, "Evading surveillance and making time," 612.
139. Collinson, "Strategies of resistance," 35.
140. See Fleming and Sewell, "Looking for the good soldier, Svejk," 865.
141. Ibid.
142. Ibid., 866.
143. See Ron A. DiBattista, "Forecasting sabotage events in the workplace," *Public Personnel Management* 25 (1996), 41; and Shari Caudron, "Fighting the enemy within," *IW* (September 4, 1995), 36–38.
144. Prasad and Prasad, "Stretching the iron cage," 396–97.
145. Ibid., 398.
146. Ibid., 395.
147. Ibid.
148. Ibid., 394–95.
149. Victor Turner, "Betwixt and between: The liminal period in rites de passage" in Victor Turner, *The Forest of Symbols: Aspects of Ndembu Ritual* (Ithaca: Cornell University, 1967). For a good overview of liminality see Graham St. John, "Alternative cultural heterotopic and the liminoid body: Beyond Turner at ConFest," *Australian Journal of Anthropology* 12 (2001), 47–68. He argues that Turner is essentialist.
150. Rosemarie Garland-Thomson, *Extraordinary Bodies: Figuring Physical Disability in American Culture and Literature* (New York: Columbia University, 1997), 22.
151. Also, the federal courts have ruled that if this move interferes with the office's seniority system and there are no special circumstances justifying a departure, an employer could let him go. The statute, however, had provided for this. See *U.S. Airways v. Barnett,* 535 U.S. 391 (2002) where the Supreme Court gave a limited perspective on what type of reassignment could be viewed as a reasonable accommodation.
152. Louise Lamphere, "Bringing the family to work: Women's culture on the shop floor," *Feminist Studies* 11 (1985), 521.
153. Ibid.
154. See Louise Lamphere, *Structuring Diversity: Ethnographic Perspectives on the New Immigration* (Chicago: University of Chicago, 1992).
155. Lamphere, "Bringing the family to work," 529.
156. Ibid., 523.
157. See Susan Ellen Bindler, "Peek and spy: A proposal for federal regulation of electronic monitoring in the workplace," *Washington University Law Quarterly* 70 (1992), 853.
158. S. Elizabeth Wilborn, "Revisiting the public/private distinction: employee monitoring in the workplace," *Georgia Law Review* 32, (1998), 825.
159. Supreme Court cases such as *National Treasury Employees Union v. Von Raab,* 514 U.S. 1029 (1994); and *Skinner v. Railway Labor Executives' Association,* 489 U.S. 602 (1989) have allowed privacy intrusions under the constitutional standards when the government demonstrated the appropriate countervailing interests. Also see *Epps v. St. Mary's Hosp., Inc.,* 802 F. 2d 412 (11th cir. 1986); *Thomas v. G. E. Co.* 207 F. Supp. 792 (W.D. Ky 1962); and *Jackson v. Nationwide Credit, Inc.,* 426 S.E. 2d 630 (Ga. Ct. App. 1992). Also see Erwin Chemerinsky, "Rethinking state action," *Northwestern University Law Review* 80 (1985), 503; Jennifer Friesen, "Shouldn't California's constitutional guarantees of individual rights apply against private actors," *Hastings Constitutional Law Quarterly* 17, (1989), 111; Scott E. Sundby, "Is abandoning state action asking too much of the constitution?" *Hastings Constitutional Law Quarterly* 17, (1989) 139; and Steven Winters, "The new privacy interest: Electronic mail in the workplace," *High Technology Law Journal* 8, (1993), 197.
160. See Lani Guinier and Gerald Torres, *The Miner's Canary: Enlisting Race, Resisting Power, Transforming Democracy* (Cambridge: Harvard University, 2002).
161. Garland-Thomson, *Extraordinary Bodies,* 46.

162. Ibid., 19.
163. Douglas Baynton notes that historians have not overlooked the fact that women have been associated with disability as a means to keep them disenfranchised. Nonetheless, he observes that different women's movements themselves have not disputed this connection. "Suffragists rarely challenged the notion that disability justified political inequality and instead disputed the claim that women suffered from these disabilities." See Douglas C. Baynton, "Disability and the justification of inequality in American history" in *The New Disability History: American Perspectives*, Paul K. Longmore and Lauri Umansky, eds. (New York: New York University, 43).
164. Gatens and Lloyd, *Imaginings: Spinoza, Past and Present*, 13.
165. Ibid., 102.

## Chapter 6: Unions: Bridging the Divide

1. Quoted from Sidney Lens, *Radicalism in America* (New York: Apollo Edition, 1969), 130.
2. Howell John Harris, *The Right to Manage: Industrial Relations Policies of American Business in the 1940s* (Madison: University of Wisconsin, 1982).
3. Christopher May, "The political economy of proximity: Intellectual property and the global division of information labour," *New Political Economy* 7 (2002), 319.
4. Michael D. Yates, "The 'new' economy and the labor movement," *Monthly Review* 121 (April 2001), 34.
5. Fourth Part, Proposition 34 in *Spinoza's Ethics*, ed. with revised trans. G. H. R. Parkinson (London: J.M. Dent & Sons, 1989), 162.
6. Two-thirds of all accommodations cost nothing; the average accommodation costs $120. Seventy percent of all accommodations cost less than $500; and only 3 percent of accommodations cost more than $1,000. Jane Bennett Clark, "Does ADA work for disabled workers?" *Kiplinger's Personal Finance Magazine* 49 (1995), 141, cites the well-known study about Sears, Roebuck. Also see Charles Young, "The value of specifying what reasonable accommodations are expected from employers," *Journal of Visual Impairment & Blindness* 94 (2000), 46.
7. Marion Crain and Ken Matheny, "Labor's divided ranks: Privilege and the united front ideology," *Cornell Law Review* 84 (1999), 1570. For a good overviews of the theory of whiteness see Adrienne D. Davis, "Identity notes part one: Playing in the light," *American University Law Review* 45 (1996), 695; Jennifer M. Russell, "The race/class conundrum and the pursuit of individualism in the making of social policy," *Hastings Law Journal* 46 (1995), 1353; Ian F. Haney Lopez, "The social construction of race: Some observations on illusion, fabrication, and choice," *Harvard Civil Rights-Civil Liberties Law Review* 29 (1994), 1; and Cheryl I. Harris, "Whiteness as property," *Harvard Law Review* 105 (1993), 1707.
8. An excellent cultural analysis of whiteness overall can be found in Vron Ware and Les Back, *Out of Whiteness: Color, Politics, and Culture* (Chicago: University of Chicago, 2002), 15–20.
9. Marion Crain, "Colorblind unionism," *UCLA Law Review* 49 (2002), 1322–29.
10. Stephen Plass, "Dualism and overlooked class consciousness in American labor laws," *Houston Law Review* 37 (2000), 830.
11. Michael Goldfield, *The Color of Politics: Race, Class, and the Mainsprings of American Politics* (New York: New, 1997).
12. Quoted in David E. Bernstein, "Roots of the 'underclass': The decline of laissez-faire jurisprudence and the rise of racist labor legislation," *American University Law Review* 43 (1993), 92. Meanwhile, organized labor attacked African-Americans for being strikebreakers, thereby undermining the labor movement.
13. Ibid. Also see David R. Roediger, *The Wages of Whiteness: Race and the Making of the American Working Class* (London: Verso, 1991). For a good overview of whiteness in the legal literature see Ariela Gross, "Beyond black and white: Cultural approaches to race and slavery," *Columbia Law Review* 101 (2001), 640.
14. Bernstein, "Roots of the 'underclass,'" 87.
15. Plass, "Dualism and overlooked class consciousness in American labor laws," 834.

16. Plass, "Dualism and overlooked class consciousness in American labor laws," 830; and Bernstein, "Roots of the 'underclass,'" 91–92.

17. Crain, "Colorblind unionism," 1322. Also see Harvard Sitkoff, *A New Deal for Blacks: The Emergence of Civil Rights as a National Issue: The Depression Decade* (New York: Oxford University, 1978), 58, for the traditional view that the New Deal "began laying the foundations for the postwar advances in Civil Rights."

18. See historian Herbert G. Gutman, "The Negro and the United Mine Workers of America, the career and letters of Richard L. Davis and something of their meaning," in *The Negro and the American Labor Movement*, Julius Jacobson, ed. (Garden City, N.J.: Anchor, 1968). While Gutman started a new school of labor history, this is not to say all historians agreed with his interpretation of American labor. Most notably, historian Herbert Hill denounced Gutman's essay for not understanding "the crucial significance of race consciousness in determining working class behavior." Hill's attack on the "New Labor History" inspired a number of other historians to re-examine this type of history. See Herbert Hill, "Myth making as labor history: Herbert Gutman and the United Mine Workers of America," *International Journal of Politics, Culture, and Society* 2 (1989), 132–200; Steven Schulman, "Racism and the making of the American working class," *International Journal of Politics, Culture, and Society* 2 (1989), 361–66; Neil Irvin Painter, "The new labor history and the historical moment," 367–70; David Roediger, "What was so great about Herbert Gutman?," *Labour/Le Travail* 23 (1989), 25–61; and Lawrence T. McDonald, "'You are too sentimental,' problems and suggestions for a new labor history," *Journal of Social History* 18 (1984), 629–53. Sean Wilentz's prize-winning book, *Chants Democratic: New York City and the Rise of the American Working Class, 1788–1850* (New York: Oxford University, 1984) received some of the same criticism. Doing what E. P. Thompson did for the English working class, Wilentz wrote about the formation of the American working class. Yet he did so without raising the riots of white workers against blacks during the Civil War draft protest of 1863. For a defense of the new labor history, see Stephen Brier, "In defense of Gutman; the union's case," *International Journal of Politics, Culture, and Society* 2 (1988), 382–95.

19. Marion Crain, "Whitewashed labor law, skinwalking unions," *Berkeley Journal of Employment and International Labor Law* 23 (2002), 221.

20. See Roediger, *The Wages of Whiteness*, 13.

21. Crain, "Colorblind unionism," 221.

22. Also see Herbert Hill, *Black Labor and the American Legal System: Race, Work, and the Law* (Madison: University of Wisconsin, 1995), 162–69.

23. Crain and Matheny, "Labor's divided ranks," 1575–77. At the same time, some industrial relations experts acknowledge that both explanations may work since capital cannot be described as monolithic.

24. Ibid., 1575.

25. Crain and Matheny, "Labor's divided ranks," 1576. Also see Elizabeth M. Iglesias, "Structures of subordination: women of color at the intersection of Title VII and the NLRA, not!," *Harvard Civil Rights and Civil Liberties Law Review* 28 (1993), 395.

26. Crain and Matheny, "Labor's divided ranks," 1574.

27. See Heidi Hartmann, "Capitalism, patriarchy, and job segregation by sex" in *Women, Class, and the Feminist Imagination*, Karen V. Hanson and Ilene J. Philipson, eds. (Philadelphia: Temple University, 1990).

28. See Iris Marion Young, *Throwing Like a Girl and Other Essays in Feminist Philosophy and Social Theory* (Bloomington: Indiana University, 1990), 32–35.

29. Ibid.

30. See Crain and Matheny, "Labor's divided ranks," 1590; and Reva B. Siegal, "Home as work: The first women's rights claims concerning wives' household labor, 1850–1880," *Yale Law Journal* 103 (1994), 1073.

31. Insisting that women maintain their gendered employment roles also meant that employers could blunt resistance to managerial control. They simply had to encourage their employees to focus on the woman's gender identity. See Crain and Matheny, "Labor's divided ranks," 1590.

32. Marion Crain, "Between feminism and unionism: Working class women, sex equality, and labor speech," *Georgetown Law Journal* 82 (1994), 42.

33. Crain, "Between feminism and unionism," 1903; and Crain and Matheny, "Labor's divided ranks," 1582. Both exploitation and domination, they argue, benefit the white men in the labor movement. Whereas exploitation requires a causal relationship between the group benefiting and the group being taken advantage of, domination means that one group deprives another group of access to productive resources. Domination differs from exploitation in that oppression does not link the deprivation of one group with the other groups' gains. Employers and white male employees benefit from both exploitation and economic oppression.

34. Ruth O'Brien, *Workers' Paradox: The Republican Origins of New Deal Labor Policy* (Chapel Hill: University of North Carolina, 1998).

35. Ibid. The concept of majority rule gained significance between 1890 and 1925 with railroad unions and then was adopted in the National Labor Relations Act.

36. Crain and Matheny, "Labor's divided ranks," 1555.

37. Ruben J. Garcia, "New voices at work: Race and gender identity caucuses in the U.S. labor movement," 54 *Hastings Law Journal* 79 (2002), 122.

38. Crain, "Whitewashed labor law, skinwalking unions," 231.

39. *Sewell Mfg. Co.*, 138 NLRB 66 (1962). In the Sewell case, the employer circulated pictures of a white woman dancing with an unidentified black man and of a white man with a caption as the union president dancing with a black woman. The implication was that the union would seek to racially integrate the work force, a situation that many southerners found alarming. They implied "unionism is a foreign, communist concept with the end objective of racial intermarriage." The NLRB was concerned with the emotional power of appeal to prejudice, suggesting that "a deliberate appeal to such prejudice is not intended or calculated to encourage the reasoning faculty." However, the NLRB included a caveat, which said as long as "a party limits itself to truthfully setting forth another party's position on matters of racial interest and does not deliberately seek to overstress and exacerbate racial feelings by irrelevant and inflammatory appeals, we shall not set aside an election on this ground." See Crain, "Whitewashed labor law, skinwalking unions," 230–34; and Daniel H. Pollitt, "The NLRB and race hate propaganda in union organization drives," *Stanford Law Review* 17 (1965), 272.

40. Crain, "Whitewashed labor law, skinwalking unions," 230.

41. Ibid., 233.

42. See *Allen-Morrison Sign Co.*, 138 NLRB 73 (1962).

43. See *Carrington South Health Care Ctr, Inc. v. NLRB*, 76 F. 3d. 802 (6th cir. 1996). Also see Crain and Matheny, "Labor's divided ranks," 1562–65; and Roger B. Jacobs, "The duty of fair representation: minorities, dissidents and exclusive representation," *Boston University Law Review* 59 (1979), 857. The one provision that protects people of color—the duty of fair representation (DFR)—is largely seen as a failure and has even backfired. Placing a union in a fiduciary-like relationship with workers, the Supreme Court has ruled that organized labor has a duty of fair representation that obligates it to represent all employees, not just the majority. First, in *Steele v. Louisville & Nashville Railroad Co.*, 323 U.S. 192 (1944) involving the Railway Labor Act and racial discrimination, the union negotiated an agreement designed to give the most desirable jobs only to whites. The Court noted that Congress conferred on bargaining representatives "powers comparable to those possessed by a legislative body both to create and restrict the rights of those whom it represents." Yet many studies show that plaintiffs have rarely prevailed with DFR claims against their unions. In *Vaca v. Sipes*, 386 U.S. 171 (1967), the Supreme Court established the standard for assessing whether a union's grievance handling procedure violates the DFR. DFR, most commentators note, is a vague principle. Some commentators argue that unions should have the same duty as a legislature with constitutional requirements of due process and equal protection. Other commentators note that due process standards used by administrative agencies should be replicated.

44. Garcia, "Other voices," 124–27. See *Emporium Capwell Co. v. Western Addition Community Organization*, 420 U.S. 50 (1975). The case referred to Section 7 of the NLRA and Title VII of the Civil Rights Act. The African-Americans had grown dissatisfied with the pace of promotions and hiring for African American employees and presented a list of grievances to

the union, which included the company's alleged race discrimination as the chief concern. Union officials reported to the company that there was a possibility of race discrimination and that "explosive" events could occur if the company did not take action. Emporium Capwell promised to look into the matter. The union called a meeting with the company officials, the California Fair Employment Practices Commission, and a local antipoverty agency. When the African-American employees were unhappy with the progress, they met with the company themselves.

45. Garcia, "Other voices," 127, 129.
46. Garcia, "New voices at work," 88.
47. Garcia, "New voices at work," 84–85, 94–95, 99–100. Although the AFL-CIO encouraged its locals and its central labor councils to cultivate the identity groups like the CBTU that emerged, there was little discussion of exactly what role these groups should play within unions themselves. With a few exceptions, most of the caucus activity centered not on demands for separate bargaining or all African-American unions, but instead on multiracial activity seeking to change the structure of union governance.
48. For example, the EEOC settled *EEOC v. Mitsubishi Motor Manufacturing of America, Inc.* In 1996, this was the largest class action sexual harassment suit—500 of 893 women in the plant suffered sexual harassment—that the EEOC had ever filed. Mitsubishi agreed to pay 300 to 400 women $34 million. It should also be noted that the union had proposed the Equal Application Agreement during bargaining, but Mitsubishi refused it. See Kim Moody, "Sexual harassment at Mitsubishi: Where was the union?" *Labor Notes* 5 (1996), 1; and Garcia, "New voices at work," 81–82.
49. Garcia, "Other voices," 124.
50. Crain and Matheny, "Labor's divided ranks," 1620.
51. Mathew W. Finkin, "The road not taken: Some thoughts on nonmajority employee representation," *Chicago-Kent Law Review* 69 (1993), 195.
52. Crain and Matheny, "Labor's divided ranks," 1619.
53. Crain, "Whitewashed labor law, skinwalking unions," 257–58.
54. Ibid., 213–14.
55. Garcia, "New voices at work," 84
56. Crain, "Whitewashed labor law, skinwalking unions," 228.
57. Mark Engler, "Yes we can!," *New Internationalist* (November 2002), 351–52.
58. Crain, "Whitewashed labor law, skinwalking unions," 213.
59. Stephen F. Befort, "Labor and employment law at the millennium: A historical overview and a critical assessment," *Boston College Law Review* 43 (2002), 353, 357.
60. Michael C. Harper, "Defining the economic relationship appropriate for collective bargaining," *Boston College Law Review* 39 (1998), 329–32.
61. Befort, "Labor and employment law at the millennium," 373.
62. Ibid., 366–67. The service industry constitutes 12 percent and the professional industry is 18 percent of the work force. Although this figure is difficult to tabulate, labor-management experts believe it is as large as 20 to 30 percent of the work force.
63. Harper, "Defining the economic relationship appropriate for collective bargaining," 333–334. The Taft–Hartley Labor-Management Relations Act was an anti-labor piece of legislation sponsored by the Republicans after World War II. This legislation gave employers the right to exclude contingent workers from the collective bargaining process. The logic underlying the exclusion of this type of worker was shored up by the legal doctrine, the "right to control," and also by the common law distinction on whether the purported employer controls or has the right to control both the result to be accomplished and the "manner and means" by which the purported employee brings about that result. It stemmed from tort law where a rational doctrine was formulated that made a distinction between a firm supervising employees and one with vicarious liability for the wrongs committed by those who may be advancing the firm's interests but were not directly employed. "A firm that surrenders the right to control how work is performed," ruled the Supreme Court, "is not in the best position to ensure that an appropriate level of care is taken to avoid wrongs." The right-to-control doctrine dictates that workers who make capital productive, yet are not supervised or controlled by employers, cannot be included in collective bargaining. Employers must have the capacity to supervise their workers given "the mischief to be

corrected and the end to be attained." In 1968, the Supreme Court upheld this in *NLRB v. United Insurance Co. of America*, 389 U.S. 1028 (1968), which distinguished between employees and independent contractors, thereby defining an employee.

64. Susan Bisom-Rapp, "Bulletproofing the workplace: Symbol and substance in the employment discrimination law practice," *Florida State University Law Review* 26 (1999), 986.
65. Crain, "Between feminism and unionism," 1956.
66. Crain and Matheny, "Labor's identity crisis," 1820; and Crain, "Between feminism and unionism," 1957.
67. Crain, "Whitewashed labor law, skinwalking unions," 213.
68. Crain and Matheny, "Labor's identity crisis," 1820.
69. Christopher May, "The political economy of proximity," *New Political Economy* 3 (2002), 319.
70. Ibid., 319, 325–27. Some information services are made routine such as the USA eLaw-Forum, an online auction site for legal services that drives down prices and increases competition in the long run.
71. On the one hand, law professor Katherine Stone envisions that the world's labor is in a "race to the bottom," as wages decrease and work conditions deteriorate. On the other hand, management historian Sanford Jacoby argues that long-term employment relations have suffered only a slight decrease under globalism. Internal labor markets, he adds, continue to represent the norm in the U.S. as well as other developed nations. See Katherine Van Wezel Stone, "The new psychological contract: Implications of the changing workplace for labor and employment law," *UCLA Law Review* 48 (2001), 519; and Sanford M. Jacoby, "Melting into air? Downsizing, job stability, and the future of work," *Chicago-Kent Law Review* 76 (2000), 1220–21.
72. Yates, "The 'new' economy and the labor movement," 29.
73. Garcia, "Other voices," 107–08, 112, 121.
74. Crain, "Whitewashed labor law, skinwalking unions," 215, 227.
75. Crain and Matheny, "Labor's divided ranks," 1542.
76. Yates, "The 'new' economy and the labor movement," 34–35.
77. Garcia, "Other voices," 118.
78. Befort, "Labor and employment law at the millennium," 380–81.
79. Age Discrimination in Employment Act, 29 U.S.C. Section 621, 1967; and Vocational Rehabilitation Act Section 791, 783, 794, 1973.
80. Befort, "Labor and employment law at the millennium," 408. Also, unions limit employee involvement plans (EIPs).
81. Julie Waters, "Does the battle over mandatory arbitration jeopardize the EEOC's war in fighting workplace discrimination?," *St. Louis Law Journal* 44 (2000), 1156.
82. Befort, "Labor and employment law at the millennium," 352.
83. Bisom-Rapp, "Bulletproofing the workplace: symbol and substance in the employment discrimination law practice," 969. Frank Dobbin analyzed data from 279 organizations after 1964.
84. Ibid., 971.
85. Ibid., 985.
86. Ibid., 965, 977, 979–80, 993, 1002, 1011. Courses like "Trends in Employment Litigation" show employers how to avoid lawsuits, though not by promoting employee rights.
87. Ibid., 976–75, 990. One practitioner said: "The single biggest advantage an employer has in employment discrimination litigation is control over the facts."
88. Ibid., 966.
89. Ibid., 969.
90. Ibid., 973.
91. Ibid., 974.
92. Ibid., 975.
93. Crain and Matheny, "Labor's identity crisis," 1801.
94. Katherine Van Wezel Stone, "Labor/employment law: Mandatory arbitration of individual employment rights: the yellow dog contract of the 1990s," *Denver University Law Review* 73 (1996), 1037.

95. For a good overview of how arbitration works and some of the main issues see Shalu Tandon Buckley, "Practical concerns regarding the arbitration of statutory employment claims: questions that remain unanswered after Gilmer and some suggested answers," *Ohio State Journal on Dispute Resolution* 11 (1996), 149; Ann C. Hodges, "Can compulsory arbitration be reconciled with Section 7 rights?" *Wake Forest Law Review* 37 (2003), 173; and Jordan L. Resnick, "Beyond *Mastrobuono*: A practitioners' guide to arbitration, employment disputes, punitive damages, and the implications of the Civil Rights Act of 1991," *Hofstra Law Review* 23 (1995), 913.

96. *Gilmer v. Interstate/Johnson Lane Corp.*, 500 U.S. 20 (1991).

97. Crain and Matheny, "Labor's identity crisis," 1803.

98. Matthew W. Finkin, "Employee representation outside the Labor Act: Thoughts on arbitral representation, group arbitration, and workplace committees," *University of Pennsylvania Journal of Labor & Employment* 5 (2002), 77–78.

99. Jesse Rudy, "What they don't know won't hurt them: Defending employment at will in light of findings that employees believe they possess just cause protection," *Berkeley Journal of Employment & Labor* 23 (2002), 311–12.

100. Steven Greenhouse, "Bill Offers Option of Compensatory Time," *New York Times*, May 10, 2003, A15.

101. Finkin, "Employee representation outside the Labor Act," 81.

102. See Ruth O'Brien "'A sweatshop of the whole nation': The Fair Labor Standards Act and the failure of regulatory unionism," *Studies in American Political Development* 15 (2001), 33–52.

103. See Ruth O'Brien, "Duality and division: The development of American labor policy from the Wagner Act to the Civil Rights Act," *International Contributions to Labor Studies* 4 (1994): 21–51.

104. See Molly S. McUsic and Michael Selmi, "Postmodern unions: Identity politics in the workplace," *Iowa Law Review* 82 (1997), 1371–72. Also see Michael Piore, *Beyond Individualism* (Cambridge: Harvard University, 1995) for a thorough, though critical, explanation of cosmopolitan unionism.

105. Michael Burawoy, *Manufacturing Consent: Changes in the Labor Process under Monopoly Capitalism* (Chicago: University of Chicago, 1979), 103.

106. Randy Hodson, "Individual voice on the shopfloor: The role of unions," *Social Forces* 75 (1997), 1184.

107. Ibid.

108. Befort, "Labor and employment law at the millennium," 360.

109. Harris, *The Right to Manage*.

110. Chester Barnard, *The Functions of the Executive* (New York: Cambridge University, 1962), 169.

111. See Oliver E. Williamson, *Markets and Hierarchies: Analysis and Antitrust Implications: A Study in the Economics of Internal Organization* (New York: Free, 1975), 81.

112. In addition to Williamson and Barnard, see Archibald Cox, who observed that the collective bargaining agreement "should be understood as an instrument of government as well as an instrument of exchange." Archibald Cox, "The legal nature of collective bargaining agreements," *Michigan Law Review* 57 (1958), 22.

113. Befort, "Labor and employment law at the millennium," 444. Two-thousand three-hundred workers in the "Worker Representation and Participation Survey" in Rogers's and Freeman's work showed that one-third of all employees would like the union form of employee representation.

## Chapter 7: Critical Care

1. Stephen Marglin, "What do bosses do? The origins and functions of hierarchy in capitalist production," *Review of Radical Political Economy* 6 (1974), 33.

2. The U.S. General Accounting Office reported that only 717 employers who were covered under the WARN Act out of 8,350 mass layoffs and plant closures in 2001, for instance, let employees know. See Margaret M. Clark, "Employers fail to give required notice in majority of mass layoffs and closures," *HR Magazine* 48 (2003), 34.

3. Doris Z. Fleischer and Frieda Zames, *The Disability Rights Movement: From Charity to Confrontation* (Philadelphia: Temple University, 2000); and Joseph P. Shapiro, *No Pity: People with Disabilities Forging a New Civil Rights Movement* (New York: Times Books, 1993).

4. *Olmstead v. L.C. by Zimring*, 527 U.S. 581 (1999), where the Supreme Court ruled that it would be discriminatory for a state not to release persons with disabilities from their institutional settings and into community-based treatment programs. Also see Ruth O'Brien, "Introduction," in *Voices from the Edge: Narratives about the Americans with Disabilities Act*, Ruth O'Brien, ed. (New York: Oxford University, 2003), 18–19.

5. See Rosemarie Garland-Thomson's books, *Freakery: Cultural Spectacles of the Extraordinary Body* (New York: New York University, 1996); *and Extraordinary Bodies: Figuring Physical Disability in American Culture and Literature* (New York: Columbia University, 1997).

6. See Rachel Adams, *Sideshow U.S.A.: Freaks and the American Cultural Imagination* (Chicago: University of Chicago, 2001). Also see Robert Bogdan, *Freak Show: Presenting Human Oddities for Amusement and Profit* (Chicago: University of Chicago, 1990).

7. Fiona Whittington-Walsh, "From freaks to savants: Disability and hegemony from *The Hunchback of Notre Dame* (1939) to *Sling Blade* (1997)," *Disability & Society* 17 (2002), 697.

8. Catherine J. Kudlick, "Disability history: Why we need another 'other,'" *American Historical Review* 108 (2003), 768.

9. "Bush" and "blind" and "deaf" yielded 64,800 Web sites on the Google search engine (visited on February 14, 2004). The description of Bush is taken from Ron Suskind, *The Price of Loyalty: George W. Bush, the White House, and the Education of Paul O'Neill* (New York: Simon & Schuster, 2004).

10. Quoted in Rosemarie Garland-Thomson, "Integrating disability, transforming feminist theory," *National Women's Studies Association Journal* 14 (2002), 6.

11. *City of Cleburne, Texas v. Cleburne Living Center, Inc.*, 473 U.S. 432 (1985), 442 and 446. Also see Ruth O'Brien, *Crippled Justice: The History of Modern Disability Policy* (Chicago: University of Chicago, 2001), 142; and Martha Minow, *Making All the Difference: Inclusion, Exclusion, and American Law* (Ithaca: Cornell University, 1990), 102. Even a disability studies expert maintains that "some forms of variation will always be associated with an irreducible negative." See Jackie Leach Scully, "Drawing lines, crossing lines: Ethics and the challenge of disabled embodiment," *Feminist Theology* 11 (2003), 270.

12. *Albertsons v. Kirkinburg*, 527 U.S. 555 (1999); *Murphy v. United Parcel Service*, 527 U.S. 516 (1999); *Board of Trustees of the University of Alabama v. Garrett*, 1531 U.S. 356 (2001); and *Toyota v. Williams*, 534 U.S. 184 (2002).

13. Richard B. Freeman and Joel Rogers, *What Workers Want* (Ithaca, N.Y.: Industrial Relations, 1999).

14. See *U.S. Airways v. Barnett*, 535 U.S. 391 (2002).

15. See Corinne Bendersky, "Organizational dispute resolution systems: A complementarities model," *Academy of Management Review* 23 (2003), 643–56.

16. Ibid., 650.

17. Randy Hodson, "Individual voice on the shopfloor: The role of unions," *Social Forces* 75 (1997), 1183.

18. Ibid., 1202.

19. Victor G. Deviatz, "Imagine that—a wildcat at Biomed! Organizational justice and the anatomy of a wildcat strike at a nonunion medical electronics factory," *Employee Responsibilities and Rights Journal* 15 (2003), 58.

20. Jane Bennett Clark, "Does ADA work for disabled workers?" *Kiplinger's Personal Finance Magazine* 49 (1995), 141, cites the well-known study about Sears, Roebuck. Also see Charles Young, "The value of specifying what reasonable accommodations are expected from employers," *Journal of Visual Impairment & Blindness* 94 (2000), 46.

21. Kathryn Abrams, "The second coming of care," *Chicago-Kent Law Review* 76, (2001), 1605. She also faults this literature for failing to come up with legal remedies.

22. Ann Vincola, "Cultural change is the work/life solution," *Workforce* 77 (1998), 70–75. "I'd like to differentiate between those that do it as a regular pattern, which I'd say is about 30 percent," says Lynne McClure, a Phoenix management consultant, "and those that do this

once in a while, which I'd say is all of us." Sabotage is very difficult to quantify and as noted in chapter 5, is not a situation that employers would like to become common knowledge.

23. Whether it is reducing hours or ergonomics, showing respect and concern for employees improves their productivity. See Juin-jen Chang, Chun-chieh Huang, and Ching-chong Lai, "Is the efficiency wage efficient when workers decide on the working time?," *Journal of Economics* 77 (2002), 267–81; Michael J. Smith and Antoinette Derjani Bayehi, "Do ergonomic improvements increase computer workers' productivity?: An intervention study in a call centre," *Ergonomics* 46 (2003), 3–18; and Robert A. Henning, Pierre Jacques, George V. Kissel, Anne B. Sullivan, and Sabina M. Alteras-Webb, "Frequent short rest breaks from computer work: Effects on productivity and well-being at two field sites," *Ergonomics* 40 (1997), 78–91.

24. Industry's rejection of standardizing the treatment of its personnel has been so categorical that some labor leaders argue that unions should stop fighting this transformation and start responding to it. One labor leader, as shown in chapter 5, advanced the argument that organized labor must negotiate individual contracts rather than collective ones, which standardize work conditions. Yet speaking alone, this labor leader would have a tough battle convincing his colleagues. See Michael D. Yates, "The 'new' economy and the labor movement," *Monthly Review* 121 (April 2001), 32.

25. Peter F. Drucker, "Knowledge-worker productivity: The biggest challenge," *California Management Review* 41(1999), 84. On page 80, he describes the twentieth century as having witnessed a 50-fold increase in the productivity of the manual worker in manufacturing, in large part because of Taylorism. "The productivity of the manual worker," he argues, "has created what we now call 'developed' economies. Before Taylor, there was no such thing— all economies were equally underdeveloped." Indeed, Drucker mentions that the term "productivity" itself is only 50 years old. Yet to maintain this high level of productivity, Drucker insists that employers should understand how to increase what he calls the knowledge worker. Between 1975 and 1993, productivity dropped to 1.4 percent annually. It picked up due to, in part, an investment boom that begin in 1993 with worker productivity at an average annual rate of 2.8 percent between 1996 and 2000. Cited from Stuart G. Hoffman and Richard Moody, "Will the capital spending slowdown affect productivity?," *ABA Banking Journal* 93 (2001), 72.

26. Drucker, "Knowledge-worker productivity," 92.

27. Ibid, 86, 89–91. He provides other examples of a company discovering what they are selling, such as AT&T realizing that it was not providing telephones, but service.

28. Ibid.

29. Louise Lamphere, "Bringing the family to work: Women's culture on the shopfloor," *Feminist Studies* 11 (1985), 538.

30. Edward Shepard and Thomas Clifton, "Are longer hours reducing productivity in manufacturing?" *International Journal of Manpower* 21 (2000), 540–41. They examine the effects of overtime hours for 18 different manufacturing industries. It lowers average productivity in almost all of them.

31. Ibid., 541.

32. Barton H. Hamilton, Jack A. Nickerson, and Hideo Owan, "Team incentives and worker heterogeneity," *Journal of Political Economy* 111 (2003), 473.

33. However, this is not to say that U.S. companies can pick and choose which practices to follow. Japanese production includes problem-solving teams, extensive orientation, training throughout employees' careers, extensive information sharing, rotation across jobs, employment security, and profit sharing. They found that the Japanese lines are more productive than U.S. since the latter only adopt a few of the practices of the former. Indeed, the Japanese factory lines were on average 7 percent more productive than American lines. Casey Ichniowski and Katherine Shaw, "The effects of human resource management systems on economic performance," *Management Science* 45 (1999), 704, 719–20.

34. Edward P. Lazear, "Hiring risky workers" in *International Labor Market, Incentives and Employment*, Isao Ohashi and Toshiaki Tachibanaki, eds. (New York: St. Martin's, 1998).

35. Hamilton, Nickerson, and Owan, "Team incentives and worker heterogeneity: An empirical analysis of the impact of teams on productivity and participation," 467. Also see Eugene

Kandel and Edward P. Lazear, "Peer pressure and partnerships," *Journal of Political Economy* 100 (1992), 801–17.

36. Hamilton, Nickerson, and Owan, "Team incentives and worker heterogeneity," 494.

37. Jaikumar Vijayan, "Downsizings leave firms vulnerable to digital attacks," *Computerworld*, 35 (June 25, 2001), 1.

38. Quoted from Carol Vinzant, "Messing with the boss's head," *Fortune* (Europe), 141 (January 5, 2000), 116. There are even Web sites where people can post their antics: A Web site devoted to sabotage at the workplace where employees can share their "stories about throwing wrenches into the work machine" can be found at <http://www.infoshop.org/sabotage.html>.

39. Ron A. DiBattista, "Forecasting sabotage events in the workplace," *Public Personnel Management* 25 (1996), 41–52.

40. Vijayan, "Downsizings leave firms vulnerable to digital attacks," 1.

41. Vinzant, "Messing with the boss's head," 116.

42. Ibid.

43. Lloyd C. Harris, "Sabotage market-oriented culture change: An exploration of resistance justifications and approaches," *Journal of Marketing Theory & Practice*, 10 (2002), 57, citing Lloyd Harris and Emmanuel Ogbonna, "Exploring service sabotage: The antecedents, types and consequences of frontline, deviant antiservice behaviors," *Journal of Service Research* 4 (2002), 163–84. Also see Michael W. Boye and Karen B. Slora, "The severity and prevalence of deviant employee activity within supermarkets," *Journal of Business and Psychology* 8 (1993), 245–54.

44. Daniel Dana, "Measuring the financial cost of organizational cost," <http://www.smart-biz.com/article/articleview/26/1/5/>.

45. Shari Caudron, "Fighting the enemy within," *IW* (September 4, 1995), 39.

46. David R. Roediger, *The Wages of Whiteness: Race and the Making of the American Working Class* (London: Verso, 1999), 8–11.

47. Stewart J. Schwab and Steven L. Willborn, "Reasonable accommodation of workplace disabilities," *William and Mary Law Review* 44 (2003), 1202.

48. Sallie Westwood, *All Day, Every Day: Factory and Family in the Making of Women's Lives* (Urbana: University of Illinois, 1985).

49. Filip Caeldries, "On the sustainability of the capitalist order: Schumpeter's capitalism, socialism and democracy revisited," *Journal of Socio-Economics* 22 (1993), 163–87.

50. Battista, "Forecasting sabotage events in the workplace," 47. Also see Caeldries, "On the sustainability of the capitalist order."

51. See Elizabeth Barham, "Social movements for sustainable agriculture in France: A Polanyian perspective," *Society & Natural Resources* 10 (1997), 239. Also see Polanyi, *The Great Transformation*; and Marc Granovetter, "Economic action and social structure: The problem of embeddedness," *American Journal of Sociology* 91 (1985), 481–510.

52. Polanyi, *The Great Transformation*, 70.

53. Joseph A. Schumpeter, *Capitalism, Socialism, and Democracy* (London: Allen and Unwin, 1976). Schumpeter argued that capitalism's economic success created social and cultural conditions inimical to its survival. This economic system has done so by disconnecting private and social concerns. As a result, the moral and ethical principles underlying capitalism—the Protestant work ethic—have been eroded.

54. Barham, "Social movements for sustainable agriculture in France: A Polanyian perspective," 239.

55. Gatens and Lloyd, *Imaginings: Spinoza, Past and Present*, 102.

# INDEX